Irish Women's Studies Reader

Irish Women's Studies Reader

Edited by
Ailbhe Smyth

Attic Press
Dublin

First published in Ireland 1993 by
Attic Press
4 Upper Mount Street
Dublin 2

British Library Cataloguing in Publication Data
Irish Women's Studies Reader
I. Smyth Ailbhe
305.42094215

ISBN 1-85594-052-3

Cover Design: Attic Press
Origination: Verbatim Typesetting
Printing: Guernsey Press

Also edited by Ailbhe Smyth

Wildish Things:
An Anthology of New Irish Writing

The Abortion Papers: Ireland

Attic Press
DUBLIN

Contents

Introduction   i

The Silencing of Women in Childbirth or
Let's Hear it for Bartholemew and the Boys
Jo Murphy-Lawless   9

'Suffrage First — Above All Else!'
An Account of the Irish Suffrage Movement
Margaret Ward   20

Political Interest and Participation of Irish
Women 1922-1992: The Unfinished Revolution
Frances Gardiner   45

The Church, the State and
the Women's Movement in Northern Ireland
Monica McWilliams   79

Women and the Law in Ireland
Mary Robinson   100

Rape: Myths and Reality
Madeleine Leonard   107

The Relationship Between
Women's Work and Poverty
Mary Daly   122

Revealing Figures?
Official Statistics and Rural Irish Women
Anne Byrne   140

Women and Poverty
Eileen Evason   162

Bringing the Margins Into the Centre:
A Review of Aspects of Irish Women's Emigration
Ann Rossiter   177

Moving Statues and Irish Women
Margaret MacCurtain   203

The Irish Travelling Woman:
Mother and Mermaid
Mary O'Malley Madec   214

Sex and Nation:
Women in Irish Culture and Politics
Gerardine Meaney   230

The Women's Movement in the Republic
of Ireland 1970-1990
Ailbhe Smyth   245

About the Contributors   270

Acknowledgements and Sources of Chapters   272

Index   273

Introduction

Feminism in all its varieties has always insisted on the importance of women's ideas, feelings and experiences. It has valued women in our own right and not according to male-defined ideas about worth. Over the years, feminists have come to celebrate women's strengths, abilities and intelligence and stressed the need for us to rediscover our past and to re-evaluate our present conditions. This process of re-education for women is called 'Women's Studies' and it represented one of the many different responses by women to the challenge of feminism (Steiner-Scott, 1985).

Feminism has been responsible for bringing about a crucial shift in the politics and practice of knowledge-making in the past twenty years or so. Feminist theorists and researchers have begun to explore the extent to which perceived differences between women and men are a consequence, not of biological 'fact' but of cultural assumptions and practices. They have shown that gender differences are not absolute and 'natural' but relative and socially constructed. But gender has had to be pushed, sometimes smuggled, on to the educational and research agendas by feminists who have begun to reveal the extraordinary omissions and distortions which occur when knowledge-makers persist in ignoring or denying the central importance of gender as a shaping force in human relations and social organisation.

Feminist inquiry, whether in the new field of Women's Studies, or working within traditional disciplines, poses funda-mental, assumption-shattering questions: What are the meanings and mechanisms of gender differentiation? How are gender differences *differently* constructed over time and across cultures, social classes and racial and ethnic groups? What are the specific reverberations of gender differences for the acquisition and exercise of social and economic power and control? What is 'gender identity' and why and how do we acquire it? What is the relation between gender and sexuality? How do different sex classes, ie women and men, differently experience that relationship? How does an understanding of the mechanisms of gender power relations enable us to change those relations?

Answering these questions — and the many others which radiate from them — involves a radical re-evaluation of the object and objectives of knowledge as traditionally constructed and defined, at least in the Western world. This obliges us in turn to confront the woeful inadequacy of the conceptual frameworks and methods of what pass for 'universal truth' and 'objective knowledge'. Hitherto 'invisible' dimensions and spheres of social, political and cultural life (and whole groups of people) are brought to light. Rooted in living social processes and always conscious of the political bases of knowledge-making, a feminist perspective continually questions the relationship between power and knowledge, theory and action, knowing and doing. It asks whether our knowledge contrib-utes positively and generously to social change, rather than serving to maintain and reproduce an oppressive status quo. It recognises that there is no such place as a 'value-free' refuge for 'knowers' (scholars, researchers, teachers) and emphasises the reality and value of the knowledge which grows out of experience. Crucially, feminism stresses the connections between the possession of knowledge and knowledge-making skills and the process of liberation:

> Feminism is the political theory and practice that struggles to free all women: women of colour, working class women, poor women, disabled women, lesbians and old women — as well as white, economically privileged heterosexual women (Smith, 1982).

Feminism is not, however, in any sense a unified, homogen-eous practice, and just as there is a diversity of feminisms, so too there is a plurality of ways of 'doing' feminist inquiry and Women's Studies. As a working definition, Women's Studies can be said to encompass at least four vital dimensions (Healy and Smyth, 1987):

1 Women's Studies is about women, and women's lives and experiences. This includes looking at power relations

between different groups of women — across race and class, between lesbians and heterosexual women — as well as between women and men, in both historical and contemporary contexts.

2 Women's Studies is an educational practice in which women themselves seek to shape and define the content, the methods and structures of the learning context.

3 Women's Studies is educational in the full sense of the word: change-oriented, liberatory, enabling us to come to a more explicitly critical awareness of the material, social and cultural circumstances of our diversely lived lives.

4 Women's Studies challenges supposedly 'universal' and 'gender-neutral' accounts of the world, which in actual fact omit or seriously distort the concerns and experiences of over half the human race. This involves developing a radical critique of knowledge and the ways in which it is made and used, right across and beyond the disciplines and institutions.

Women's Studies in Ireland
Just a decade and a half ago, Women's Studies in Ireland was largely unmapped terrain. The pioneering collection of essays, *Women in Irish Society: The Historical Dimension* (MacCurtain and Ó Corráin, 1978) marked out some of the most significant scholarly and critical directions for the study of the historical and contemporary realities of women in Irish social, political and cultural life for, as Margaret MacCurtain commented in her preface: 'Many Irish women find it difficult to learn about their historical identity, or their role in the life of the country because they have neither the information readily available nor the skills of evaluation at their disposal.' Since then, the work of feminist scholars and researchers has immeasurably enriched our knowledge of Irish women's contribution in many spheres and begun to identify and explore the complexities of gendered power relations.

Establishing Women's Studies as an important and 'legitimate' field has, of course, been an uphill struggle. The odds are stacked in any case against educational activities and approaches which the mainstream sees as a threat to its established values and methods, and are all the greater in a time of extreme economic crisis, when resources have been pruned to an absolute minimum. The repercussions of the recession in Ireland have been severe throughout the educational system but are especially acute in adult education, which has always had to struggle for even basic recognition. It is no coincidence that this sector is the one where women are in a large majority as both 'providers' and 'consumers', and where demand for women-centred education has grown dramatically over the past decade. Resistance to the emergence of Women's Studies has been especially marked in Ireland where the struggle between the opposing forces of traditionalism and modernisation has been so significantly fought over the socially prescribed 'place' of women in the state (Smyth, 1992).

However, building on the vitality of the women's move-ment in Ireland and their own active participation in its campaigns and struggles, feminists in both the third-level and adult education sectors have developed feminist perspectives in their work, introducing new materials and courses into the curricula and exploring new areas and methods of research. Since the 1980s, Women's Studies has gone from strength to strength and now exists in a plethora of different forms and settings. Almost all of the universities throughout the country offer postgraduate, undergraduate and/or non-graduate courses in Women's Studies, while there are at least a hundred community or locally-based women's educational projects. Anne Mulvey (1992) comments:

> Because of the commitment of a few academic women to include community and grassroots groups and issues in their work, and the tenacity of feminists doing community-based [education] who demand inclusion in academic Women's Studies, there seems to be quite good communication and co-operation between the grassroots women's movement, community-based education for women, and Women's Studies in academia. This is not meant to suggest that there are no conflicts between these groups . . . [but rather] to highlight the visible and

ongoing bridging of community-based formal and informal women's groups and academic Women's Studies.

Feminist research in Ireland covers a large and rapidly-growing range of areas and disciplines, with particular emphasis on and interest in Irish historical, social and cultural studies. Feminist research, however, continues to suffer from generalised highly conservative funding policies which lay heavy stress on economic issues to the detriment of the exploration of crucial social and political topics. As a non-exhaustive minimum, a research agenda for the 1990s in Irish Women's Studies needs to include a more developed and institutionally-resourced focus on the following: differences between women, whether of class, religion, ethnicity, race or sexuality: for example, the needs of poor and unemployed women, women in rural areas, traveller women and women with disabilities; the impact of economic and social policies on women's lives in a range of different circumstances; increased entry into the labour market, and the impact of changes in the labour market on women; the impact of 'Europeanisation' on Irish women; the construction of sexuality and, in particular, the experiences of lesbians; the social control of women through sexuality and reproduction; the nature, extent and effects of male violence on women; the meaning of emigration in women's lives; the reverberations for women of the political division of Ireland into two separate parts; the evolution and impact of the women's movement and women's mobilisation in the sphere of 'public' politics.

Women's Studies, responsive to the changing educational needs and demands of women, is also — and by no means less importantly — making a vital contribution to our understand-ing of the Irish social, political and cultural systems, at a time of especially rapid and far-reaching change. It is to the benefit of everyone that its development should be fully supported and properly resourced.

The *Irish Women's Studies Reader*
The *Reader* provides a sampling of the challenging work being done by Irish feminist scholars and researchers. It brings together previously dispersed essays on topics in a range of disciplines from history through sociology, social policy and political science to literary and cultural studies and is intended primarily for use as a textbook by students in higher and adult education. While it does not replace earlier excellent Irish collections, nor lessen the usefulness of the general textbooks in Women's Studies published in North America and the UK, the *Reader* aims to be an up-to-date and convenient source book of Irish materials and perspectives for students who have a special interest in Ireland. The *Reader* makes no claim to be exhaustive — a very much larger book would be needed now before we could even begin to reach that point — and there are especially regrettable 'absences', including work on education, sexuality, disability, health issues, and developments in the labour market. Nevertheless, I hope that the suggestions for further reading will stimulate more in-depth investigation and exploration of the increasingly rich and invigorating field of Irish Women's Studies.

Ailbhe Smyth
July 1993

References and further reading

AONTAS Women's Education Group. 1991. *From the Personal to the Political: A Women's Education Workbook.* Dublin, Attic Press.

Byrne, A. 1992. 'Women's Studies in Ireland'. Paper presented at WISE seminar, Brussels.

Canadian Journal of Irish Studies. 1992. Special Issue: Women in Ireland. Vol 18, No.1.

Cullen, M. 1986. 'Redefining Knowledge: Women's Studies in Ireland'. In *Council News.* Council for the Status of Women, Dublin.

Cullen, M. (ed). 1987. *Girls Don't Do Honours.* WEB, Dublin.

Curtin, C., Jackson, P., O'Connor, B. (eds). 1987. *Gender in Irish Society.* Galway University Press, Galway.

Drew, E. 1993. 'Country Case Study on Women's Studies in the Republic of Ireland'. Paper presented at the UNESCO-KEGME Seminar: Gender Studies: Towards the Year 2000, Athens, Greece.

Healy, G. and Smyth, A. 1987. 'Women's Studies: Irish Style'. In RFR/DRF, Vol. 16, No. 4, Toronto.

Mulvey, A. 1992. 'Irish Women's Studies and Community Activism: Reflections and Exemplars'. In *Women's Studies International Forum*, Vol. 15, No. 4, 1992.

Ní Chuilleanáin, E. (ed.) 1985. *Irish Women: Image and Achievement.* Arlen House, Dublin.

Smith, B. 1982. 'Racism and Women's Studies'. In Hull, G. T., Bell Scott, P., and Smith, B. (eds.), *All the Women are White, All the Blacks are Men, But Some of Us are Brave: Black Women's Studies.* The Feminist Press, New York.

Smyth, A. (ed.). 1992. *The Abortion Papers: Ireland.* Attic Press, Dublin.

Steiner-Scott, L. (ed.). 1985. *Personally Speaking: Women's Thoughts on Women's Issues.* Attic Press, Dublin.

UCG Women's Studies Centre Review. 1992. Vol. 1. University College Galway, Galway.

The Silencing of Women in Childbirth
or
Let's Hear it From Bartholomew and the Boys

Jo Murphy-Lawless

Recently I was re-reading Helen Roberts' 1981 paper, 'Women and their Doctors: Power and Powerlessness in the Research Process', in which she was speaking of the importance of research which not only makes the problem of women's subordination visible and analysable but which also contributes to an integration of feminist theory and practice. I was struck by one footnote to the article which reads:

> Margaret Stacey has suggested that during their reproductive years, women may well establish a particular relationship with and reliance upon doctors because of the medicalisation of childbirth which has occurred over the past 50 to 100 years (Roberts, 1981: 27).

This statement encapsulates for me a number of dilemmas and contradictions which are inherent in much of the feminist writing about childbirth, contradictions which impelled me some years ago to begin digging through eighteenth- and nineteenth-century obstetric texts. This is not because my own initial training as an historian made me a stickler for 'the facts' but because I am committed to the position that the analysis of the historical specificity of the concrete forms of women's subordination is crucial for feminist theory.

Quite early on, I encountered the reports, or clinical records, of a Dr Johnston who was Master of the Rotunda during the 1870s. This was during a period when the hospital was subject to a series of severe puerperal fever epidemics, with consequent loss of life for many of the women so afflicted.[1] The following extract stopped me cold. Johnston is relating the account of one woman who came up to Dublin to the Rotunda to give birth to her first baby:

. . . a case of acute bronchitis, aged 25; as she was suffering from great dysponea, she was delivered [by forceps] when the os was 2/5 dilated; the child weighed 6 lbs 5oz which died on the third day, the mother not being able to nurse it. She was at once put under treatment for a chest complaint. The following morning, Dr H Kennedy was kind enough to see her with me. She had a pulse of 130; tongue dry, brown crust — in fact all the signs of typhus fever. At noon, she was again visited when she was found crying; and on being asked why she was doing so, she stated that she had been seduced, turned out by her parents, she had nowhere to go and did not know what would become of her, that she had twice attempted suicide, but was prevented. We told her make her mind easy that we would befriend her and get a home for her. From this, she began to mend. She was sent to No. 11 the chronic ward, on her tenth day [after giving birth], a week after which she took the place of a wardmaid where she continues ever since. This is a remarkable instance of the wonderful influence of the mind over the body (Johnston, 1875: 142).

Medical power in childbirth: problems of definition

First of all, returning to Roberts' quote, what constitutes medicalisation: how is that being defined? What does the process entail: is it synonymous with the establishment of maternity hospitals in which case how can it be dated as a process going back only fifty to one hundred years? Lying-in or maternity hospitals are not a recent phenomenon. They date back to the eighteenth century. On the other hand, does every woman have to be hospitalised before childbirth can be defined as medicalised in which case we can only talk about medicalised childbirth existing since 1972 when rates of hospitalised childbirth in Britain and Ireland finally encompassed the majority of childbearing women. (The rate currently stands at 99.9 per cent of all births here in Ireland.)

And what about the issue of power? Within the context of the counselling and support work I have done with pregnant women over the last fourteen years, it had long impressed me that the subordinate relationship established between women and doctors has had more to do with the issue of power than with medicalisation as such, and that it is an issue which is not immediately easy to analyse. It also struck me that the medicalisation of childbirth has been itself a more complex social and historical process with more far-reaching consequences for women than has hitherto been recognised.

The necessity to establish what the relationship is between the historical process which subsumed women as subordinate within the medical hierarchy and our contemporary struggle to gain control of our bodies in the area of reproduction was the starting point for Ehrenreich and English's classic pamphlet: *Witches, Midwives and Nurses* (1973). Yet from that point, the struggle for power in the birthplace has been presented in feminist writing as one between women practitioners and the emerging profession of male midwives, with the latter gradually gaining control at the expense of the former, and also at the expense of labouring women themselves. The argument about women's oppression at the hands of male medicine is one which sees medicalisation as a cumulative process over a long period of time and which has increased as the technical and pharmacological prowess of science has increased. Haire (1974) and Oakley (1980), for instance, argue that medicalised childbirth, as distinct from hospitalised childbirth, has existed for the last fifteen to twenty years.

Reading women's past

I was not at all certain about that hypothesis when I first began to read the works of men midwives. The opposition between men and women practitioners seemed too simple a dichotomy resulting in an explanation which was insufficient in relation to the radical break in social practices surrounding childbirth that male midwifery represented. I was also uneasy about the difficulty of reconstructing the voice of female experience in all this. Ehrenreich and English, for instance, wrote that their work could only be a fragmentary effort because women's written records were so minimal. At that time in the women's movement, during the early 1970s, there seemed a real possibility that we could deconstruct male historical 'facts' about us and

11

reconstruct women's experience by reconstructing their voices which had been silenced for so long.

This was a theme carried through in a number of fields in Women's Studies, not just the medical one, as the work of Dale Spender on women in history, Virago Press's reprints of little-known women writers, and the excellent research on working class women in nineteenth-century Britain by Judith Walkowitz, for example, all testify. But in this crucial effort to valorise women's experience under patriarchy in its many guises, what we could see by the end of the 1970s was that women's past had been assigned a kind of fantasy voice, a fantasy status for us. On this point, Meaghan Morris writes that feminist analysis of patriarchy could too often be reduced to the obvious explanation of a 'continuous and evenly distributed, consistently significant oppression of the eternal object "woman" or "women" through the ages' (Morris, 1979: p151).

There is a continuing problem here, as feminists such as Rowbotham (1973) have argued, as to how we can actually make women audible and visible in history thereby establishing a female consciousness of our history.

The female body and historical specificity

Nowhere can this be more acute than in the problematic set by the female body itself, for not only have women written relatively little in comparison with men, but also the subject of childbirth itself is dominated by male discourse. In relation to the childbirth issue, what struck me was that the Ehrenreich and English thesis, subsequently built on by Donnison (1977), Rich (1977), Wertz and Wertz (1977) and others, in focusing on the suppression of female midwives as the most visible and analysable aspect of the male takeover resulted in a tendency to romanticise women midwives and woman-controlled childbirth as a natural historical entity, positing a Golden Age of childbirth (Macintyre, 1977; Callaway, 1978; Radford, 1984).

The argument centred on the suppression of female practitioners and woman-controlled childbirth did little, for instance, to address the current micropolitics of the individual pregnant woman trying to deal with the realities of power she confronts with her doctor. Too often, it left women regretting a hypothetical vision about childbirth they could not achieve, while diverting attention from the realities of current obstetric provision (Macintyre, 1977). At the level of theory, it left wide open the space through which Shorter (1983) galloped with his thesis about how women were the natural victims of their reproductive functions until male science rescued them with its increasing skill and wisdom, whereupon men 'changed . . . from being women's enemies to being their best friends' (Shorter, 1983: 286).

It also inadvertently submerged from view the specificity of the female body in childbirth by drawing our attention away from how male science had sought to systematise that body as distinct from suppressing woman-controlled childbirth, so that the problem of reconstructing or uncovering the silent female voice in childbirth remained.

A resounding silence

This was the background for me when I began my research. I knew that the Rotunda Lying-in Hospital in Dublin was the first maternity hospital in the British Isles, and so I began reading the works of those men midwives who had been connected with the Rotunda, most usually as master, that is, head man midwife or obstetrician. This was when I came across the extract from Johnston's clinical records. I was haunted by it, not least by the reported conversation between the woman and the two men midwives. For all her anguish, it was as close as I, another woman coming across those dusty records over a hundred years later, could get to this nameless woman. Yet the account revealed an appalling personal tragedy.

Here was a woman who had travelled to Dublin to the one hospital in Ireland which would give her shelter as an unmarried woman while she laboured to give birth. Not only was she already ill and greatly distressed emotionally, bereft of any family support when she entered the Rotunda, she was then subject to an instrumental delivery of her child when her cervix was barely dilated and, subsequently, to the death of her child. Little wonder that the woman was found weeping. Perhaps she really had considered herself fortunate to have the offer of work and shelter in the harsh economic climate of post-Famine Ireland, where women's value extended only as far as their dowry upon marriage, and illegitimacy was socially even less acceptable than it was elsewhere in Britain or Europe. I found I was somewhat mollified by the fact that she had finally been treated in a kindly manner by these men midwives, even though such paternalism exposed the reality of the woman's powerlessness. But I kept asking myself what had she thought about her situation as she did the rounds of the wards, cleaning up after women whose circumstances were in all probability little better than hers but whose babies were alive. What had she felt about the physical assault she had suffered in having the forceps applied to her, when her labour was still at such an early stage.[2] And, as ill as she had been, how had she gathered her strength a bare fortnight after her ordeal to begin working.

Of course, she made me no answer; there was no answer from any woman about that climate, that hospital regime, their own lack of power. As close as I could get to women's experiences was through the texts of the men midwives, I kept saying in frustration until suddenly I realised the implication of male medical discourse. The history of women giving birth in institutions like the Rotunda can only ever be read through male medical discourse which itself has created that history, both at the level of individual experience and social reality.

'Public virtue, public love': Speaking through Bartholomew and the boys

The establishment of male midwifery and its institutional base, the lying-in hospital, must be viewed as part of that vast movement beginning in the eighteenth century that Foucault (1981) terms 'bio-politics' in which the economic and political potential of women as reproducers was recognised and which by the 1760s, as Badinter (1981) has ably shown, began to put such emphasis on the maternal duty of breastfeeding to preserve infant life. The intentions to preserve maternal and infant life because of their economic potential were publicly articulated here in Ireland between 1745 and the 1760s when the main buildings of the Rotunda were erected. Its founder, a self-styled man midwife named Bartholomew Mosse, was considered a great philanthropist for taking account of the needs of 'poor women' giving birth in the overcrowded slums that characterised eighteenth-century Dublin. Indeed the extent of poverty in Ireland, considered by contemporaries to be far worse here than elsewhere in the British Isles, led to state support for the Rotunda as a worthy and important public charity for what were known as 'poor lying-in women'. A plaque inscribed by a local sculptor in 1749 to the founder of the hospital drives home this message:

A public Virtue in thy Founder blaz'd,
A public Love thy sacred Mansions rais'd,
Mansions by Charity herself design'd,
The sure Asylum of the suff'ring Kind.

But even the most benign account of the Rotunda's history, say by its latest apologist, Ross in his book entitled *Public Virtue, Public Love*, does not attempt to deny the, 'desire of doctors to have a steady supply of cases for clinical study and the instruction of (male) students' (1986: 151) and what is perfectly clear from the clinical records is not just the attempt by male medicine to establish the 'speaking eye' of clinical discourse which could formulate definitive truths about the body (Foucault, 1976: 114) but a very specific application in relation to the female body. Badinter argues that there has been a 'perfect continuity' in constructing motherhood as a social institution from the middle of the eighteenth century down to the present and that much of the work contemporary feminism has had to undertake is to examine critically the impact of those discourses on women and how they see their role as mothers over that long historical epoch.

It seemed to me that male-controlled childbirth as women currently experience it, with its focus on women as essentially passive objects, at the same time has shared many of the same ideological premises about women and motherhood and that the two are not unconnected. The Rotunda Lying-in Hospital is the institutional expression of a series of economic and philosophical arguments about the importance of women as reproducers. It is, however, equally the institutional expression of the desire of male medical discourse to control the female body in labour. But total hospitalisation of the childbearing population, a relatively recent achievement, was not necessary to effect that control. The importance of those male texts as a discursive structure lies in the fact that they have themselves shaped for women the experience of how and when women give birth. The central argument of male medical discourse is not just that 'poor women' of the lower classes needed their assistance but that all women in labour were 'poor suffering women'. Their texts resonate not with the voices of women who labour strongly and well to give birth but with their version of women's voices as poor, weak and feeble, in a word incompetent to undergo birth without male intervention. Obstetric science has consistently used this theory of female incompetence not only to justify the necessity of its presence at birth, but also as the basis of its clinical practice and herein lies its power. It claims a definitive knowledge about the female body but that knowledge is premised on the 'fact' of women's feebleness and incompetence. If we return to the extract from Johnston's clinical records we find the detail, 'she was delivered when ... 2/5 dilated'.

What we are actually hearing about is the clinical practice of an eminent obstetrician, the Rotunda's master, who argued that the hospital's high rate of puerperal fever sprang from the women themselves and not from the men midwives spreading infection. Johnston argued that puerperal fever was the result of the high rate of admissions of unmarried women who were suffering remorse because they were pregnant which emotional frailty left them more open to infection. The application of the forceps (with resulting damage to cervical and vaginal tissue) became routine practice for unmarried mothers during his mastership for Johnston reasoned that it would preserve them from a lengthy labour which in their enfeebled state would further endanger them. The fact that the rate of death from puerperal fever was significantly higher amongst this group of women only served as further proof for him of his theory rather than an indication that his intervention had introduced infection leading to puerperal fever.

The continuity in this theory of female incompetence extends from the eighteenth-century text of the Dublin man midwife and Master of the Rotunda, Fielding Ould, who developed the technique of episiotomy, to Johnston, to the early twentieth-century American obstetrician, De Lee, who believed in delivering babies by means of the 'prophylactic forceps operation' while the mothers were heavily drugged (De Lee, 1920) to the current enthusiasm for 'active management of labour' with the use of oxytocic infusions (again, I regret to say, an Irish development — see O'Driscoll and Meagher (1980) where they claim that women's emotional state is such that they cannot survive a long labour without permanent damage and therefore require their labours to be shortened by pharmacological control). The power that doctors wield over women in childbirth is *par excellence* the power of the written word to shape the way our bodies function as we actually give birth. Our reliance upon them can be brought to an end only as and when we construct a discourse about the female body which contests their theory of female incompetence.

Notes

1 Puerperal fever was the name given to the infection which too often proved fatal to women in childbirth. Mary Wollstonecraft, for instance, died from puerperal fever. With the growth of lying-in hospitals, the infection was rife until the distinction between sepsis and asepsis was finally accepted. See Rich (1977: 139—142) and Shorter (1983: 103—108).

2 With the cervix less than half open, the damage to the vaginal and cervical tissue is immense, ranging from badly torn tissue to the cervix detaching and being sloughed off. In Johnston's time, before the introduction of aseptic measures, it also greatly increased the chance of contracting puerperal fever.

References and further reading

Badinter, E. 1981. *The Myth of Motherhood: An Historical View of the Maternal Instinct.* Souvenir Press, London.

Callaway, H. 1978. 'The Most Essentially Female Function of All: Giving Birth'. In Ardener, S. (ed.), *Defining Females: The Nature of Women in Society.* Croom Helm, London.

Davis, K. 1988. *Power Under the Microscope.* Foris Publications, Dordrecht, Holland.

De Lee, J. 1920. 'The prophylactic forceps operation'. In *American Journal of Obstetrics and Gynaecology,* 1: October.

Donnison, J. 1977. *Midwives and Medical Men.* Heinemann, London.

Ehrenreich, B. and English, D. 1977. *Witches, Midwives, and Nurses: A History of Women Healers.* Feminist Press, Old Westbury, New York.

Foucault, M. 1976. *The Birth of the Clinic: An Archaeology of Medical Perception.* Tavistock, London.

Foucault, M. 1981. *The History of Sexuality, Volume One: An Introduction.* Penguin, Harmondsworth.

Haire, D. 1974. *The Cultural Warping of Childbirth.* International Childbirth Education Association, Hillside, New Jersey.

Johnston, G. 1875. 'Clinical Report of the Rotunda Lying-in Hospital for the year ending 5 November, 1874'. *Dublin Quarterly Journal of Medical Science,* Volume LIX, January and June,1875.

Macintyre, S. 1977. 'Childbirth: the myth of the Golden Age', *World Medicine.* Vol. 12, No. 18.

Morris, M. 1979. 'The Pirate's Fiancée. In Meaghan, M. and Patton, P. (eds.), *Michel Foucault: Power, Truth and Strategy.* Feral Publications, Sydney.

Murphy-Lawless, J. 1992. 'The Obstetric View of Feminine Reality: A Nineteenth-Century Case History of the Use of Forceps in Ireland'. In Smyth, A. (ed.), *The Abortion Papers: Ireland.* Attic Press, Dublin.

Oakley, A. 1980. *Women Confined: Towards a Sociology of Childbirth.* Martin Robertson, Oxford.

O'Driscoll, K. and Meagher, D. 1980. *Active Management of Labour.* Saunders, London.

Ould, F. 1742. *A Treatise of Midwifry in Three Parts.* Dublin.

Radford, L. 1984. 'Review: *A History of Women's Bodies* by Edward Shorter'. *Feminist Review,* Summer.

Rich, A. 1977. *Of Woman Born: Motherhood as Experience and Institution.* Virago, London.

Roberts, H. (ed.) 1981. 'Women and their Doctors: Power and Powerlessness in the Research Process'. In *Doing Feminist Research.* Routledge and Kegan, Paul, London.

Ross, I. C. (ed.). 1981. *Public Virtue, Public Love: The Early Years of the Rotunda Lying-in Hospital.* O'Brien Press, Dublin.

Rowbotham, S. 1973. *Woman's Consciousness: Man's World.* Penguin, Harmondsworth.

Shorter, E. 1983. *A History of Women's Bodies.* Allen Lane, London.

Smith, D. E. 1988. *The Everyday World as Problematic: a feminist sociology.* Open University Press, Milton Keynes.

Spender, D. 1982. *Women of Ideas: and what men have done to them from Aphra Benn to Adrienne Rich .* Routledge and Kegan Paul, London.

Walkowitz, J. R. 1980. *Prostitution and Victorian Society: women, class and the state*. Cambridge University Press, Cambridge.

Wertz, D. and Wertz, R. 1977. *Lying-in: A History of Childbirth in America*. Free Press, New York.

Discussion Topics

1 The sociologist, Dorothy Smith (1988), explains how the writing and speech of men have been the basis for constructing authority in larger social structures. By contrast, although women have 'been at work' in the making of modern bourgeois society, we have been 'largely excluded from the work of producing the forms of thought and the images in which thought is expressed and ordered.' Does this argument link up with the writer's position that the history of childbirth in modern society begins with the obstetrician and his texts, not with our experiences, hence with what appears to be our silence?

2 Davis (1988) has argued that benevolence constitutes the 'Janus-face of paternalism', making it difficult for women to control their medical encounters on their own terms. Analyse how this 'Janus face' works for the writer who tells us she is moved by the kindliness shown by Johnston to the woman who has given birth in such difficult circumstances.

3 Is the Foucauldian notion of bio-politics useful in accounting for why childbirth becomes institutionalised towards the end of the eighteenth century?

4 In the chapter, there is an argument that medical theories about women's bodies are based on a principle of female incompetence, that the female body cannot work without scientific assistance. Does this argument help to analyse women's powerlessness in the obstetric and gynaecological setting ?

5 How does the chapter seek to establish that the scientific 'facts' about women are ideological in nature?

6 Write a critique of two recent articles on childbirth from popular women's magazines with reference to how women's subjective experiences are determined by obstetric practices.

'Suffrage First — Above All Else!'
An Account of the Irish Suffrage Movement

Margaret Ward

Historical research is not only concerned with discovering the past — it should also help us to understand our failures, and maybe even suggest strategies for the future. In this respect, the Irish suffrage movement retains its immediacy. The manner in which the suffragists attempted to deal with the consequences of acute political divisions throws light upon the contemporary debates concerning the degree to which women will mobilise to fight against their oppression, regardless of the fact that this sexual oppression is mediated by class, race, and religious differences. And if women do unite on specific issues, the question then arises as to whether this recognition of common needs can spill over into other areas, so that political disagreements will eventually be transcended. This is a fundamental issue amongst Northern Irish feminists. The evidence of history does not give us cause for optimism — the suffragists certainly failed — but we can at least learn from the reasons for their failure. Can it be attributed to external factors, rather than to any internal contradictions within feminism? This discussion does not provide any ready-made answers, it simply raises some of the questions.

The national question
Political life in Ireland was concerned with one issue only: Ireland's domination by Britain and whether or not to fight for independence. Attempted rebellions had all been defeated, but by the end of the nineteenth century physical force no longer appeared necessary as Prime Minister Gladstone declared his conversion to the principle of home rule in Ireland. Ulster unionism was now the only stumbling block: the Unionists declared themselves to be utterly opposed to any diminution of the British connection, and when the House of Lords vetoed the Home Rule Bill of 1893, they were triumphant; as long as the House of Lords existed, their position was

impregnable. But in the first decade of the twentieth century, two events occurred which altered this comfortable calculation, giving renewed spirit to the Irish nationalists. The general election of February 1910 left the nationalists (the Irish Party) holding the balance of power between the Liberal government and the Conservatives and the Unionists: they were therefore able to pressurise the Liberals for another Home Rule Bill as the condition for their continued support. This unexpected advantage was reinforced the following year by the passing of the Parliament Act (a reprisal for the rejection of Lloyd George's budget), reducing the Lords' power to obstruct to a mere two years. For the first time, home rule for Ireland appeared more than possible — it could surely only be a matter of time before all the constitutional niceties were disposed of.

By January 1913 the Home Rule Bill had finally passed through the House of Commons, but resistance to its implementation had grown to hysterical proportions in the North. Under the leadership of Sir Edward Carson and James Craig a quarter of a million Protestants had, in September 1912, pledged themselves with a solemn league and covenant to resist home rule by any means. By the beginning of the following year, the Ulster Volunteer Force had been formed to defend the union by force of arms. Their coup in the Larne gun-running of April 1914, when over 24,000 German guns were spirited into the country, made it plain that there would be no peaceful solution of the Irish question. In retaliation to the unionist display of militarism, militant nationalists formed the Irish Volunteers in 1913, as an avowal of their determination to achieve independence. The Howth gun-running, although only contributing 1000 guns, showed that the nationalists meant business also. And the determination was not limited to the men — both unionists and nationalists formed women's sections for the purposes of fund raising and first aid. 234,406 Ulster women signed a female counterpart to the covenant and women from the Ulster Unionist Women's Council, formed in 1911 (Kingham, 1975: 20-1) who trained as despatch riders and nurses, made, as the *Times* correspondent remarked 'an almost greater appeal to one's imagination even than the men' (*Belfast Newsletter* 21 January 1914). Cumann na mBan (The Irish Women's Council) was not formed until April 1914; its eventual formation was a compromise between those women who argued for equal rights for women within the volunteers, and those men who could not countenance women's presence within a political organisation (Ward, 1980). The role of Cumann na mBan will be referred to in more detail later.

Within this polarised situation there were two obvious paths of intervention for women anxious to make their own political claim: either to put pressure exclusively upon the faction they identified with politically — home rulers or unionists — in order to ensure women's enfranchisement would be included within any constitutional settlement; or to campaign whole-heartedly for one faction, in the expectation that once the crisis had been resolved their victorious allies would reward their zeal. Both of these courses of action were indeed taken, but there was another group of women — the suffragists — who rejected such one-sided stratagems. Their dissension introduced a distinctively feminist voice into Irish politics. Although some suffrage groups (for example, the Irish branch of the Conservative and Unionist Women's Suffrage Association) had undeniable political links, many suffragists refused to align themselves to any side. They believed that the suffrage banner was powerful enough to unite women of different political persuasions: once that had been achieved, the expectation or hope must have been that political differences would melt away, dissolved in a new spirit of mutual cooperation and understanding.

The Irish Women's Franchise League

From the outset, the two issues of home rule and votes for women were hopelessly entangled. As the support of the Irish MPs was vital to the minority Liberal government, they were in a strong position to put pressure on the government for reform. But Prime Minister Asquith was a declared opponent of female suffrage, threatening to resign if such a measure were passed. As the collapse of the Liberals would signal the end of any hope for home rule, John Redmond, the leader of the Irish nationalists, was able to use this threat as justification for his resistance to the appeals of the various suffrage delegations. He was, in any case, utterly opposed to women's enfranchisement. As the likelihood of home rule increased, so too did Redmond's antipathy towards the feminists, whose agitation threatened to divide the nationalist ranks.

Irish politicians had never been renowned as supporters of women's claims. Despite the union with Britain there had been a time-lag of twenty years before Irish women also won the right to become Poor Law Guardians and only in 1898 did they gain the local government vote. These reforms had been fought for by a small group of women and men calling themselves the Irish Women's Suffrage and Local Government Association (ISLGA), formed by Anna Haslam, a Quaker, in 1876. The sedate campaigning of the ISLGA, with its petitions and drawing-room meetings was much too genteel for the new generation of women, who were (as Hanna Sheehy Skeffington wrote on the eve of her imprisonment in 1912) 'somewhat in a hurry with reform' (Sheehy Skeffington and Owens, c. 1975: 11). But no other model presented itself until 1903, when the Pankhursts established the Women's Social and Political Union (WSPU), whose militancy and passion were to provide inspiration for feminists throughout the world. Hanna remembered 'a responsive chord' being struck in 'Irish feminist breasts'. (Sheehy Skeffington and Owens, c. 1975: 12) which eventually resulted in the formation in 1908 of the Irish Women's Franchise League (IWFL).

The members of the IWFL were a well-educated group — exceptionally so, in comparison with the average Irish woman. Hanna Sheehy Skeffington, its secretary, was a graduate of Trinity College Dublin, now teaching German; Margaret Cousins, the treasurer, had a degree in music, and the president, Mrs Charles Oldham was wife of a Trinity College Dublin professor. In contrast, the majority of women had few educational opportunities and most of those in paid employment worked as domestic servants. Irish life was predominantly rural with the economy structured around small farms where members of the family worked without a wage — an insularity reinforced by the conservatism of the Roman Catholic religion. Women in the few urban centres were only marginally better off. For example, in Dublin at this time, of the twenty to twenty-five age group, only 553 were teachers or governesses, while 2,500 were domestic servants. A further 1,500 women worked in the sweated trade as milliners and shirtmakers, 810 were shop assistants, while a mere 453 worked in factories. Various other semi- and unskilled jobs provided employment for the rest of the 9,500 women of this age group who were listed by the 1911 Census as working. And only in 1911 did women workers begin to organise, with the formation of the Irish Women Workers' Union (IWWU), established by Larkin in Dublin and by Connolly in Belfast.

The eager new generation of suffragists had much to contend with, but a spirit of change was in the air, a feeling that Ireland might at long last be about to leave the burden of history behind. The IWFL held weekly meetings in Dublin's Phoenix Park and organised speaking tours around the countryside. Margaret Cousins claimed that although their receptions were uniformly hostile, their ability to engage in quick-witted repartee at least allowed them their right to be heard. That much an Irish crowd would usually allow, but they made few converts. Although by 1912 the IWLF was listed as having some 1,000 members, thus making it the largest suffrage society, Cousins estimated the active membership as around fifty (Cousins and Cousins, 1956: 166).

In England the WSPU had decided upon a policy of opposing Liberal candidates at by-elections, a tactic regarded as anti-Irish by many people in Ireland, who feared it would lead to the defeat of the government and consequently the defeat of their hopes for home rule. Convincing people of the legitimacy of the suffrage demand was therefore doubly difficult in Ireland: feminists faced an anti-woman prejudice which was able to hide hypocritically behind a nationalist face.

From the beginning, the IWLF was absolutely clear on what their strategy would be: they were going to ensure that votes for women were incorporated within the proposed Home Rule Bill. Irish MPs were also to be urged to support any woman suffrage bill that might be presented to the House of Commons; such a bill would have positive benefits for Irishwomen as there would then exist a precedent which could hardly be ignored by the framers of any Home Rule Bill. With their defiant slogan of 'Suffrage First — Before All Else!' they made it clear that all other issues would be subordinated to this one end. At the same time, their acceptance of home rule as a political aim defines the IWFL as nationalist in orientation. While they were prepared to abstract the principle of women's enfranchisement from any political group, thus establishing their autonomy, their mobilising cry was 'Home Rule for Irishwomen as well as Irishmen!' As the complexities of the situation developed, suffragists were forced to define their objective more clearly: the vote, regardless of context, or the vote in an independent Ireland. The later intervention of the Ulster Unionists was to provide an additional complication.

The strategy of the IWFL

As Irishwomen, the IWFL recognised that, much as they admired the WSPU, they would have to modify their tactics to take account of the difference in circumstances. As Margaret Cousins explained, they had to work out a programme of action which would be 'suitable to the different political situation of Ireland, as between a subject-country seeking freedom from England, and England, a free country' (Cousins and Cousins, 1950: 164).

One important difference concerned whether or not the vote would be extended on the existing property qualifications. The WSPU, in campaigning for the vote to be given to women on the same terms as men, was in effect campaigning on behalf of a small élite. But in Ireland, the main beneficiaries of such a reform would be the women of the Anglo-Irish ascendancy, and middle-class Catholic women were not fighting on their behalf.

Their demand was for the local government register to become the basis for electoral eligibility, a demand supported by the labour movement.

The initial reasoning behind the militancy of the WSPU was that if life was made utterly intolerable for the rich, they would pressurise the government into conceding the women's demands. No one in Ireland carried that much weight, and Irish women had to be careful not to alienate already antagonistic people through indiscriminate acts of violence. Political power was clearly located in England, not Ireland: there were no cabinet ministers to plague, few by-elections in which to intervene. At first, therefore, the IWFL confined itself to basic propaganda work, holding meetings and lobbying politicians. However, they did not rule out the possibility that militant action might be necessary in the future — this recognition of the validity of violence in certain circumstances set the IWFL apart from the suffrage groups formed in its wake: all the others remained strictly non-militant.

Strong links were forged between the IWFL and the WSPU in these early days. In 1910 Margaret Cousins was one of a contingent of Irish delegates who joined a suffrage deputation to Asquith. The women joined in all the WSPU activities, some even going to jail in consequence. It was regarded as excellent training for the time when the movement would begin militant activities in Ireland (Cousins and Cousins, 1950: 175—82). And as a morale booster, Emmeline and Christabel Pankhurst, the Pethick-Lawrences and Mrs Despard all came over on speaking tours.

Other suffrage groups, often catering for women with specific political opinions, soon formed. Eventually in 1911 Louie Bennett and Helen Chenevix established the Irish Women's Suffrage Federation (IWSF) as an umbrella group to link up the various, often painfully small, groups. The federation was firmly non-militant, so the IWFL remained outside. It was also non-party, determined to speak for all women, regardless of political beliefs. An important constituent body of the federation was the Irish Women's Reform League, also formed by

Louie Bennett, which campaigned not only for the vote, but also worked to publicise the situation of working women. Bennett came from a well-to-do Protestant family from the exclusive Dublin suburb of Rathmines; it was to take the trauma of the 1916 Rising before she developed any sympathy with the aims of nationalism (Fox, *c.* 1958: 50). In later years both Bennett and Chenevix became full-time organisers for the Irish Women Workers' Union (IWWU), both also becoming Presidents of the Irish Trades Union Congress.

The anti-feminism of the Irish Party

An all-party Conciliation Bill which provided for a limited franchise was introduced into the House of Commons in 1910. It failed, but the following year a revised Bill was submitted, passing its second reading by a vote of 255 to 88, with thirty-four Irish MPs voting in favour and only nine against. This was the last occasion the House of Commons was to prove sympathetic to women's claims until 1918. On March 28, 1912, in the second session of Parliament, after the government had promised that the bill would receive time to go through all the necessary stages, it was defeated by fourteen votes — and this time, only four Irish MPs had voted in its favour. Sylvia Pankhurst was convinced that the wrecking of the Bill was a direct result of this unexpect-edly large reversal in the Irish voting pattern (Pankhurst, 1977: 381). There was another reason for this abrupt change of heart: Redmond's realisation of the reper-cussions involved in franchise reform. If the franchise was extended, this would have to occur along with general electoral reform, including redistribution of seats. Giving the vote to the working class and women would assist the rise of Sinn Féin, while a redistribution of seats would strengthen the Unionists in Ulster. The Irish Party was confronted by 'the devil of Sinn Féin and the deep sea of Ulster machinations inside the Unionist party' (Morgan, 1975: 147). Redmond was painfully aware that any measure of female suffrage was an opening of the floodgates.

Redmond's opportunism came in for increasing

criticism, and not only from suffragists. C P Scott, editor of the *Manchester Guardian*, tried to urge him to reconsider his attitude by pointing out the inconsistency of a home rule party betraying the very principle of home rule — 'that emancipation for Irish men (would be) purchased at the cost of its refusal for English women' (Morgan, 1975: 113). It was only with considerable reluctance that many Liberals continued to support the aspirations of the Irish Party.

This dilemma was resolved by many women through a decision to fight exclusively for their own interests, now that it had become apparent that their MPs would not. Anticipating the result of the vote, the Irish Women's Suffrage Federation had already written to the *Manchester Guardian*, saying that nationalist opposition to the principle of women's suffrage contained in the Conciliation Bill would be 'an act of hostility to Irish women', forcing them to subsequently place suffrage before home rule (Morgan, 1975: 98). It was not only the militants of the IWFL who were now estranged from male-defined political concerns. Women who had initially been moderate in their plea to have women included within home rule provisions, were being forced to lay exclusive emphasis upon their demand for enfranchisement. But Christabel Pankhurst went even further — she sent a poster parade to Parliament Square, which announced 'No Votes for Women', No Home Rule', a policy her sister Sylvia considered 'fantastic' and doomed to failure (Pankhurst, 1977: 403). Sylvia tried to persuade the WSPU to leave the Irish question to Irish women, and Liberals sympathetic to the WSPU tried to persuade them that one movement for liberation could not be counterposed to another. Despite this advice, the WSPU decided there would be 'a fight to the finish between suffragists and the Nationalist Party' (Rosen, 1974: 166). There was a crucial difference between this policy and that of the majority of the Irish suffragists — one declared itself opposed to home rule, while the other demanded the inclusion of women within the constitutional settlement. The IWFL and the Federation continued their campaigning, refusing to support any political group, but the logic of the WSPUs' position was to move them inexorably into the Unionist camp.

An historic meeting

The main brunt of the IWFL campaign was now directed against what was regarded as the principal enemy — the Irish Party. In February 1912 they demonstrated outside the Gresham Hotel, Dublin, while Redmond addressed a meeting, carrying banners demanding 'Home Rule for Irish women as well as men'. Two months later they met Redmond in deputation, only to be informed that he would never, under any circumstances, support female suffrage (*The Irish Citizen*, 4 January 1913). His antagonism was revealed in the voting, in November 1912, on a motion introduced by Philip Snowden to include female suffrage within the proposed Home Rule Bill. Only five Irish MPs were in favour, with seventy-one against, making this the largest anti-vote on the issue that the Irish Party ever mobilised (Harrison, 1978: 28-30).

Redmond organised a national convention in April 1912 to rally support around the Home Rule Bill. No women were admitted. Tom Kettle, husband of Hanna's sister Mary and an ally of the IWFL, reneged on his promise to move a resolution that votes be given to women under the new parliament; he was also an MP, and unwilling to oppose Redmond, his leader. *The Irish Citizen* (the suffrage paper edited by Francis Sheehy Skeffington and James Cousins, husbands of IWFL members) reliably reported that Kettle felt obliged to choose the preservation of nationalist unity, once Redmond had made plain his feelings (3 August, 1912).

In retaliation, a mass meeting of women was held in the Antient Concert Rooms on 1 June. Nineteen organisations sent delegates from all parts of Ireland to demand the inclusion of female suffrage in the Home Rule Bill. Mary Hayden, Professor of Modern Irish History in University College Dublin (UCD), and a member of the ISLGA, chaired the meeting. Her address summed up most people's feelings: that the new Ireland to be initiated would be a sham if it was based on the unjust principle of the exclusion of women. A more war-like note was struck by Hanna Sheehy Skeffington, who warned that if the resolution was ignored, women would 'find other ways' of pursuing their claims. She emphasised the urgency of the occasion by stressing the fact that if the franchise remained as it was, then under the provisions of the Home Rule Bill, it would remain so for the first three years of the new state's existence. This was women's last chance for constitutional agitation to prevent the establishment of a wholly male legislature.

This mobilisation of feminist opinion was a unique occasion in Irish political life. At a time of enormous tension, unionist and nationalist came together to voice women's outrage at this cavalier dismissal of their demand for equal citizenship. Mary Hayden made the point that all joined together on this one issue without sacrificing their individual political opinions — what was being demanded was a point of principle, not home rule. Mrs Cope, of the Armagh Suffrage Society, summed up this remarkable degree of unity:

> I write from the purely Unionist point of view. But it seems to me imperative that all women, of whatever political party, should now stand for a great principle — the principle that no democratic Government can be considered complete which ignores not only a class but a whole sex. It is because I know we are one in standing for this that I would gladly have joined you on your platform tonight (*The Irish Citizen* 15 June, 1912).

The resolution was sent to all Irish MPs and to the cabinet. It was ignored. No one held out hopes that the last resort of a private member's amendment would succeed.

The Liberal Government and the Irish Party had decided the terms of Irish independence; they were terms that completely excluded women, denying them citizenship. They would neither voice their opinion on the Home Rule Bill, nor participate in the new legislature. As all methods of peaceful persuasion had now failed, the IWFL decided it was time for militant action. In the early hours of 13 June, eight members of the IWFL symbolically struck out against the government by smashing the windows of the General Post Office, the Custom House and Dublin Castle. Two of the women received sentences of one month, the other six received six months in jail. There was little support from the public. As Hanna later explained 'Not only were we enemies of Home Rule, but rebels as women' (Sheehy Skeffington and Owens, *c.* 1975: 20). Undeterred, others followed: in the next two years there were thirty-six convictions for suffrage militancy in Ireland (Owens, 1977).

The WSPU comes to Dublin

This supposed connection between suffragism and anti-nationalism was bolstered by the activities of two members of the WSPU — Mary Leigh and Gladys Evans — who travelled over to Dublin in pursuit of Asquith, who had arrived in Ireland in July 1912 to reassure people of the Liberal determination to achieve home rule. He was to have a memorable visit. Irish suffragists met his boat, shouting slogans through megaphones and showering him with Votes for Women confetti as he and Redmond took part in a procession through the streets. All women and anyone known to have suffragist sympathies were barred from attending the Asquith meeting at the Theatre Royal, Dublin, although Francis Sheehy Skeffington, disguising himself as a clergyman, succeeded in evading the stewards. Before being thrown out he managed to shout 'Give votes to women. Stop forcible feeding of women prisoners. Put votes for women in the Home Rule Bill' (Cousins and Cousins, 1950: 187). But for WSPU activists, the time for heckling at meetings had long since passed. As Asquith was returning to his carriage, a small blunt hatchet was thrown at him; later that night, Leigh and Evans attempted to set fire to the theatre.

The furore aroused by the grazing of the Prime Minister's ear led to mob hysteria as news of the incident spread. Members of the IWFL who were holding a protest meeting nearby while the Asquith meeting proceeded, suddenly found themselves attacked by angry crowds. Many people made no distinction between the acts of Leigh and Evans and the less violent protests of the IWFL. The IWFL itself lost members, and the pages of *The Irish Citizen* were soon full of debate. The Cork branch of the Munster Women's Franchise League, in a letter written by its secretary, Mary MacSwiney, (in later years to be one of the most vehement of republicans) proclaimed its 'abhorrence of the wicked actions of the English suffragettes' (3 August, 1912). More surprisingly, the National Council of Sinn Féin defended the women, stating 'a principle is not to be condemned because of the methods of any of its advocates' (*Sinn Féin* 27 July, 1912). James Connolly made a special trip from Belfast to speak in solidarity at the next weekly meeting of the IWFL.

However, when Leigh and Evans came to trial, Arthur Griffith, founder of Sinn Féin, took the opportunity to hammer home his insular form of nationalism, complaining of the exploitation in political affairs of Irish women by English women. For this intervention he was soundly rebuked by Jenny Wyse Power, a veteran of the Ladies' Land League of the 1880s, and also an executive member of Sinn Féin: it was a 'woman's question' and one which would be resolved without men. She also cleverly appealed to the nationalist conscience by suggesting that those who had suffered at British hands should be 'slow in blaming women who have been goaded into revolution by the tactics of the present government' (*Sinn Féin* 24 August, 1912). Mary Leigh was given a three-year sentence, Gladys Evans a year's hard labour. Although the IWFL did not support their action, they refused to utter any condemnation because, as women, they were 'strictly within their rights' to use any means they considered effective (Sheehy Skeffington and Owens, *c.* 1975: 22). Four imprisoned IWFL members decided to hunger strike in sympathy, although almost at the end of their sentences. Leigh and Evans were force-fed, having immediately embarked on a hunger strike. They were eventually released on convict licence, although many more court appearances were to follow before they were able, in December, to return to England.

The Cat and Mouse Act
In England, the well-publicised horror of force-feeding was generating a sympathetic response to suffragette agonies and there were repeated calls for the government

to abandon the practice. In order to outwit the hunger-striking tactic and to circumvent the necessity for forcible feeding, Home Secretary McKenna in March 1913 introduced the Prisoners' Temporary Discharge for Ill-Health Act — aptly nick-named the Cat and Mouse Act, as by its provisions a prisoner could be released and re-arrested almost indefinitely. Of all the members of the Irish Party, only Tim Healy (the barrister who defended Leigh and Evans) voted against its enforcement. A storm of protest in Ireland led to a huge meeting in the Mansion House, at which women and men of many political persuasions gathered in condemnation of what chairman Tom Kettle described as 'a dangerous weapon of political oppression in the hands of any Government' (*The Irish Citizen*, 5 July, 1913). The Act was never enforced in Ireland, and released suffragists rejoiced 'that Irish public opinion will not tolerate prison cell persecution' (*The Irish Citizen*, 13 July, 1913). It was certainly true that the Irish, for historic reasons, had (and still have) strong feelings about the kind of treatment sustained by prisoners, but the non-implementation of the Cat and Mouse Act probably owed less to popular pressure than to the government's desire to avoid too much controversy while the home rule issue remained unresolved.

The WSPU arrives in Ulster

As we have seen, the WSPU began to take an interest in the Irish situation as a reaction to the nationalist refusal to support the suffrage movement. Ulster unionism was initially irrelevant, but by virtue of their increasing hostility towards the party of home rule, they now discovered an affinity with the women of the north-east of Ireland. It was a mirror-image of the WSPU's estrangement from Labour and the Liberals and subsequent wooing of the Conservatives — it was, after all, the joint Conservative *and* Unionist Party, and Bonar Law, Conservative leader, was a strong supporter of Ulster unionism.

Suffrage societies in the north were non-militant and generally careful to abstain from comment on the future of the province — although some groups, such as the Whitehead branch of the Irish Women's Suffrage Federation, were reported to have concluded their meetings with the singing of the national anthem, a jingoistic procedure not normally associated with suffrage activities (*Belfast Newsletter* 5 February, 1914). But the groups were small, particularly in comparison with the numbers who flocked to join the Ulster Unionist Women's Council, the majority of whom were decidedly anti-feminist, disregarding 'the offer of citizenship, even when put before them by their own leaders', as a correspondent in *The Irish Citizen* indignantly remarked (9 May 1914). Yet suddenly, in this unpromising atmosphere of self-sacrifice and militarism, it seemed as if women's demands were finally going to be granted.

In September 1913 Dawson Bates, secretary of the Ulster Unionist Council, informed the Ulster Unionist Women's Council that the draft articles for a provisional government (which would be set up in protest if home rule was implemented) included provisions for the enfranchisement of women (Rosen, 1974: 229). This completely unexpected move quickly led to congratulations, with *The Irish Citizen* rather naïvely predicting that an additional benefit of the gesture would be a decrease in nationalist hostility towards Ulster secession, because of their overwhelming desire to see at least some Irish women obtaining the vote. Some claimed this change of heart to be a belated recognition of the hard work of the women auxiliaries; the more cynical saw in it a pre-emptive move to ensure that they remained within the ranks. For its part, the IWFL attributed the credit to Mrs Priestly McCracken, who had devoted considerable energy to arguing with unionist women that they had a right to expect recognition as citizens. The WSPU however had their own views and announced that they were responsible for the decision because the week before Dawson Bates' letter was made public, the organisation had declared its intention of initiating a campaign in the north in order to coerce Carson into giving women the vote.

This assumption of WSPU superiority provoked an angry reaction in Ireland and letters poured into the offices of *The Irish Citizen*. Mrs Chambers of the Irish Women's Suffrage Society wrote to say she considered their presence in Belfast to be 'wholly superfluous', and even the mild-mannered Louie Bennett was incensed enough to declare:

> We Irish women must all resent the independent interference of any English organisation in our political affairs. English suffragists cannot do any work for us in Ireland unless they co-operate with us and allow themselves to be guided by our more intimate knowledge of the Irish people and Irish affairs (20 September, 1913).

Despite these reactions, the WSPU appointed Dorothy Evans, an experienced activist, as Ulster organiser and a branch was established in Belfast. Mrs Priestly McCracken was an early recruit and by the following April the Irish Women's Suffrage Society had been disbanded as so many of its members had joined the WSPU.

It soon appeared that Dawson Bates had been premature in making his generous proposal. Carson had never made a secret of his implacable opposition to female suffrage, and when he was challenged he revealed the disunity that existed. Evans revealed a series of letters with Carson, reminding him of his 'solemn pledge' to the women of Ulster. She demanded an assurance that no matter what the final constitutional settlement, be it a maintenance of the union, or a separate Ulster government (significantly, not home rule), the enfranchisement of women would be an integral part. Carson eventually replied, stating that as his party had divergent views on the question, he had no authority to give any such assurance. A deputation from the northern committee of the Irish Women's Suffrage Federation also met Carson, receiving the same reply (*Belfast Newsletter* 7 and 24 March, 1914). The following day, Dorothy Evans led a deputation of Ulster women to London, where they camped outside Carson's house. He declared himself to be ill and unable to meet the women, although not ill enough to turn away male colleagues. Evans had warned of the consequences if the pledge was broken. After the deputation had sat on camp stools in the pouring rain for several days, it became obvious that the promise had been retracted.

The WSPU declares war on the Ulster Unionists

The WSPU response was swift and unambiguous: war was declared upon the Ulster Unionists. A week later, on 27 March, they set fire to Abbeylands, in the grounds of which the Ulster Unionists held their military drill. The cost was reckoned at £20,000. Of the seven arson attacks committed by the WSPU between 10 April and 3 May, five occurred in Ulster (Rosen 1974: 230).

On 22 July, Dorothy Evans, Madge Muir and Mary Lamour were tried for possession of explosives and for committing arson. As they refused to cooperate with the court, they were remanded in custody, but released after hunger striking (*Belfast Newsletter* 22 July, 1914). After a small explosion at Lisburn Cathedral, Mrs Metge, Dorothy Evans, Maud Wickham and Miss D. Carson (no relation!) were all hurriedly rounded up by the police, but again released after hunger-striking.

Despite this non-use of the Cat and Mouse Act, the WSPU came in for harsh treatment by the law, with thirteen of its members arrested in a six-month period (Owens, 1977). A blind eye was, however, turned towards the posturings of the Ulster Volunteer Force, reflecting both the hysteria created by the activities of the WSPU, and the influential friends of the Ulster unionists. For example, while the WSPU offices in Belfast were raided and the women held on conspiracy charges, the UVF leaders could with impunity threaten armed resistance to any constitutional settlement. The WSPU, along with all the suffrage groups, had been banned from holding meetings in the parks of central London, yet the Ulster Defence League was given permission to hold a rally in Hyde Park. In protest, the WSPU held a counter demonstration. Mrs Pankhurst remarked bitterly that 'The militant men were allowed to speak in defence of bloodshed but Mrs Drummond was arrested before she had uttered more than a few words' (Pankhurst, 1979: 346). Christabel began calling for the arrest of Carson and Bonar Law, arguing that if they were not arrested, then the sentences on the women should be cancelled, as both groups were calling for their right to be British citizens (Rosen, 1974: 230).

While Christabel's logic was incontrovertible, not all feminists were calling for the right to be British citizens. The IWFL might insist that their demand concerned the principle of equal citizenship for women and men, regardless of political context, but their political practice had demonstrated the impossibility of abstracting the issue from current events. Hanna Sheehy Skeffington in fact admitted that in Belfast they were regarded as 'tainted with Nationalism' (Sheehy Skeffington and Owens, c. 1975: 16), and the IWFL had not been able to establish branches of their organisation in the north. The difference not only in tactics, but also with regard to ultimate objectives, was becoming increasingly evident.

The disintegration of the feminist movement

By 1914, the partition of Ireland was being suggested as a solution to the political impasse. James Connolly predicted 'a carnival of reaction' north and south if this occurred (Berresford Ellis, 1973: 275). The unity of all progressive forces was an urgent necessity, but the divisions were surfacing. Unionist women were predictably aghast at those who had 'not patriotism enough' to stand up for their country 'in this awful crisis', instead of going to London to argue with Carson, as 'Common-Sense Ulsterwoman' complained, angry at the temerity of Dorothy Evans (*Belfast Newsletter* 24 March, 1914). But instead of feminists uniting to justify their campaign for the vote, regardless of the political situation, the IWFL now felt itself forced publicly to disassociate itself from the WSPU by taking to court Lelia and Rosalind Cadiz after the sisters refused to accept expulsion. The executive of the IWFL affirmed in court that the women were working 'entirely' for the WSPU, whose militancy they considered 'ill-judged, misdirected and ineffective' (*Belfast Newsletter* 24 March, 1914).

But the WSPU was not to remain in Ireland much longer. At the outbreak of war, the WSPU's offices were hastily abandoned in an obedient response to the Pankhurst directive to suspend militancy in order to fight 'the German peril'. Other feminists were infuriated that the avowedly feminist organisation should show such a 'lack of political acumen' as to express an opinion on a war that was undertaken without any consultation of women and, having expressed that opinion, simply to leave when the suffrage and home rule issues were still 'matters of eager controversy'. Now that the WSPU was no longer part of the Irish women's movement, all constraints on voicing the extent of the rupture had disappeared. English intervention was condemned as interference, undertaken 'without regard to the welfare of its Irish members or the actualities of the Irish situation'. The sudden withdrawal of the WSPU 'amply justified' these objections and angered many of its former members (*The Irish Citizen* 22 August, 1914). It was never made clear what policy they intended to pursue, but by this stage there were few opportunities for suffrage propaganda in any part of the country.

The Home Rule Bill finally became law in September, but was immediately shelved until the end of the First World War. The problem of Ulster had still not been resolved and armed conflict appeared ever more likely as men continued to join the Ulster Volunteers and the Irish Volunteers. Political allegiances had no convenient geographic delineation: there were unionist women in the south of Ireland, nationalist women in the north. Would it be possible for them to retain (or develop) feminist sympathies while faced with the prospect of incorporation into a new state they opposed? Francis Sheehy Skeffington saw the two ideologies of feminism and pacifism as indivisible entities: their antithesis the male cult of violence. He was prepared to admit that feminism did not necessarily entail holding the same political views, but affirmed his belief in the potentially constructive qualities of feminism. In this hope, he began to urge unionist women in the south to adopt a realistic approach to the situation: accepting that home rule was on the cards, they should now work to ensure representation of women in the new parliament. And Ulster women should also continue to work for the suffrage cause, as insurance policy (if Ulster did opt out of home rule) against being abandoned by Carson as nationalist women had been by Redmond (*The Irish*

Citizen 1 October, 1914). Militarism on the other hand not only reinforced divisions between people, it meant also that women were fighting for objectives that had not been defined by them. This was evident in the war fever surrounding the conduct of the First World War. The Munster Women's Franchise League decided to devote its energies into forming an ambulance corps and banned *The Irish Citizen* — the only woman's paper in Ireland — from its office because of its anti-war views (*The Irish Citizen* 25 November, 1914). Nationalists like Mary MacSwiney resigned from the group, which now became entirely unionist in sympathy.

Cumann na mBan: The Irish Volunteers and the feminists
Cumann na mBan had been formed for the purpose of 'advancing the cause of Irish liberty and assisting the arming and equipping of Irishmen for the defence of Ireland' (Ward, 1980: 101). The women were not given seats on the Volunteer executive, but had their own executive. This 'separate but equal' formula gave rise to absolute inequality as women were regarded as subordinates and excluded from the decision-making process. Sheehy Skeffington, in an open letter to his friend Thomas MacDonagh, director of training of the Volunteers, had polemicised against the exclusion of women, believing that such a dismissal summed up the reactionary nature of the movement: formed to fight for Irish freedom, but not prepared to extend the concept to women (*The Irish Citizen* 22 May, 1915). It was this relegation of women that so infuriated feminists — not the fact that women were involved in the nationalist movement. In itself, this was a tacit acceptance (by some feminists at least) of the inevitability of extra-parliamentary means to resolve the nationalist question — and many feminists had by now lost all faith in the parliamentary process. But the Volunteer movement refused to commit itself to support for women's enfranchisement as it was a broadly-based movement and amongst its members were some notorious anti-suffragists. In June 1914 Redmond managed to inveigle control over the Volunteers (in order to preserve unity, militant nationalists remained silent) and feminist fury

exploded. Not only were women excluded from the Volunteer executive, and were confined to meekly raising money for the men, but they were actually working for the man who had opposed women being given the vote in the new Ireland. Hanna Sheehy Skeffington in exasperation dismissed Cumann na mBan as merely an 'animated collecting box for men', whose 'blind sacrifice' was accustoming men to 'acquiesce in women's enslavement' (*The Irish Citizen* 12 June, 1915). During the internal manoeuverings of the Volunteers, Cumann na mBan remained neutral; only one prominent member publicly denounced her executive for not opposing Redmond's leadership.

Some leading members of Cumann na mBan had been active suffragists, but now that nationalist women had acquired a public identity, they withdrew from the suffrage movement: women could only be emancipated *after* the national issue had been resolved. To ask Britain for the vote was to accept Britain's right to rule (although it did not appear to be anti-nationalist to ask Britain for home rule). Even Countess Markievicz, President of Cumann na mBan, admitted that the organisation's main function was 'to collect funds for the men to spend', a process which she believed demoralised women and deprived them of initiative and independence (*The Irish Citizen* 23 October, 1915). At this time she was far more involved in Connolly's Citizen Army, which accepted women and men on an equal basis. Markievicz did not take Cumann na mBan seriously until after the 1916 Rising, by which time the organisation had changed considerably as the new recruits took on a much more active military role in response to the demands of guerrilla warfare.

War and its aftermath

Feminists had lost the battle as far as the Home Rule Bill was concerned. They had also failed to maintain unity amongst the various suffrage groups, which disintegrated under the combined impact of world war and threatened civil war. The appeal to women's specific interests turned out to be too fragile to withstand these competing interests. Although the IWFL and the Irish Women's

Reform League retained a pacifist stance, seeking to unite women of all nations, and an Irish section of the Women's International League for Peace and Freedom, they were by now a tiny grouping. The Irish Women's Reform League remained hostile to nationalist claims, but an important event occurred which reconciled at least one section of the suffragists to the nationalist movement, in the process vindicating their single-minded campaign of the last decade: the Republican Proclamation of 1916, read out by Pearse in front of the GPO at the start of the Easter Rising, affirmed the equal citizenship of Irish men and Irish women. Hanna Sheehy Skeffington was informed of this by Connolly before the Rising took place and although it was obviously Connolly who insisted on its inclusion; the groundwork for its acceptance had been achieved through the work of the feminists (Fox, 1935: 140). A measure of the esteem in which Hanna Sheehy Skeffington personally was held is evident from the fact that republican plans for a civil provisional government, should the Rising be protracted, included Hanna as one of the five members (O'Shannon 1959: 68). The proclamation, through the martyr's death of its signatories, became a revered document amongst nationalists: there was no way the new leadership could renege on this promise.

Although Cumann na mBan never became a feminist organisation, its emphasis changed under the impact of the realisation that they were fighting for the freedom of women as well as the 'nation'. Their Convention in 1918 reflected this, as the aims were altered to state that the funds they collected were now to be used for the arming and equipping of the men and women of Ireland.

The antagonism between the IWFL and Cumann na mBan dissolved in the trauma of the Rising, while the brutal murder of Francis Sheehy Skeffington, killed although a non-combatant, contributed towards his widow's deepening identification with the nationalist cause. When the British government gave women over thirty the vote in 1918, Cumann na mBan and the IWFL joined together to campaign for the imprisoned Countess Markievicz, who became the first woman to be elected to Westminster — but as a Sinn Féin member, she boycotted

Westminster in favour of the Republican Dáil Eireann, the provisional Irish Parliament. Louie Bennett took over editorship of *The Irish Citizen*, which now became a forum for all women's organisations, particularly trade unions. When the Black and Tans smashed up the type in 1920, Irish women lost their only means of communication. The small, autonomous women's movement gradually disappeared, its only sign of life being occasional reunions of the old IWFL members. Cumann na mBan absorbed most of the politically active women while some of the Citizen Army members now turned their attention towards building up the Irish Women Workers' Union.

The early years of the new state's life were difficult times: the war with Britain had ended only to be followed by a civil war which divided families and friends. The six northern counties, formed in 1921 into a 'Protestant Parliament for a Protestant People', withdrew into a bitter, sectarian isolation — Hanna Sheehy Skeffington was to serve a short jail sentence in 1931 for daring to defy an exclusion order served upon her by the unionists. And although the twenty-six-county state gave women over twenty-one the vote after the Treaty election, in recognition of women's work during the War of Independence, and in accordance with the provision of the 1916 Proclamation, it was a bitter victory. This was in fact the last piece of progressive legislation concerning women that would be passed until a new generation of Irish feminists began to raise insistent voices fifty years later.

Conclusions

Was the 1922 extension of the franchise a recognition of women's right to equal citizenship, or an attempt to cajole the irreconcilables of Cumann na mBan into acceptance of the Treaty? In other words, had the suffrage movement succeeded in establishing the principle that women were to be given full political rights in an independent Ireland? The work performed by Cumann na mBan is often considered to have been the decisive factor, but while it was obviously instrumental in convincing some of the diehards that women were actually capable of working outside the domestic sphere, it was the feminists who had insisted that this was their right. Their campaign ten years earlier had forced the issue into the political vocabulary of the current nationalist leaders: feminists had defined the terms of reference and in extracting a later commitment to reform, Cumann na mBan simply restated the arguments.

The disintegration of the suffrage movement was not unique to Ireland; confronted with the obscenity of the First World War, feminist and socialist movements world-wide had crumbled in horrified confusion. What is remarkable is the fact that the Irish movement had remained united for so long under the most difficult of circumstances. But Ireland was also a country torn apart by internal political conflict and it would have been wholly artificial to have insisted upon the preservation of a movement whose only demand was a woman's right to vote. The pity was that in losing the suffrage movement, Irish women lost their only independent voices as nothing emerged in its place. With no organisation to give priority to women's needs, post-partition Ireland was able to implement, with little resistance, highly reactionary policies in relation to women, whose domestic role within the family became endowed with almost sacramental qualities. Only now is the confessional nature of the Irish state undergoing serious re-examination. It is a challenge which has coincided with the emergence of a regenerated Irish feminism that has learned the necessity of maintaining an autonomous organisation.

References and further reading

Berresford Ellis, P. 1973. *James Connolly: Selected Writings*. Pelican, London.

Cousins, J. H. and Cousins, M. E. 1950. *We Two Together*. Talbot, India.

Fox, R. M. *Rebel Irishwomen*. 1935. Talbot, Dublin and Cork.

Fox, R. M. *c.* 1958. *Louie Bennett*. Talbot, Dublin.

Harrison, B. 1978. *Separate Spheres: The Opposition to Women's Suffrage in Britain*. Croom Helm, London.

Kingham, N. 1975. *United We Stood*. Appletree, Belfast.

Luddy, M. and Murphy, C. (eds). 1989. *Women Surviving*. Poolbeg Press, Dublin.

Morgan, D. 1975. *Suffragists and Liberals*. Blackwell, Oxford.

Murphy, C. 1989. *The Women's Suffrage Movement and Irish Society in the Early Twentieth Century*. Harvester Wheatsheaf, Brighton.

O'Shannon, C. 1959. *Fifty Years of Liberty Hall*. Four Candles, Dublin.

Owens, R. C. 1984. *Smashing Times: A History of the Irish Suffrage Movement*. Attic Press, Dublin.

Owens, R. C. 1977. 'Votes for Women: Irish Women's Campaign for the vote 1876-1915'. MA Thesis, University College, Dublin.

Pankhurst, E. 1979. *My Own Story*. Virago, London.

Pankhurst, S. 1977. *The Suffragette Movement*. Virago, London.

Rosen, A. 1974. *Rise Up Women*. Routledge and Kegan Paul, London.

Sheehy Skeffington, H. *c.* 1975. 'Reminiscences of an Irish Suffragette'. In *Votes for Women: Irish Women's Struggle for the Vote*. Edited and published by A.D. Sheehy Skeffington and R. C. Owens. Dublin.

Ward, M. 1980. 'Marginality and Militancy: Cumann na mBan 1914-1936'. In Morgan A. and Purdie, B. (eds.), *Ireland: Divided Nation, Divided Class*. Inklinks, London.

Ward, M. 1991. *The Missing Sex: Putting Women into Irish History*. Attic Press, LIP Pamphlet, Dublin.

Ward, M. 1983. *Unmanageable Revolutionaries: Women and Irish Nationalism*. Brandon, Dingle/Pluto, London.

Discussion topics

1 How did the Home Rule question affect Irish women's campaign for the vote? Consider the impact of the issue upon nationalist and unionist women as well as the various suffrage groups.

2 What were the main differences between the IWFL and the WSPU? Were these differences over tactics, or did they have wider political implications?

3 How important was the Irish Party in determining the likelihood of franchise reform passing through the House of Commons?

4 Consider the arguments put forward in justification of suffrage militancy. How effective were the actions of the IWFL in the South and the WSPU in the North?

5 What was the impact of the First World War on the different suffrage organisations?

6 What do you think were the reasons for Irishwomen over the age of twenty-one obtaining the vote in 1922?

Political Interest and Participation of Irish Women 1922 — 1992: The Unfinished Revolution

Frances Gardiner

In common with international experience, Irish women are underrepresented in decision-making fora, be it national parliament, civil service, trade union, employer or farmer organisations. This gendered hierarchy of power is equally evident in the media, educational and legal institutions. It is usual to regard the Dáil, the lower house of the Irish parliament, as the main policy-making arena. While women TDs have always been few in number, the early 1980s brought an increase, with women winning 14 of the 166 Dáil seats in 1982. This modest figure slumped in the 1989 election, but was recently reversed in the first election of the 1990s (November 1992) to reach its highest level in seven decades.

The comparative context

Discussion of women's political representation inevitably looks to the Scandinavian countries, for long a reference point for pioneers of political equality. In Northern Europe, the Republic of Ireland remains a Catholic anomaly in a predominantly Protestant cultural environment. But, as one of the smaller democracies of Europe, relative geographical adjacency, and formative historical Viking links, combined with early enfranchisement and use of proportional representation in multi-member constit-uencies for elections, mark some points of similarity between Ireland and the Nordic countries. Surprising, perhaps, but almost half a century ago, more than twenty years post-suffrage, Irish women's parliamentary representation exceeded that of Danish and Norwegian women (see Table 1).

Table 1: Women as % Lower House 1943

Ireland	Iceland	Denmark	Norway
2.2	0.0	1	1

Sources: Haavio-Mannila, 1985; Dept. of the Environment, Dublin.

Fifty years later, this coincidence seems like an historical illusion. A cursory look reveals strikingly different advances in the comparative position of Irish and Scandinavian women (see Table 2). Ireland, which up to and during the 1980s occupied a median position in the hierarchy of female parliamentary representation, then fell back to a residual category with only one woman for every thirteen legislators.

It could be argued that this comparison is unfair, that most European countries fall far short of the success of the Scandinavians. Yet the degree of disparity in many cases was not as great as in Ireland prior to the 1992 election. Of nineteen Western democracies, few shared the distinction of having fewer women parliamentarians entering the 1990s than the 1980s, most countries showing an upward trend. In Luxembourg, Spain, Italy, West Germany (as it then was), as well as Canada and New Zealand, percentages went from single to double figures. While Ireland joined this latter group in the last election, the Scandinavian lead cannot be ignored.

Table 2: Women as % Lower House, April, 1992

Ireland	Iceland	Denmark	Sweden	Norway	Finland
7.8	20.6	33.7	37.8	35.8	38.4

Sources: Embassies; Dept. of the Environment, Dublin; Gallagher, Laver and Mair (1992).

Clearly some facilitating mechanisms present in these countries must be absent in Ireland, or conversely, some impediments peculiar to Irish society function to bar women's entry to political elites.

Suffrage and separatism: A zero-sum experience
Irish women experienced a double incentive to political mobilisation — as suffragists and freedom fighters — in the early years of the century. Yet these causes evinced contrary reactions. On the one hand, antipathy to women's suffrage was expressed by the churches, political parties and their leaders, and public opinion, including some women. Owens (1984: 45) documents the Catholic Church's view that 'allowing women the right of suffrage is incompatible with the Catholic ideal of the unity of domestic life'. Deportation for militant suffrag-

ettes was advocated in a Protestant church gazette in
1914. Hanna Sheehy Skeffington, an Irish suffragist,
recalls the Irish MP John Dillon arguing that giving
women the right to vote would be the ruin of western
civilisation, destroying the home, and challenging the
Godgiven headship of man within the home (Sheehy
Skeffington and Owens, 1975: 18).

Militant activity by suffragists was severely sanctioned, imprisonment of the women contrasting with the
treatment of women's activism in the national struggle,
which gained total acceptance. Nationalists opined that it
was unpatriotic of the suffragists to seek the vote whilst
Ireland remained under British rule, promising that once
home rule was attained suffrage would be granted by an
Irish, not a foreign, parliament.

It would be misleading, however, to equate popular
hostility to women's suffrage simply with revulsion at its
concession from a British parliament. Overt verbal and
physical intimidation of suffragists, imprisonment of
women for acts of civic disobedience such as breaking
windows in government property, the force-feeding of
some suffragists who resorted to hunger strike as protest,
all reflected rising tensions in which national, industrial
and gender struggles overlapped. For separatist nationalists, denunciation of suffrage misdemeanours ironically
coincided with their own preparation for markedly
stronger forms of violence (see Owens, 1984).

Of course, opposition to enfranchising women was not
unique to Ireland. In some countries the suffrage struggle
was more strongly militant than was the case in Ireland.
But few simultaneously endured a divisive national
independence struggle. Ultimately, at least on the surface,
both appeared to triumph. In reality, a budding feminist
political consciousness was subsumed by nationalist
hegemony.

Irish women over thirty years of age and men over
twenty-one were enfranchised from Westminster under
the Representation of the People Act 1918. Women over
twenty-one were fully enfranchised under the Irish Free
State Constitution of 1922, on achieving independence
from Britain. Most commentators tend to overemphasise
the breakthrough that getting the vote represented. It

was, as was realised later, but the first small step in political liberation for women.

Women candidates: why so few ?

The number of women seeking political office in Ireland in the decades following independence was minimal. There were five women in the Dáil (lower house) in 1923, two more than in 1943. In 1952, thirty years after independence, there were still fewer women in elected politics than in 1922 (Manning, 1987:156). Four decades later, in early 1992, the Dáil had but thirteen women deputies, while only forty-four different women deputies had ever been elected since the foundation of the state (Gallagher 1990: 87).

Table 3: Women in Irish General Elections by decade

	Candidates			Elected		
Year	Total N	W cands	W as %	Total N	W	W as%
1923	377	7	1.9	153	5	3.3
1933	246	6	2.4	153	3	1.9
1943	354	9	2.5	138	3	2.2
1954	303	6	1.9	147	5	3.4
1969	373	11	2.9	144	3	2.1
1977	375	25	6.6	148	6	4.1
1982b	365	31	8.5	166	14	8.4
1989	371	53	13.8	166	13	7.8
Total	2764	148	5.3	1215	52	4.2

Sources: Dept. of the Environment; Nealon, T. 1974. Ireland: A Parliamentary Directory 1973-4; Nealon's Guide to the 25th Dáil & Seanad; Nealon's Guide to the 26th Dáil & Seanad; Magill Book of Irish Politics, 1983; *Political Parties.*

It has been noted that, following enfranchisement, women's political activity often seemed to recede, as if the effort of getting the vote had left suffragists temporarily exhausted. But, in many countries, within a matter of decades a remobilisation occurred. This contrasted with the Irish experience, where women appeared to lose motivation to reinstate feminist concerns on the political agenda, or to participate in the shaping of the new state. Several reasons can be identified to account for this:

1 Nationalism had split the suffragists, diminishing their personal ambition, with republican sympathies further

strengthened by the execution of leaders of the 1916 Easter rebellion.

2 Connolly, the Labour leader and arguably the most ardent supporter of the suffragists outside their immediate families, was among those executed, thereby removing a significant constituency of support. Connolly's death, and the decision by Labour not to contest the 1918 election in order not to split the nationalist vote had far-reaching effects on women's political future. The weakness of the Left in Ireland today has been linked with this failure to jump on the political roundabout at this historically significant time. If the Lipset-Rokkan hypothesis (1967) can help analyse the cleavages in Irish politics (Sinnott, 1987), and there is no universal consensus that it does (Carty, 1983), it might also help to explain why such a vibrant feminist political activism apparently atrophied after 1918. Gender, as a cross-cutting cleavage, was of insufficient significance at that historically vital juncture, fragmented as it was by nationalism, and was 'frozen out' of the mould of Irish politics afterwards. However, women's activism in the election of that year was vital, both as voters and party workers (Owens, 1984: 127). It is evident in the election results, with the newly expanded electorate returning a landslide victory for Sinn Féin and the women's vote reacting against the Irish Parliamentary Party (IPP), which had vigorously opposed women's suffrage. Up to then the IPP had been the main organ of political representation in Ireland, as well as holding the balance of power in Westminster after the 1910 election. As MacCurtain puts it, Irish women had a 'political education over the previous twenty years not often afforded to a generation of women' (1978: 54-55).

3 The debate over the Anglo-Irish Treaty in 1922 further divided women, with their speeches showing 'inflexible and doctrinaire republicanism'. Five of the six women in the lower house in 1919 were related to men executed in 1916, so the sublimation of feminism into nationalism was an easy step. The abstentionist policy of the anti-Treatyites after independence from Britain prevented those female deputies from taking their seats until 1927, depriving them of the first-hand experience of govern-

ment essential to developing parliamentary skills. The dissolution and reorganisation which characterised party activity in the late 1920s also dislodged women from traditional political affiliations.

4 This diminishing public visibility was aided by the sociological changes wrought on the new state. The first decade of independence saw ethnocentric suspicion of foreign influences, especially in matters of morality, with films already under censorship by 1923, and the passage in 1929 of the Censorship of Publications Act. (Ward, 1983). This social caution was mirrored by increased conservatism towards women. The Conditions of Employment Bill 1935 deliberately sought to exclude women from areas of the labour force because they might take work away from men.

5 Not one woman took part in drafting the 1937 Irish Constitution, *Bunreacht na hEireann*. The now famous Article 41 can be regarded as an implicit denial of freedom of choice to women in personal matters.

> 1.1 The State recognises the Family as the natural primary and fundamental unit group of Society, and as a moral institution possessing inalienable rights, antecedent and superior to all positive law.

> 1.2. The State, therefore, guarantees to protect the Family in its constitution and authority, as the necessary basis of social order and as indispensable to the welfare of the Nation and the State.

> 2.1 In particular, the State recognises that by her life within the home, woman gives to the State a support without which the common good cannot be achieved.

> 2.2 The State, shall, therefore, endeavour to ensure that mothers shall not be obliged by economic necessity to engage in labour to the neglect of their duties in the home.

Scannell (1988: 125) sees it, at worst, as the 'grossest form of sexual stereotyping', or at best 'rationalised by an attitude of romantic paternalism'. Although it invoked heated protests from women, Eamon de Valera, the Taoiseach, refused to delete it. This constitutional vision of the role of woman in Irish society as fulltime wife and mother in an indissoluble marriage tallies with the earlier resistance to the enfranchisement of women. Political activism would be completely at variance with this comfortable homemaker role. Even work outside the home, as Scannell points out, was regarded as a selfish distraction from home duties.

6 A public furore greeted the Mother and Child Scheme in the late 1940s, a plan to provide state health care for pregnant women, construed as an intrusion by the state into the privacy of the family, and rejected by the government of the day. Its failure was later viewed as reflecting church dominance over the social policy of the state (Whyte, 1971; Lee, 1985). The Civil Service Act 1956 was to provide that the majority of women in the civil service would be required to resign on marriage, crowning almost four decades of increasingly authoritarian legislation, which curbed women's self-determination to the extent that political involvement wsa severely curtailed, if not actually impossible, for most women, save as political wife, sister or mother.

It was not until 1969, over fifty years after getting the vote that the number of women candidates reached double figures, 11 contesting the election of that year. In Denmark, by contrast, 164 women contested the 1968 election, and 354 women contested the 1969 election in Norway.

Feminist issues on the political agenda
Women's political remobilisation in Ireland was catalysed during the 1970s. The virtual absence of women among the legislative élite, with only three female deputies among the 144 in the Dáil in 1970, awakened a resolve that women should be encouraged to participate in the running of public affairs. At the same time, in common with most Western democracies, the second wave of the women's movement boosted political consciousness regarding specifically female issues. From now on, women's pressure groups highlighted legal, educational, political and social as well as economic inequalities, and lobbied for reform.

It was in 1970 also that the Irish government set up a commission on the status of women, chaired by Dr Thekla Beere, the only Irish woman ever to reach top office in the civil service, then Secretary of the Department of Transport and Power. This initiative, a response to the UN Decade for Women, was symbolic in legitimating women's claims of injustice, its report three years later cataloguing the anomalies governing women's lives. Its moderate tone pleased both government and public alike (Arnold, 1987), and marked a watershed in the development of women's rights, and their admission to the political agenda. The Council for the Status of Women, an umbrella group for women's organisations, was established in 1973.

Of these groups, the Women's Political Association, a voluntary organisation formed to educate and support aspiring women politicians, proved itself a training ground for some women, whose leadership experience and taste for politics were to lead to Dáil careers. Pursued by the parties as electoral assets, many joined the established parties and got selected as candidates, or were imposed on constituencies by the party hierarchies. Sections on women's issues graced election manifestoes. For a while it seemed that concern for women's issues would perpetuate this novel platform for women activists, and retain legislators' goodwill.

As in other areas of government, it was easier to exact reforms that did not involve financial outlay. In 1974 the Supreme Court ruled that the ban on the importation of contraceptives was unconstitutional. The 1927 Juries Act was also successfully challenged in the Supreme Court that year. Women would now be eligible for jury service. Judicial review in Ireland is a legal route used by women where the frequency and success of their constitutional cases has been impressive.

In 1976 a report held that thirty-six of the forty-nine recommendations of the Commission on the Status of Women had been effected. Membership of the European Community enforced implementation of some other equality measures for women, creating the illusion, following *de jure* legislation, that equal opportunity now prevailed.

The propensity for women to organise around issues of importance to them is a striking feature of Irish politics in the broad sense. Bearing in mind the trend over the past two decades among Europeans to resort to social movements as a method of expressing dissatisfaction with political parties in meeting their needs (Steiner, 1991;

Gallagher, Laver and Mair, 1992), Irish women's activism follows a similar path. The Council for the Status of Women (CSW) encompasses almost one hundred women's organisations, representing a broad range of views and issues. Constituent organisations themselves lobby individually on their own behalf also. The writing of letters and visiting TDs at their clinics suggest that women have utilised the existing clientelist framework to highlight their interests, although some would say not forcefully enough. It is largely due to the efforts of the CSW and the persistence of individual women's groups that there is a growing awareness of the ubiquity of inequality.

The 1980s witnessed the empowerment of community groupings to articulate general interests. Women have been to the fore in these mainstream lobbies for community amenities, including a marine rescue service, various environmental issues, and an army wives lobby on behalf of their soldier husbands who lacked a representative organ. Some groups formally disbanded once their demands had been met by government.

The influence of these pressure groups raises the question of the decline of parliament as a policy shaping forum (Gardiner, 1992a). It further suggests that pressure from the outside is essential to influencing decision makers, especially given the dearth of women within parliament. The signals imply that, as far as women's interests are concerned, in Ireland pressure on the Dáil from the outside, whether from women's groups or the European Community has achieved more than legislative pressure within (Gardiner, 1992b).

Labour force v legislature

Participation in the paid workforce has frequently been linked with heightened political consciousness. The bar on married women working in the public service was removed in 1973, and the Employment Equality Act, 1977, prohibited discrimination on grounds of sex or marital status in recruitment, training or provision of opportunities for promotion. In 1961, only 29 per cent of all women and 5 per cent of married women were in the labour force (Blackwell, 1982: 49). The most striking change in the intervening thirty years is the increased number of married women working. While women comprised 31.6 per cent of the total labour force in 1990, and 33 per cent of the employed labour force, married women's share increased fivefold to 25 per cent (ICTU, 1992). Married women now form 41.5 per cent of the female labour force.

But if their workforce participation continued to increase, it remained difficult for women to obtain satisfactory access to the competitive arena of electoral politics. The high point for women during the 1980s came in November 1982, when 14 women were elected to the Dáil. The increase in parliamentary seats, from 148 to 166 in 1981 may have widened electoral opportunity for women in the 1981/82 elections. But almost immediately, the impact of worldwide recession and spiralling public debt reclaimed legislators' attention and dominated the party manifestoes at election time, relegating women's issues and their espousers to the sidelines. Parties now seemed less open to women candidates focusing on women's concerns alone.

Even as recently as 1989, of the 53 women contesting the election of that year in Ireland, 14 stood as Independents (26 per cent), indicating either inability to get selected by the parties or disillusion with party politics in Ireland. Nevertheless, the scarcity of women candidates is also evident. That only 40-odd women candidates should have been nominated to contest 41 multi-member constituencies begs the question of whether the onus lies with the parties or women themselves. It would seem that women are reluctant political debutantes. Whether this is due to lack of political interest on the part of women themselves, as voters and candidates, rather than party hostility to selecting women candidates is not clear.

Voting intentions

The importance accorded to the act of voting varies, some interpreting the simple gesture as a socially conditioned response, requiring little real effort from the elector, and therefore of marginal consequence as an index of political participation. Others, including the suffragists, viewed the right to vote as a basic democratic freedom, exercise of which represented an important civil liberty. It is not my intention here to peruse the arguments, except to acknowledge that at least as an index of some level of political interest it is of value in estimating whether Irish women exercise the franchise as frequently as, and hold partisan views similar to, men.

Irish women, following an early propensity to turn out to vote, and despite decrease in overall turnout over the years, have continued to vote with increasing frequency. A gender gap of 9 per cent was noted in the June 1977 pre-election poll. This would seem to be at least partially confirmed by the response to the 1981 question asking respondents whether they voted in the 1977 election (see Table 5).

Table 5: Likelihoood of voting

	May 1977			June 1977		
	Total	Male	Female	Total	Male	Female
% Certain to vote	76	78	74	83	87	78
% Certain not to vote	3	4	2	2	1	3

Source: IMS, 1977.

Table 6: Whether voted in 1977 election

	Total	Male	Female
% Saying no	24	21	26

Source: IMS, 1981.

In the 1977 election turnout was 75.5 per cent on the day, which invites speculation on whether the gender gap simply reflects a more honest response from women. In recent elections turnout has fallen further, to 67.7 per cent in 1989. Yet women's propensity to vote has increased, and disinclination to vote decreased. By 1989, the poll closest to election day produced a reverse gender gap: 3 per cent of women as against 6 per cent of men indicated they would not vote in the forthcoming election, although statistically, allowing for margin of error none of these differences are significant (see Table 7).

Table 7: Current Voting Intentions (1977—1989)

%Will not Vote	1977(a)	1977(b)	1981	1982	1987	1989(a)	1989(b)
Total	4	2	2	3	4	9	5
Male	5	2	2	2	4	9	6
Female	3	3	1	3	4	8	3

Sources: IMS, 1977, 1981; MRBI 1987, 1989.

Indications of Irish women's increased voting frequency are reinforced by the Eurobarometer 1987 findings, when intention to vote at the next general election was explored. It was found that the number of 'certain' intentions to participate in a national election was equal for men and women in the Netherlands, Greece, Ireland and Germany, women in all the other EC member states expressing less certain voting intentions (*Women of Europe*, 1988).

If we can accept a hierarchy in degrees of political participation, then next to voting comes expressing interest in politics and political discussion, participation in public meetings or demonstrations, membership, active or passive, of a quasi-political or political organisation, and ultimately seeking or holding political or administrative office (Rush and Althoff, 1971: 76).

Political interest among Irish women

This section explores some of the literature on political interest, from Almond and Verba (1963) through Inglehart (1981), combining these with other Eurobarometer (1988, 1991) and Irish studies, e.g. Raven and Whelan's (1976) research on Irish political culture, and also contemporary opinion poll data on political interest.

Inglehart's study of West European women (1981) was among the first to incorporate data on gender differences in Irish political attitudes. Her conviction was that specific historical events had an 'enduring impact on the political culture of given nations', which could still be measured at the individual level, even centuries after key events had caused one nation's history to diverge from another's (1981: 300).

Focusing on the relative politicisation of women today as a reflection of historical shaping by Catholicism or Protestantism, the imprint of which affected both sexes, in eight countries overall, women emerged as substantially less interested in discussing political matters.

Through time series data, certain countries ranked consistently high: the Netherlands, Denmark, Germany and France, while others ranked consistently low:

Belgium, Italy and Ireland. Britain tended to occupy a median position between these two groups. Compared with a 1977 Netherlands level of 77 per cent, the highest expressed level of Irish interest — that of 1977 — was 53 per cent, and this decreased further to 43 per cent in subsequent surveys. Ireland ranked consistently low in discussion levels, and ranked high when the mean differences between male and female frequency levels were charted. Not only, then, did Irish people display a low level of interest in politics, but Irish women were much less inclined than men to discussion. Irish women ranked low, also, compared with other European women, as did Irish men compared with their peers.

Table 8: Mean frequency of political discussion between the sexes and mean difference in political interest

Nation	1973-1978			1989		
	Male %	Female %	Mean Diff. %	Male %	Female %	Mean Diff. %
Italy	74	48	26	68	44	24
Germany	88	67	21	91	79	12
Ireland	67	48	19	67	51	16
Belgium	56	38	18	56	40	16
France	76	61	15	71	64	7
Britain	73	59	14	72	64	8
Denmark	77	64	13	85	75	10
Netherlands	77	69	8	78	69	9
Spain	-	-	-	53	31	22
Portugal	-	-	-	55	36	19
Greece	-	-	-	90	71	19

Sources: Inglehart, 1981; Eurobarometer, 1987, 1991.

Furthermore, even if in every country the women discussed politics less than the men, the disparities were more significant between women of different countries than between men and women of the same country. So, while women were substantially less interested in politics than men, sex, per se, was not the dominant influence. Nationality emerged as the most important factor in explaining a person's interest in politics, followed by education, sex and age.

Recent findings from a follow-up Eurobarometer poll

show the Irish gender gap to have narrowed, with Irish women's political interest increasing from 38 per cent (mean) in the 1973-1978 data to 51 per cent in 1989. Nevertheless, while compared with Irish men Irish women discuss politics more frequently than they did previously, this is still a somewhat lower level than that which prevailed for Irish women in 1977 (53 per cent).

But at higher levels of education, the pattern reveals that Irish women are ahead of Irish men in their propensity to discuss politics. In Ireland, where 36 per cent of men and 60 per cent of women never have exchanges about matters political, if they have left school at fifteen years of age, the figures are 43 per cent and 31 per cent when they have been educated up to twenty years of age or beyond (Mossuz-Lavau, 1992: 13). The proportion of women who do not talk about politics decreases by half, and as Mossuz-Lavau puts it 'distinctly fewer women than the men are willing to be silent in politics'. This is only one of several instances where Irish women have outscored Irish men, according to Eurobarometer surveys.

Patterns observed in an earlier study by Almond and Verba (1963) tend to reinforce the theory that although women are less politically competent, aware and active than men, this decreased as education level increased. Acknowledging that low socio-economic status predicted less involvement in politics, the impact was neither as strong nor as clear as that of education, allowing them to conclude that with expanding educational opportunity 'the traditional female status would weaken', and gender differences become less evident (1963: 399). Almost thirty years later, their predictions appear to be authenticated.

Nevertheless, it is striking that the gap between Irish and German or Danish women in political discussion is almost twice as large as that between Irish women and men. Clearly, the suggestion by Inglehart (1981) that nationality played a significant part in promoting such discussions is worthy of note. Here, Inglehart's theory that the influence of hierarchical and authoritarian social structures could be applied to both the Catholic Church and a powerful national army (for she also found a significant gender gap in the German data), was based on the patriarchal characteristics which promoted a traditional role for women. Almond and Verba, in *The Civic Culture Revisited* (1980), describe this classic 'Kinder, Kirche und Küche' orientation in German society, which could equally validly be applied in the Irish context, albeit mediated via the Catholic Church rather than the army. Inglehart sees the male monopoly of the Catholic Church, with its inhibiting orientation to women, as formative, in that those countries most closely adhering to the Catholic faith are the same countries which have been 'the most niggardly in granting rights to women, and where women remain the most timid in enjoying what rights they have received — including the right to vote and to discuss politics' (1981: 316). Many Irish women might add contraception and divorce to this list. (For a fuller treatment of the influence of the Catholic Church on Irish women see Mahon, 1987.)

The question of how frequently politics is discussed inevitably meets the criticism that it can be construed differently by different people. Some may see it as referring to national affairs only, or foreign policy issues, while others may see it as referring to informal political gossip. It has been suggested that women tend to underestimate the frequency with which they actually do discuss political matters, whereas men may overestimate their frequency.

Table 9: Political interest between the sexes

		1983 %		1987 %	
		Male	Female	Male	Female
Irish affairs	Interested	72	73	70	78
	Not interested	6	2	4	3
World affairs	Interested	46	52	51	55
	Not interested	11	9	8	8
European affairs	Interested	46	42	49	45
	Not interested	14	13	11	11
Current affairs	Interested	76	74	70	69
	Not interested	13	13	21	20

Source: MRBI, 1983, 1987.

Furthermore, as has been mentioned in the Euro-barometer publications, women tend to discuss 'social' affairs more frequently, among which are listed human rights, poverty, and the Third World. That these do not merit being graded as 'political' seems strange, for they surely rank among the world's most pressing problems, and have been somewhat arbitrarily consigned to a 'social' category. Allied to this methodological problem of what should be considered political is the semantics of 'expressed interest' and 'partaking in political discussion'. For an interesting example of how critical the phrasing of questions can be in this type of research, see the MRBI findings in Table 9, where respondents were asked if they were interested in specific areas of politics.

Here we find women's expressed *interest* in *specific* political topics evincing a substantially higher level of response than the *discussion* question. In the Inglehart study 48 per cent of Irish women on average between 1973 and 1978 said they discussed politics. This figure increased to 51 per cent in 1989. By contrast, in 1987, according to MRBI, while 51 per cent of men expressed an interest in world affairs, 55 per cent of women did so; and 78 per cent of women compared with 70 per cent of men avowed an interest in Irish affairs. A major difficulty, of course, surrounds the verification of such polls. At least pre-election intentions to vote can ultimately be tested against the real turnout. And if Table 5 suggests that women's voting intentions tallied more closely with eventual turnout in the subsequent election than men's, further research is needed to ascertain the extent to which some people may overestimate their interest in and discussion of politics.

One might wonder why interest in European affairs evokes a lower response rate than world affairs. Yet, on reflection, much of the discourse on Europe during the 1970s revolved around the Common Agricultural Policy (as far as Irish people were concerned), and talk of the Green Pound, and Monetary Compensation Amounts, topics of more interest to farmers, and less likely to engage popular interest compared with more easily comprehensible international affairs.

However, that Irish women should express such differing levels of political *interest* compared with frequency of *discussion* invites speculation as to why this might be. Could it be the authoritarian atmosphere that Inglehart suggests is linked with Catholic cultures? Are Irish women less confident in expressing political opinions in company, especially male company, giving the mistaken impression that they are not interested in politics?

Conversely, Inglehart suggests, women in predominantly Protestant countries scored consistently higher in discussion of politics, partly explained by the prevalence of a more egalitarian outlook on women in those cultures. Catholic countries, then, granted suffrage rights, in general, later to women, did not promote an atmosphere of equality wherein women were encouraged to participate in political discussion and activism, and indeed promoted a traditional environment such that women's interest in political matters was retarded.

In Ireland, the European Value Systems Study (Fogarty et al, 1984) included some data showing that 83 per cent of Protestants compared with 76 per cent of Catholics regularly read a daily paper; that 52 per cent of Catholics compared with 62 per cent of Protestants are interested but not active in politics; that 44 per cent of Catholics compared with 38 per cent of Protestants are 'not interested' in politics; and that 26 per cent of Catholics are either party members, voluntary workers for a party, or 'close' to a party, while no Protestant is recorded in any of these categories. 72 per cent of Protestants discuss politics with friends compared with 50 per cent of Catholics, and only 27 per cent of Protestants never discuss politics with friends compared with 49 per cent of Catholics. So, even within a predominantly Catholic culture such as the Republic of Ireland, Protestants from this survey seem to exhibit higher levels of interest in matters political, supporting the Inglehart hypothesis, but are not active participants in the system.

Irish women's civic participation
Given the suggestion that Irish women seem to be highly

interested in politics, yet tend not to engage in open discussion as frequently as their male peers, how does this affect their civic participation patterns?

Raven and Whelan's study on Irish political culture (1976) links Irish adults' perception of civic institutions with Almond and Verba's (1963) research on subjective competence. In the former, a large majority of respondents felt they were unable effectively to influence legislation at either national or local levels. Almost three-fifths at national level, and half at local level felt that there was nothing they could do to influence an unjust or harmful regulation. (See Table 10.) Notable here is the striking lack in women's sense of efficacy when the ability to influence legislation is examined. Only 46 per cent of Irish women compared with 62 per cent of Irish men felt efficacious regarding a very unjust or harmful local law.

Like some of the earlier data, there is a larger gap between women in different cultures in their personal sense of efficacy, eg between Irish and American women, 46 per cent and 74 per cent than between Irish women and Irish men, 46 per cent and 62 per cent. Also, a sense of efficacy in national matters is likely to be less strong than that pertaining in local affairs, so Irish women's subjective competence would fall further if tested at the higher political level.

Table 10: % who say they can do something about a very unjust or harmful local law, by gender.

Nation	Total %	% Male	%Female
USA	77	80	74
GB	78	83	73
Germany	62	72	53
Ireland	53	62	46
Mexico	53	63	46
Italy	51	62	47

Sources: Raven and Whelan, 1976; Almond and Verba, 1963.

Raven and Whelan found that the vast majority of Irish respondents did not believe that the most effective way of preventing an unjust or harmful local regulation was by working through a formal organisation. The authors found this surprising, since the influence of these groups which include trade unions, educational, social and cultural groups is well recognised in Ireland. Even among those who felt they could do something about an unjust local law, a lower percentage would enlist the aid of an informal group than in the USA or Britain.

There is much here to provoke reflection on Irish political culture, be it the low sense of personal influence regarding unjust laws or lack of trust in the efficacy of informal groups. Scholarly work abounds on the factors which lead Irish citizens to resort to elected politicians, notably TDs, to make representations on their behalf to the public administration even over small matters like pensions, or social welfare entitlements (Carty, 1983; Chubb, 1963; Farrell, 1985; Roche, 1982).

The studies surveyed also highlight features of Irish political culture that resemble aspects of those cited by Almond and Verba. For example, the low levels of political discussion and sense of efficacy among Irish people closely resemble the Mexican and Italian patterns for men and women, which contrasted with their American or British counterparts. The authors accepted that in Britain and the USA the family appears to merge with the system of political communications, suggesting that a high level of involvement in the community on the part of families tended to transmit the issues and events of the polity into the family for discussion. Political discussion tended to be frequent and reciprocal, rather than male dominated.

On the other hand, in Italy, for instance, where the rate of political discussion is low, it is particularly low among women. It would appear that when men engage in political discussion, they tend to do so outside of the home, in the café, on the street, or in their place of work (1963: 391). It could be argued that when Irish men discuss politics it tends to occur in pubs or at work, or even at spectator sports, areas where women are still a minority. In 1987 MRBI found that among weekend leisure activities, visits to pubs were recorded by 44 per cent of men, and 22 per cent of women. Likewise, among those saying they were spectators at an outdoor sport, men outnumbered women by 19 per cent to 9 per cent. But, notwithstanding these insightful snapshots of Irish political culture, and regardless of methodological shortcomings of data or questions, Irish women's political interest emerges as substantial. Mossuz-Lavau (1992: 9) identifies 'a two-speed Europe, that of the North and, in certain aspects, of the centre, where the process (women's interest in politics) is quite firmly underway, and a Europe of the South joined by Belgium and Ireland, where they are just beginning to emerge from a long prehistory'. But in some respects Ireland shows more similarity with the North European pattern than the Mediterranean trends, which will be discussed later.

Party loyalty by gender

The breakdown by party of women TDs between 1922 and 1977 corresponded roughly with the proportionate strength of the parties over the years: twelve Fianna Fáil, five Fine Gael and two Labour (Manning, 1978: 93). The third Sinn Féin party had five women Dáil members. It is not therefore surprising to find that a majority of women voters did support Fianna Fáil.

In the light of the landslide victory of the Fianna Fáil party in 1977, women's contribution to this success should be assessed. Opinion polls show a record level of 54 per cent of women supporting Fianna Fáil, compared with 42 per cent of men, which suggests that the women's vote may have been a significant factor in 1977, although a poll nearer to election day indicated women's support had dropped to 44 per cent

With Fianna Fáil support on the day reaching 50.6 per cent nationally, and deliberate campaign propaganda tactics to attract women and youth, it seems likely that the women's vote was an important component of Fianna Fáil success. Lynch, the Taoiseach of the day, exercised his prerogative in adding six women candidates to the list selected at conventions, indicating his support for political women, which was reinforced later by his nominating three women among his list of eleven nominees to the Senate. Fianna Fáil support among women was lower during the elections of the 1980s, with 32 per cent in 1982, peaking to 41 per cent before the 1987 election, to fall again to 37 per cent before the 1989 election. With a coalition government of Fine Gael and Labour in power from 1982 to 1987, the institution of a Ministry for Women's Affairs, and some feminist coalition policy initiatives, Fianna Fáil must have suffered voter leakage. Fine Gael seems to draw greater support from women than men, but at a lower level of popularity overall than Fianna Fáil. Labour, the Workers' Party and the Progressive Democrats normally draw less than 10 per cent of the vote, and are marginally less popular with women than with men. (See Table 11.)

Table 11: Party affiliation by % voting intentions

Party	1982	M	F	1987	M	F	1989	M	F
Fianna Fáil	36	40	32	40	39	41	38	39	37
Fine Gael	35	32	37	19	18	19	23	21	25
Labour	8	9	7	4	3	5	6	6	6
Workers' Party	2	4	1	2	3	2	4	5	4
Progressive Dem.	-	-	-	11	13	9	5	5	4
Will not vote	6	6	6	5	6	3	5	6	3
Don't know	9	6	12	16	13	20	13	9	17

Source: IMS, selected years.

As to whether party support is simply a voting act, a once-off gesture at elections, or more permanently anchored in dues paying membership, the records are incomplete and therefore unreliable. Fine Gael seems to attract more women among its members than Fianna Fáil, although the latter is a larger and more popular party nationally.

Candidate selection
At elections, which party puts forward the most candidates? It might be expected that Fianna Fáil, commanding such extensive voting support from women, would

also run more women candidates. But, as can be seen from Table 12, Fianna Fáil over the five elections during the 1980s nominated a total of 48 women compared with Fine Gael's 60. Bearing in mind the national strength of each party, Fianna Fáil with 44 per cent support countrywide nominated 25 per cent fewer women than Fine Gael, which then drew but 29 per cent of the national vote. The Labour Party, with less than 10 per cent support nationally, nominated fewer women at successive elections during the 1980s and had not elected a woman TD from 1982 until the 1992 election. The Progressive Democrats, with just over 5 per cent of the vote, nominated proportionally more women in the two elections fought since its inception than Fianna Fáil, Fine Gael or the Labour Party. The Workers' Party and the Green Party had yet to elect a woman deputy. The weaker of the two main parties, then, selects and elects more women members of parliament, yet its own lack of electoral clout proves disadvantageous for the party's women candidates. The strongest Irish party, on the other hand, enjoying traditionally wider popular support nationally, seems more hesitant regarding women's candidature, yet does not seem to lose women voters because of this policy.

Table 12: Women candidates and women elected by party affiliation over five general elections in the 1980s.*

Party	June '81		Feb '82		Nov '82		Feb '87		June '89		Total	Total
	Cand.	El.	Cand.	El	Cand.	El.	Cand.	El	Cand.	El.	Cand.	El
Fianna Fáil	10	4	11	2	7	4	10	5	10	5	48	20
Fine Gael	16	6	11	5	11	9	11	5	11	6	60	31
Labour	10	1	5	1	5	1	3	-	3	-	26	3
Prog. Dem.	-	-	-	-	-	-	7	4	7	2	14	6
Workers' Party	-	-	-	-	-	-	4	-	4	-	8	-
Green Party	-	-	-	-	-	-	4	-	4	-	8	-
Other	5	-	8	-	8	-	12	-	12	-	44	-
Total	41	11	35	8	31	14	66	14	53	13	210	60

Sources: Political Parties; Nealon's Guide to the 26th Dáil; Magill Book of Irish Politics, 1984.

* A discrepancy arises where a woman candidate stands in more than one constituency, thus increasing the overall number of women candidates.

Challenges of the 1990s

Given this strong loyalty of Irish women for Fianna Fáil, it was natural that the 1990 presidential election would pose a dilemma for those with feminist instincts within the party. The government candidate was a longstanding and popular male member of the Fianna Fáil party. The Labour Party, supported by the Workers' Party, nominated a woman lawyer, a feminist senator from a middle-class background with a record in representing minority rights. The third candidate was nominated by Fine Gael.

The electoral musical chairs which this contest evinced illustrates that cross-party voting is more acceptable at a presidential than at a general election. The polls close to election day showed that the government candidate would hold just under three-quarters of his own party's vote, with no other source giving him even as much as 20 per cent. They also predicted that the Left candidate would not only retain over four-fifths of her own parties' support, but draw almost three-quarters of the Progressive Democrat vote (the junior government partner), and over half the Fine Gael vote. While the male government candidate, outside of his own party, did not achieve higher than 18 per cent support from any source according to the polls, the now incumbent president's support in only one instance went as low as 18 per cent, and that was from Fianna Fáil.

The shock win which brought the first woman president to Ireland precipitated media speculation that it was a massive women's vote that had swung the election (O'Reilly, 1991). But opinion poll data challenges this suggestion. Between October and November the polls showed the women's vote changing from 30 per cent to 41 per cent in favour of Mary Robinson, and from 44 per cent to 40 per cent in favour of the government candidate. This is hardly a strong feminist statement. There has never been a massive women's vote in Ireland, and 'Robinson's Rainbow' (O'Malley, 1990) best describes the Left, liberal, feminist (male and female) and minorities' cohesion, which together with cross-party and catch-all 'top-up' brought victory for the Left. Postmaterialists might be tempted to see in this election some evidence of 'quality of life' campaign strategies emerging in an Irish context (Gardiner, 1991). That it represented a coup for women as voters and credible candidates remained to be tested at the next hustings.

Table 13: Women candidates and elected councillors Local Elections 1991

Party	Candidates			Elected		
	Total	F	%	Total	F	%
Fianna Fáil	643	71	11.0	358	22	6.2
Fine Gael	472	70	14.8	270	31	11.5
Labour	200	29	14.5	90	14	15.6
Prog. Dems.	122	25	20.5	37	12	32.4
Workers Party	80	20	25.0	24	4	16.7
Green Party	59	19	32.2	13	5	38.5
Sinn Fein	57	2	3.5	8	0	0.0
Independ	308	34	11.0	82	11	13.4
Others	12	0	0.0	1	0	0.0
Total	1953	270	13.8	883	99	11.21

Sources: Dept. of the Environment 1992; The Irish Times, 1991; Author's calculations.

The subsequent 1991 local elections provided an opportunity to gauge the parties' rating of women as electoral assets. Table 13 reveals the willingness of the parties to select women candidates. Again, Fianna Fáil, potentially the party with the greatest opportunities for women due to its wide electoral appeal, nominated a lower percentage of female candidates than any other mainstream party. The Workers' Party, the Progressive Democrats and the Green Party nominated the most women. The latter two also achieved the greatest success with 32 per cent women among the Progressive Democrats' elected councillors, and approximately 39 per cent of women among the Green Party councillors. Because these parties command low levels of national support the numbers of women elected are correspondingly small. General concern was expressed at the low percentage of women elected, but at 11.2 per cent it represents a substantial increase on the previous election (see Randall and Smyth, 1987: 206).

Summary
Electoral competition in the Irish political system poses

an arduous challenge to aspiring politicians, not least to women. It is not within the scope of this paper to explore all the factors which influence women's access to local and national parliament (such a study is forthcoming by the present author). Personal, party and constituency factors as well as electoral formula are some of the criteria impacting on political careers. There are, moreover, social structural variables that can make public careers more difficult for women to pursue than men.

In recent decades it has become apparent that for women, the political battle starts at an earlier stage than sheer party or constituency dynamics. Various structural elements in the economic, legal, social and domestic context impinge on women's eligibility not just for political life, but also for many other forms of public office. Some of these are more rigid in Irish society than elsewhere. And while a parliamentary career presents special problems of access, women are under-represented in virtually every other Irish power élite too. Whether in education, law, religion, trade unions, the civil service or business, the nearer the top the greater the invisibility of women (Gardiner, 1992b).

The indications are that women participating in the paid workforce are more politically aware, having a stake in the system, so to speak. On the other hand, the double or triple burden facing women who combine family and paid work, and also aspire to build a political career is well documented. This triple commitment results in many women abandoning rewarding careers as public representatives. On the one hand, lack of economic independence curtails the possibility of running an election campaign. On the other hand, involvement in the world of work, for women, means attending to domestic responsibilities in what men customarily regard as their rightful leisure time.

In Ireland, traditions of high marital fertility have coexisted with Catholic prohibition on contraception. Recent developments reveal a rapid convergence towards the lower fertility levels found in almost all western countries (Clancy, 1991: 16). Concern over the declining birth rate throughout Europe has been expressed by policy makers. All twelve member states of the EC now have a total fertility rate below the replacement rate of 2.15 (Kiely and Richardson, 1991: 3). In 1989, which Clancy sees as an important transition in Ireland's demographic history, the total Irish fertility rate went below the replacement rate. Yet, looking at Table 14, there seems an enduring ambivalence regarding preferred family size. Where most other countries favour two or three children, 51 per cent of Irish respondents still apparently favour four, five or more. Unfortunately, there is no gender breakdown for these figures, to check whether the gap already identified between Irish men and women's attitudes on questions discussed earlier holds also for ideal family size.

Table 14: Ideal number of children : Comparative survey data

No. of Children	Britain %	USA %	West Germany %	Hungary %	Republic of Ireland %
None	1	1	1	1	-
1	2	2	9	3	-
2	79	54	66	59	20
3	14	25	20	33	30
4	3	14	4	2	38
5 or more	-	5	1	2	13

Source: Harding, 1989.

Without a national policy on childcare, the ideal family size espoused in this table by Irish people seems to assume a fulltime mother working within the home exclusively. This is in keeping with the perception of the role of women in the constitution.

Irish women have one of the lowest labour force participation rates in the EC. The choices facing women wishing to participate in public life may be reduced to (a) foregoing motherhood, or (b) returning after childrearing. The latter route has been well trodden by women in political life. It is, however, an increasingly tenuous option, whether applied to political office or other labour force sectors. De-skilling accompanies long periods out of the workforce, making re-entry difficult. In politics, the childbearing and rearing years for women are exactly those when aspiring candidates join a party and build up a constituency profile. Many societies, especially those with falling birth rates, practise positive discrimination to attract women to stay in or return to the labour force, and increasingly favour family policies designed to increase population also. They also use quota systems to try to equalise the gender balance of selected candidates. Policy makers, especially in the larger Irish parties, are slow to adopt such strategies, and women themselves are divided on these issues.

Looking at the marital status of the newly elected deputies in the 1989 Dáil, of the nineteen single parliamentarians, five were women. There were only thirteen women deputies altogether, which means that almost 40 per cent of them were single. The comparative rate for men was 9 per cent single. And if the most common family size overall was four children, among women deputies it was two.

The extent to which Irish women feel treated equally with men can be gauged from the response to an MRBI poll in 1987 (see Table 15).

Table 15: Irishwomen are treated equally with men

	Total %	Urban%	Rural%	Male %	Female %
Agree	29	26	32	38	20
Disagree	57	61	53	45	68
No opinion	14	13	15	17	12

Source: MRBI, 1987.

It could be argued that it is equally difficult for both sexes to engage in party politics. Building up a constituency profile in a culture that values a public representative with local roots entails evening party political commitments, which for both men and women is voluntary activity. Research in 1987 in the EC member states clearly showed that the model of the home where the man is the only member to exercise a profession, and where the woman does the housework is still very strong in Luxembourg, Ireland and Germany (*Women of Europe,* 1987). This impression of traditional roles was confirmed in another section of the 1987 study. When asked to state confidence in a man or woman in different jobs, such as bus or train driver, surgeon or barrister, Denmark and the Netherlands were the most egalitarian while Ireland and

Italy were the most traditional. The profession that caused the biggest difference between men and women was that of bus or train driver, where the gap between men and women was zero in Denmark, and highest in Ireland, Spain and Portugal.

Of more significance as far as women's role within the home is concerned, Ireland was one of only three countries where a majority of married men preferred their wives not to work. But although the study placed Ireland in the bottom group of the European scale for equality of the sexes, in that there was less acceptance of equal roles within the family, in several instances the divergence between Irish men's and women's responses was noted. Women tend to be more liberal-progressive, converging on the north European attitude model, whereas Irish men tend still to hold traditional attitudes.

It was most striking when the question 'would things be better or worse if there were more women in parliament?' was put to respondents. Ireland led the group of countries professing that things would be better, 36 per cent responding positively. Women were more than twice as likely as men to give a positive response. Bearing in mind the Mossuz-Lavau findings (1992) that at higher levels of education Irish women outscored men regarding political discussion, here is another indicator of a gender gap in liberal attitudes in Ireland.

Table 16: Confidence in a man or woman as a member of parliament, % responding 'More confidence in a man'

	Men				Women			
Country	1975	1983	1987	Diff'ce	1975	1983	1987	Diff'ce
Denmark	20	9	7	13	15	8	7	8
UK	37	27	15	22	31	27	17	14
Netherlands	28	19	16	12	23	16	12	11
Ireland	42	38	33	9	33	20	17	16
France	35	28	24	11	28	22	20	8
Italy	47	39	31	16	41	34	22	19
W.Germany	53	45	30	23	37	30	19	18

Source: Eurobarometer, 1987; Men and Women of Europe, 1987.

Here, the difference in attitude between Irish men and women is again clear. In 1987, Irish men scored highest in having more confidence in a man than woman parliamentarian, whereas Irish women occupied a median position between the liberal Danes and the Dutch, on the one hand, and the more conservative French, West German and Italian women on the other. And, whereas in 1975 Irish men and women were more alike in attitude, in 1987 the gap between them was much larger. Clearly, Irish women are becoming more liberal minded on a range of issues, moving ahead of Irish men, many of whom still cling to traditional attitudes. There is evidence, however, that traditional attitudes still prevail among many women, highlighting a generation as well as a gender gap.

The coexistence of liberal and conservative strains in Irish culture is outlined by O'Leary and Hesketh (1988) and developed in Gardiner (1991) to explain the surprise outcome of the presidential election in 1990. The Europeanisation of Irish attitudes regarding women's role is likely to become more evident in coming years, with differences between southern and northern European mores adding to the complexity.

Postscript: Earthquake election 1992

The snap general election of November 1992 occurred at a time when media focus on Irish women was at its highest ever. Three major moral issues dominated the political agenda in the leadup to the election. First, the increasing incidence of reported sexual crimes against women and children, and the perceived leniency of sentencing policy in the courts created public outcry during the preceding year. Second, the events surrounding the X case in early 1992, the protocol that had been attached to the Irish document for the Maastricht Treaty, and the divisive abortion debate that followed, highlighted anomalies regarding women's rights, particularly those relating to pregnant women. The urgency of these issues was reinforced due to the coincidence at international level of similar perceived affronts to women. In the USA, fallout from the Smith case and heightened feeling over the Clarence Thomas/Anita Hill hearings were intensified by claims that rape was being used as a strategy in ethnic cleansing in Bosnia. Media coverage ensured that these issues stayed at the forefront of public debate. Finally, a scandal relating to alleged corporate fraud which involved leading politicians exploded, culminating in the calling of an election at short notice.

From the perspective of women candidates, the adversity of the circumstances for women's rights afforded a centre stage spotlight on such issues, since three referenda were held in conjunction with the general election. These related to the right to travel, the right to information, and the substantive issue of abortion itself (Smyth, 1992). A record eighty-nine women stood in the Dáil election, and twenty were elected. A substantial swing to the left saw five Labour Party women and one Democratic Left woman elected, as well as four for the Progressive Democrats. Fianna Fáil and Fine Gael returned five women each to the 27th Dáil.

However, without the swing to the left, the gender profile of the Dáil and Seanad would not have been much different to its outgoing status. The main parties nominated few women among their lists of candidates. A Fine Gael incumbent deputy and former Minister for Women's Affairs did not contest the election, while two other Fine Gael women deputies lost their seats. The party however, returned two new faces to the Dail, although one of these was a former TD, who had lost her seat in the 1989 election. Fianna Fáil returned all their incumbent women deputies. Nevertheless, without the six new women TDs from the Labour and Democratic Left parties, the total in the new Dáil might have been the same as in 1982 and 1987, a modest fourteen out of the total 166.

The subsequent Seanad election brought three Labour women, one each from the Progressive Democrats, Fianna Fáil and Fine Gael, as well as an Independent woman candidate from the Dublin University panel, bringing the total elected to seven. When the Taoiseach included only one woman among his eleven Seanad appointees there was understandable consternation. The ink on the report of the Second Commission on the Status of Women was hardly dry, and the Taoiseach's public commitment to nominate more women among his appointments hot off the press. Overall the Oireachtas now includes 28 women among the 226 deputies and senators. At 12.4 per cent, while nowhere approaching that of Denmark or the Netherlands, it makes a sizeable difference to the gender content of both houses, where issues raised, style of debate and legislative output will be monitored with interest.

Conclusion

Irish women profess a strong interest in political affairs, if less prone to discuss politics as formally defined, a growing trust in their own ability, and awareness of domestic and global problems. Their contribution to public life in Ireland is thwarted due to obstacles which prevent them gaining access to decision-making centres. Political parties, especially the larger ones, select few women election candidates. Only twenty of the 166 members of the Dáil are women. Much of women's political participation has been through pressure group activity, albeit mostly concerned with women's issues or community concerns, and not in the mainstream powerful interest organisations. Nevertheless, women's effectiveness in social movement politics is a testament to their flexibility in attitude and approach to problem resolution, if reinforcing the outsider status of such activity.

It is mainly due to this pressure from the outside, and EC influence, that gender equality in Ireland has so far been addressed. But outside pressure should be balanced by a critical mass of women parliamentarians on the inside. Since the 1992 election, an upward shift in women's Oireachtas visibility is evident. But, at 12 per cent, this still leaves the ratio less than half way to reaching even a quarter of the Dáil. Until this equation approaches one third, women's contribution to the wider agenda of democratic government will remain difficult to effect.

References and further reading

Almond, G. and Verba, S. 1963. *The Civic Culture.* Princeton University Press.

Almond, G. and Verba, S. (eds.) 1980. *The Civic Culture Revisited.* Princeton University Press,

Arnold, M. 1987. *Irishwomen into Focus.* Office of the Minister of State for Women's Affairs, Dublin.

Blackwell, J. 1982. 'Government, Economy and Society'. In Litton, F. (ed.) *Unequal Achievement*.

Bogdanor, V. (ed.) 1985. *Representatives of the People:* Gower, London.

Bunreacht na hEireann: Constitution of Ireland. Stationery Office, Dublin.

Carty, R. K. 1980. 'Women in Irish Politics'. *Canadian Journal of Irish Studies*, Vol.6. No.1.

Carty, R. K. 1983. (2nd. ed.) *Electoral Politics in Ireland*. Brandon, Dingle

Chubb, B. 1970. *The Government and Politics of Ireland.* Oxford University Press, Oxford.

Clancy, P. 1991. 'Irish Nuptiality and Fertility Patterns in Transition'. In Kiely, G. and Richardson, V. (eds.), *Family Policy: European Perspectives*, Family Studies Centre, University College Dublin.

Claffey, U. 1993. *The Women Who Won*. Attic Press, Dublin

Darcy, R., Welch, S. and Clark, J. 1987. *Women, Elections and Representation*. Longman, London.

Duverger, M. 1955. *The Political Role of Women*. UNESCO, Paris.

Eurobarometer. Commission of the European Communities, Brussels. 1987.

Farrell, B. 1985. 'From Friends and Neighbours to Clients and Partisans'. In Bogdanor, V. (ed.), *Representatives of the People.*

Farrell, B. and Penniman, H. (eds.). 1987. *Ireland at the Polls.* American Enterprise Institute.

Farrell, B. (ed.) 1988. *De Valera's Constitution and Ours.* Gill and Macmillan, Dublin.

Fogarty, M, Ryan, L. and Lee, J. 1984. *Irish Values and Attitudes: The Irish Report of the European Value Systems Study.* Dominican Publications, Dublin.

Gallagher, M. 1985. 'Social Backgrounds and Local Orientations of Members of the Irish Dáil'. In *Legislative Studies Quarterly.* X, 3.

Gallagher, M. 1990. 'The election results and the new Dáil'. In Gallagher, M. and Sinnott, R. (eds.), *How Ireland Voted.*

Gallagher, M. and Sinnott, R. (eds.), 1990. *How Ireland Voted.* Centre for the Study of Irish Elections. University College Galway.

Gallagher, M., Laver, M., and Mair, P. 1992. *Representative Government in Western Europe.* McGraw-Hill, London.

Gardiner, F. 1991. 'The Irish Presidential Election — a Feminist Triumph?' Paper presented to the European Consortium for Political Research, Joint Sessions of Workshops, Bochum, Germany.

Gardiner, F. 1992a. 'Reshaping the Political Agenda: A Push-Pull analysis'. Paper presented to the ECPR Joint Sessions of Workshops, Limerick, Ireland.

Gardiner, F. 1992b. 'Gender: the democratic deficit in the Irish political system'. Paper presented to the Political Studies Association, Cork.

Haavio-Mannila, E. 1985. (ed.) *Unfinished Democracy.* Pergamon, London.

Harding, S. 1989. 'Interim Report: The Changing Family'. In Jowell, R., Witherspoon, S. and Brooks, L. (eds.), *British Social Attitudes: Special International Report*, Gower, London.

Inglehart, M. 1981. 'Political Interest in West European Women'. In *Comparative Political Studies*, Vol. 14, No. 3.

Irish Marketing Surveys. 1977, 1981, 1982.

Kiely, G. and Richardson, V. 1991. 'Some Issues in Family Policy'. In Kiely, G. and Richardson, V. (eds.), *Family Policy: European Perspectives*, Family Studies Centre, University College, Dublin.

Lee, J. J. 1989. *Ireland 1912-1985*. Cambridge University Press, Cambridge.

Lipset, S. M. and Rokkan, S. 1967. 'Cleavage Structures, Party Systems and Voter Alignments: An Introduction'. In Lipset, S.M. and Rokkan, S. (eds.), *Party Systems and Voter Alignments*, The Free Press, New York.

Litton, F. (ed.) 1982. *Unequal Achievement*. Institute of Public Administration, Dublin.

Lovenduski, J. and Hills, J. 1981. (eds.) *The Politics of the Second Electorate*. Routledge and Kegan Paul, London.

MacCurtain, M. 1978. 'Women, the vote and revolution'. In MacCurtain, M. and O Corráin, D. (eds.) 1978. *Women in Irish Society: The Historical Dimension*.

MacCurtain, M. and O Corráin, D. (eds.) 1978. *Women in Irish Society: The Historical Dimension*. Arlen House, Dublin.

Mahon, E. 1987. 'Women and Catholicism in Ireland'. In *New Left Review*.

Manning, M. 1978. 'Women and Politics in Ireland'. In MacCurtain, M. and O Corráin, D. (eds.) *Women in Irish Society*.

Manning, M. 1987. 'Women and the Elections'. In Penniman and Farrell (eds.) *Ireland at the Polls*.

Market Research Bureau of Ireland. Various polls, 1983, 1987, 1989.

Mossuz-Lavau, J. 1992. *Women and Men of Europe Today*. Commission of the European Communities, Brussels.

Nealon, T. 1974. *Ireland: A Parliamentary Directory. 21st, 22nd Dáil and Seanad*. Platform Press.

Nealon, T. 1987. *Nealon's Guide: 25th Dáil & Seanad*. Platform Press, Dublin.

Nealon, T. 1989. *Nealon's Guide: 26th Dáil & Seanad*. Platform Press, Dublin.

Norris, P. 1987. *Politics and Sexual Equality*. Wheatsheaf Books Ltd., London.

O'Leary, C. and Hesketh, T. 1988. 'The Irish Abortion and Divorce Referendum Campaigns'. In *Irish Political Studies* 3: 43-62.

O'Malley, J. 1990. *The Sunday Independent*, 11 November.

O'Reilly, E. 1991. *Candidate: The Truth Behind the Presidential Campaign*. Attic Press, Dublin

Owens, R. C. 1984. *Smashing Times*. Attic Press, Dublin.

Putnam, R. D. 1976. *The Comparative Study of Political Elites*. Prentice Hall, Englewood Cliffs, New Jersey.

Randall, V. 1987. (2nd ed.) *Women and Politics*. Macmillan, London.

Randall, V. and Smyth, A. 1987. 'Bishops and Bailiwicks: Obstacles to women's political participation in Ireland'. In *Economic and Social*

Review, Vol. 18, No. 3.

Raven, J. and Whelan, C. T. et al. 1976. *Political Culture in Ireland.* Institute of Public Administration, Dublin.

Roche, R. 1982. 'The High Cost of Complaining Irish style'. In *Journal of Irish Business and Administrative Research,* 4, (2).

Rush, M. and Althoff, P. 1971. *An Introduction to Political Sociology.* Thomas Nelson and Sons, London.

Scannell, Y. 1988. 'The Constitution and the Role of Women'. In Farrell, B. (ed.) *De Valera's Constitution and Ours.*

Sheehy Skeffington, A. D. and Owens, R. C. 1975. *Votes for Women.* Dublin.

Sinnott, R. 1987. 'The Voters, the Issues, and the Party System'. In Farrell and Penniman, *Ireland at the Polls.*

Smyth, A. 1992. *The Abortion Papers: Ireland.* Attic Press, Dublin.

Steiner, J. 1991. *European Democracies.* Longman, London.

Ward, M. 1983. *Unmanageable Revolutionaries.* Brandon Books, Dingle.

Whyte, J H. 1971. *Church and State in Modern Ireland 1923-1970.* Gill and Macmillan, Dublin.

Women of Europe, 1987, 1988, 1991. Commission of the European Communities, Brussels.

Discussion Topics

1 How important was the interplay between nationalism and suffragism in the early years of the century?

2 'Getting the vote was only the first step, and perhaps the easiest, towards women's political participation in Ireland.' Discuss.

3 Why do some cultures seem to foster political interest more than others?

4 Does working within the political party system offer a realistic route to equality in decision-making for women?

5 Can 'women's interests' be represented as well by a feminist male politician as by a female politician? Or is this an outdated concept in any event, as suggested by some people?

The Church, the State and the Women's Movement in Northern Ireland

Monica McWilliams

The role played by both church and state in Northern Ireland has shaped not only the more traditional thinking behind some of the major institutions but has also been responsible for the extremely conservative ideology for which the province has become infamous. The intention of this chapter is to illustrate how church and state have combined together at various times to ensure that the prime role for women was as home-makers and mothers. It will also show the extent to which it has proved extremely difficult for women to organise around issues which are of personal and political importance to them in the face of such traditional religious ideology. Even raising issues relating to sexuality, the dissolution of marriage or women's rights has meant that feminists have faced opposition, not only from clergy and politicians, but also from within their own communities. The fact that they have gone some way down this road in organising and politicising around such 'controversial' issues is a testimony to the strength and determination which women in Northern Ireland have to 'drag the country kicking and screaming into the twentieth century'.[1]

Alongside the issue of religion in Northern Ireland, the other dominant factor which has created divisions within the women's movement is the extent to which women prioritise the nationalist question. On the difficult question of political affiliation, this chapter will also assess the extent to which safe spaces have been found in Northern Ireland where women can organise together on issues of common interest whilst tentatively moving forward on the more divisive ones.

Legislative change

The backwardness of the Northern Ireland state can best be seen by the reaction to legislative change in the province, particularly on issues of sexual morality and domestic violence. The Free Presbyterian Church organised a campaign to 'Save Ulster From Sodomy' to counteract Jeff Dudgeon's case to the European Court in 1982 which resulted in homosexuality being decriminalised. Despite this move, the Catholic Church still holds the view that 'objectively, homosexual acts are intrinsically and gravely immoral' (Irish Catholic Bishops, 1985: 9). Divorce on the grounds of irreconcilability was eventually made legal in Northern Ireland in 1978 — ten years after the rest of the UK. The Democratic Unionist Party, and in particular Ian Paisley, used the 'sanctity of marriage' argument to obstruct the legislation. In the end they succeeded in introducing amendments which made 'quickie' postal divorces impossible and divorce itself more expensive. It could only be obtained through High Court proceedings.[2]

Such hostility to social change was strongly evidenced not only by the Free Presbyterians but by the Catholic Church. In a pastoral letter the bishops wrote: 'The concept of irretrievable breakdown in marriage is the basis for the most restrictive form of divorce in the world today. It can be imposed on an innocent and unwilling partner by an unfaithful spouse and the innocent partner can do nothing to prevent it. The remedy for a minority of marriages which fail, itself becomes a factor causing more marriages to fail. A divorce mentality spreads through the community' (Irish Catholic Bishops, 1985: 9). In a similar vein to Bowlby's maternal deprivation thesis of the 1950s which was instrumental in making women feel guilty for going out to work and leaving their children in the care of others, the bishops argue that 'reliable studies indicate that children prefer even an unhappy marriage relationship to divorce of their parents. Divorce is always a disaster for children.' (Irish Catholic Bishops, 1985: 5). Such sweeping generalisations were to be taken as fact by the Catholic laity and the 'reliability' of the studies uncontested.

Despite these views, in July 1978, the judiciary had the responsibility of introducing legislation allowing divorce in Northern Ireland. This was seen as the culmination of many years of campaigning by groups such as the

Women's Law and Research Group and the Northern Ireland Women's Rights Movement. Lord Justice McDermott, however, did not share the views of the women's groups. He was more in tune with church thinking on the subject when he remarked that such laws were 'perils to family life'. Again in 1980, when the domestic violence legislation was being amended to bring it into line with similar legislation in Britain, this was also adapted to fit the more conservative views on the subject.

Consequently, the 1980 order specified that it should be applied to married couples only and not to cohabitees. Some elements of the judiciary were once again appalled by the 'perils to family life', this time in the shape of exclusion orders. One local magistrate was forced to adjourn court proceedings, until he read the actual order and was convinced that in his words 'a man could be put out of his own home'.[3] Other barristers recall magistrates speaking of their regret that a time had come once again to Ireland when men could be 'thrown out on to the street'.[4] Not being disposed to understanding the reasons for introducing such legislation on domestic violence, some magistrates in Northern Ireland were erroneously equating exclusion orders with the penal evictions of the nineteenth century.

Interestingly, the issue of domestic violence throws up some contradictions in the Northern Ireland context. Although women protested vociferously against the violence of the British Army throughout the 1970s, particularly at the time of internment, they were less likely to protest against the violence of their male partners in their own homes. The traditional link between nationalism (both orange and green) and their respective churches has ensured that the ultra-conservative view of women as both the property of, and the inferior of, men remains strongly entrenched in Irish society. When the question of domestic violence as a specific campaigning issue arose in the late 1970s in Derry, it brought Women's Aid there into conflict with both the churches and the republican movement. The Catholic Church disagreed with the women's campaign to end the cohabitation rule and was initially opposed to the provision of women's refuges on the grounds that they split up families. The republican paramilitaries, on the other hand, became angry with the women's group when they refused to distinguish between violence involved, on the one hand, in 'political punishments' (tarring and feathering of women) and the violence inflicted by state forces or husbands on the other (Harkin and Kilmurray, 1985).

Irish images of motherhood

Over the past twenty-five years of campaigning and mobilising for social change, women in Northern Ireland have had to be extra sensitive to the beliefs and traditions operating in the community. There is a view that to move too quickly down the feminist road, in the light of such church opposition, may only alienate some women or prevent a more progressive consciousness from developing. Beth Rowland was involved in an education project for women and holds the view that some of the tenets of the feminist movement strike at the very heart of the women's religious beliefs. She questions whether or not feminists have any right to challenge the traditional role of women since it has so often provided them with their only real identity. She goes further by arguing that these 'religious beliefs are a fact of life which the education/ community worker must accept' (Rowland, 1985).

However, the majority of politically active women have come up against this hurdle before. Women's groups have begun to enquire about the origins of these religious beliefs. They do not accept that their traditional role within the family giving them their only identity as mothers and wives cannot be changed. It is difficult, often painful, to challenge beliefs which have been so strongly inculcated through the education system. Education in Ireland has almost an adhesive effect between church, state, women and morality. Inglis (1987) quotes from a parliamentary commission report: 'The civilisation of Irish society depends not just on giving more power to the Catholic Church but on the transformation of Irish women into good mothers.' The Church through the schools became providers of education while parents became providers of children who are faithful members of the Catholic Church. Not only were Catholic girls to model themselves on the image of the Virgin Mary by maintaining their chastity and purity, but equally they were called upon to adopt the mother's passive, unquestioning role. Mary Holland, in particular, has commented on this image of motherhood which runs through our popular culture. 'We have apostrophised the country itself as a mother. The concept of Mother Ireland has met with wholehearted national approval. The message has been unequivocal. The proper place for a woman apart from the convent is the home, preferably rearing sons for Ireland.' (1988) When the Pope visited Ireland in 1979, his more conservative orthodox views on women (not to mention women's rights) became enshrined in his appeal to young Irish women: 'May Irish mothers, young women and girls, not listen to those who tell them that working at a secular job, succeeding in a secular profession is more important than the vocation of giving life and caring for this life as a mother . . . I entrust this to Mary, bright Sun of the Irish Race.' (Pope John Paul II at Limerick, October 1979).

Marina Warner traces the history of the Marian devotion (1985). She argues that by making the virginity of Christ's mother an article of faith, the Catholic Church has quite consciously separated sex from motherhood. This is an important distinction and one which many young women in Ireland are familiar with. In fact, Mary Holland holds the view that by passing this philosophy on through the Catholic education system, it has taught Irish women to hate their bodies (1988).

Throughout the late 1970s (particularly at the time of the hunger strikes) wall murals began to appear on the Falls Road in nationalist West Belfast depicting the anguish of Mary as she stands over her martyred son. The pictures were meant to convey a symbol of Mother Ireland where the crucifiers were, of course, British imperialists. Whilst the Catholic Church shows a good deal of antipathy towards such portraits, they have no problems with the Catholic Church, in the form of the Virgin Mary, being represented on the side of the oppressed. More recently some politically active women in Northern Ireland were asked to discuss in a television documentary, what this imagery of 'Mother Ireland' meant for them. Bernadette McAliskey saw herself as a 'daughter of Mother Ireland' whilst Mairéad Farrell exhorted Mother Ireland 'to get off our backs'.[5] Róisín McDonagh, writing in *Women's News*, argues that she initially had some sympathy with such a rejection identifying the image with 'a crass, sentimental and ultimately offensive stereotype of Ireland as a tragic but stoically dignified woman whose honour was/is defended by her brave sons fighting against perfidious Albion' (1989). However, an identification with the Irish culture and the Irish language is beginning to take root amongst a group of feminists in Belfast and within this, they argue, there is room for different Irish mythological images of the Great Mothers of our culture — images of mothers as warriors, clever, imaginative, strong, cunning, wise and compassionate.[6] McDonagh argues that these are precisely the ideological images of Mother Ireland which have been trampled down by the imposition of a narrow, patriarchal, colonial culture.

The state approach to childcare and women's work
In the case of the Protestant churches, the veneration of Mary as a mother figure is anathema to the teachings of Free Presbyterianism. The patriarchal nature of Protestantism leaves out the imagery of women and in turn women become invisible. Where it does refer to women, its more Calvinistic theology calls upon them to be obedient and subservient — again emphasising their prime role as home-makers. This was more noticeable in the post-war period when the state's alignment with the churches helped to institutionalise some of the most extreme forms of patriarchy. Examples of these were investment for male but not female employment, the exclusion of women from certain occupations through marriage bars and the closure of day nurseries. The Ministry of Education refused to provide funding for the well established and efficiently run workplace nurseries which had allowed the skilled labour of married women

to be used so profitably in the linen mills. Their labour was to be expendable since the Stormont administration refused to subvent the linen industry, which would have enabled it to compete with foreign competitors. The same rule did not apply to the shipbuilding industry since these men's jobs, which were also predominantly Protestant, had to be protected at all costs (Morrissey, 1980).

The two religious traditions adopted a similar line in the post-war period on women's domestic role. They exhorted mothers to take responsibility for their children by looking after them at home. The churches felt threatened by the provision of day care for children since it assumed intervention by the state in family life and posed a threat to the concept of the family wage. Liz McShane shows that in 1945 both Catholic bishops and Unionist MPs agreed with the closure of day nurseries in the province, arguing that they destroyed 'the natural and divinely ordained traditional family' (1987). Both class and sex bias is revealed in the lack of understanding of the impoverishment from which women suffer. In preventing women's emancipation by opposing nursery facilities, church and state oppressed women by keeping them isolated in the home on a full time basis. 'The proper place for the baby is in the home and the proper guardian is the mother. Nature decided that and God approved of that decision of Nature'. (Bishop McGean, 1945, in McShane, 1987.) Childcare either at the work-place or state-provided, presented a challenge to the traditional ideology which supports the segregated division of labour in the home. The opportunity was also lost for a child-centred educational and welfare rationale for day nurseries which would have dramatically increased the opportunity of women to participate in employment.

From the Second World War onwards, the consistently higher levels of unemployment and the decline in the manufacturing industry encouraged the government in Northern Ireland to pursue a development strategy which would attract investment for male employment. Not only did female workers lose their jobs in the clothing and textile industries, they also lost the possibility for women to combine work, marriage and motherhood. The marriage bars, operating in the civil service, teaching professions and banking were not abolished until the late 1960s. These had a profound effect on married women's employment in the province and undoubtedly help to explain why, in 1971, only 29 per cent of married women were economically active. This contrasts sharply with the figure of 42 per cent for Great Britain in 1971. Only in the mid-to-late-1980s were Northern Irish married women beginning to catch up with their counterparts in the rest of Britain.[7]

Social change
The other major factor which helps to explain the lower economic activity of married women in Northern Ireland is their higher fertility rates. The province has one of the highest child dependency ratios in Europe, exceeded within OECD countries only by Turkey. In 1990, the birth rate was 17.5 births per thousand population compared to 12.5 for Britain. As one would expect, family size remains consistently larger and stands unchanged since 1983 at 2.2 children.[8]

Although Protestant family size is greater than the British average it is undoubtedly the case that the number of children in Catholic families is larger than in Protestant. However, the birth rate for both is declining due to an increasing use of contraception and a demand for females to remain in the labour force. Despite the Catholic Church's strong views on contraception, younger married women in Northern Ireland are making up their own minds. This does not mean that they are no longer practising Catholics. Contrary to the Church's view that the demands for contraception and sterilisation are a result of 'modern society organised on the basis of sex without control', women are very much in control (Irish Catholic Bishops, 1985). As Nell McCafferty believes, Irish women pick and choose with intelligence among the rules drawn up by the holy men for the best expression of that belief (McCafferty, 1989).

Young people, however, still have the most difficulty

in obtaining contraception as is revealed by the high rates of births outside marriage to women under the age of 20.[9] In 1979, in the Republic of Ireland, 'an Irish solution to an Irish problem,' was found in the Health (Family Planning) Act which legalised the distribution and use of contraceptives — but only to persons with *bone fide* family planning purposes'.[10] Prior to 1979, many women from the Republic travelled to Northern Ireland to avail of contraceptives. One of the first women's groups in the north (the Socialist Women's Group formed in 1975) highlighted this anomaly by taking a supply of contraceptives to Dundalk (on the southern side of the border) and freely handing them out. Their mode of transport became known as 'the condom train'. In 1985 in the Republic of Ireland, the sale of contraceptives was legalised but, as in Northern Ireland, this did not solve the problem. Like sterilisation, and reproductive technology, the availability of contraception depends a great deal on one's social class and place of residence. The problem for women in the North is that although family planning is free, the clinics themselves may not be easily accessible — particularly for those living in rural areas. It is also the case that women in predominantly Catholic areas cannot freely avail of contraceptives because doctors will not prescribe them and chemists will not stock them. Single women and men, and married couples who have a social relationship with their doctors still feel a certain stigma. They know they are deviating from the 'moral' code. Perhaps they are still reeling from the words of the Catholic bishops who, as late as 1985, were able to write: 'Every age has had its surfeit of sin, but it can hardly be denied that our contemporary Western society has seen an unprecedented breakdown of what were once universally accepted moral standards, especially in the sphere of sexuality. It is as though our whole civilisation is aphrodisiac.' (Irish Catholic Bishops, 1985). To counteract such views feminists have formed supportive collectives around the issues of family planning and women's health.

Although the Protestant churches do not agree with the Catholic Church's teaching on birth control and divorce, they have been extremely adept at incorporating Protestant practice into Northern legislation when the opportunity arose. One of the most sectarian debates in Stormont took place over the allowances paid to families for their children in 1954.[11] The Unionists wished to stop all payments to Catholics with more than four children. Such statements that there 'was little poverty under the blanket' often coloured their arguments. McGivern and Ward further argue that the Protestant churches' apparent liberality on the issue of birth control may be questioned 'in that the more ultra-Protestant advocacy of contraception is not posed in terms of women's emancipation but rather stems from a fear of being outbred by feckless Catholics' (1982).

Liam O'Dowd claims that 'the ideology of their [Protestant] intellectuals is largely the product of men who have either ignored or marginalised the social role of women or alternatively consigned women to a servicing and largely invisible role outside history and politics' (1987). It could be argued that by their very exclusion, women in Northern Ireland have been discriminated against. It is less a case of what is said about them, than what is not said. By leaving things alone discrimination occurs in itself because existing models derive totally from a male representation of reality. These male models have for so long shown a determination to preserve community and family rather than the individual as the basic unit of society. In Northern Ireland, models can have a very long life in situations where they are taken as given. Women are now succeeding in challenging their lack of position, their very exclusion from this 'malestream' way of life, and they are having some success in doing so. However, there still exists a good deal of hysterical negativism by church and state when women do speak out. On the issue of abortion not only is there a lack of rational debate but those associated with the campaign are publicly denounced. As the Northern Ireland Abortion Law Reform Association (NIALRA) testified in a tribunal in Belfast in 1987, there is so much fear and secrecy around abortion that women are afraid to even debate the issue publicly (NIALRA, 1989). As a result of the legal situation, certain simple and relatively risk-free ante-natal tests, which are commonly available in Britain, are not routinely offered in Northern Ireland. Because doctors have no clear guidelines under the 1861 Offences Against the Person Act (amended by the 1945 Criminal Justice (NI) Act) there are inconsistencies within the medical profession. Where a woman conceives as a result of rape or incest, termination of the pregnancy is left to the doctor's discretion.

Abortions are performed, though not guaranteed in all such circumstances, and fear of legal reprisal leaves the medical profession unwilling to discuss their practice. Again doctors are often left to impose their own legal and moral judgements upon women. When trade unionists and members of the health and medical professions attempt to raise some of these concerns they are reminded that if they are Catholics they should be guided by the tenets of Catholic teaching. In as much as Irish political parties have divided within themselves for religious reasons on moral issues, so have trade union movements, legal organisations, medical professions and even women's groups working in the community. Giving prior allegiance to one's religious beliefs can cause conflict amongst individuals. Many women become so concerned about their family and relatives or friends and neighbours that they do not feel at liberty to speak out or to be seen as betraying their 'religion'. In publicly deploring the organisation of small groups of women around issues of personal concern (particularly when they relate to 'sexual morality'), the Catholic Church can be seen as adopting a strategy of alienating those who raise these issues from the rest of the community and consequently preventing any discussion on the subject. It remains the case that in Ireland, the Catholic Church in putting forward its 'option for the poor' is much more comfortable with Marx than with Freud (Healey and Reynolds, 1987).

Political change
From the civil rights days of the late 1960s and early 1970s, to the organisation of women's centres in the mid-

1970s and 1980s, feminists in Northern Ireland have played a central role. A great deal has been learned along the way. Initially, in the civil rights movement, men and women marched together demanding 'One Man, One Vote'. The chant was given without any consideration to its sexist connotations and it was only later that the women who joined the Women's Rights Movement were able to reflect on the irony of this. The civil rights movement was the backdrop against which many woman activists cut their political teeth. Some of these women went on to put much of their energy into what was then, in the mid-1970s, a relatively new women's movement in Northern Ireland. In April 1975, female students at Queen's University came together to hold the first public meeting on women's rights. They helped to form an action group with the intention of bringing the role of women in Northern Ireland into line with that of women in Britain. This group later became the Northern Ireland Women's Rights Movement and its first campaign was to have the Sex Discrimination Act extended to Northern Ireland. Although a split occurred with the Socialist Women's Group over the question of anti-imperialism, there are still many issues around which women's groups in Northern Ireland find common ground. Given the relatively small size of the country, many women know and readily acknowledge the political affiliations of those with whom they work. Similarly, it is not uncommon for a woman in Northern Ireland to be active in her women's group, her trade union and her local community so that a good deal of crossover occurs on various issues making the lobbying of political parties and/or statutory bodies so much easier. Unlike Britain, however, women's groups receive little official recognition and much less funding. As a consequence of their grassroots involvement, trade union women have established an extremely healthy relationship between the Irish Congress of Trade Unions (Northern Ireland Committee) and the women's movement in Northern Ireland. Different styles of working are, of course, operated by the two very different organisations. The women's movement tends to be less formally structured and a good deal more spontaneous in its campaigning and advice work whilst it benefits from the direct negotiations which the ICTU has from time to time with various government ministers. Female trade unionists have become particularly active on a variety of social and health issues — holding meetings of local women in various towns throughout Northern Ireland. Equally, on the issue of strip-searching, trade union women's conference resolutions meant that ICTU officials were asked to negotiate with Nicholas Scott (then the Minister responsible for prisons in Northern Ireland).[12]

The women's movement in Northern Ireland has been most influential in effecting political change in working-class communities and in this respect it differs greatly from its more middle-class contemporaries in other countries. It is creating structures which enable un-employed and low-income women to have some measure of control over their lives. This can be particularly noticed in the work of umbrella organisations such as 'The Women's Information Day'.[13]

Other women's groups which deserve credit in this field are Women's Aid, the Women's Education Project and the large number of local community women's groups which are now organising together through the Women's Support Network. All of these work in a non-sectarian way — holding meetings in both nationalist and loyalist areas and raising controversial issues in a way which is sensitive to one another's beliefs. The support of the Protestant working-class women who came together with Catholics in these groups is far from fictitious. On one occasion in 1985, when campaigning on changes to the benefit system, a group of Protestant and Catholic women travelled to London where they lobbied their MPs to oppose the Social Security Bill which was going through Parliament at that time. They were appalled to find that their own political representatives were more interested in opposing the Anglo-Irish Agreement and refused to meet them given their preoccupation with this agreement. The women remained undaunted and before they left Westminster they had successfully lobbied MPs from outside of Northern Ireland by recalling their own personal experiences as claimants. They returned home to Belfast more convinced than ever that their political representatives were *least* interested in the social and economic issues which concerned them as women. The Protestant women in the group had little difficulty in publicly criticising the role of their political representatives which is an increasing feature of Protestant activists in the women's movement in Northern Ireland. [14]

For women campaigning on changes to their social security benefits, one of the most glaring features of life is the hardship of poverty — with all its social, financial and psychological repercussions. Everywhere it is good to be at the top of the economic ladder — in terms of household income, earnings, standards of housing — women in Northern Ireland find themselves at the bottom. Where it would be preferable to be at the bottom — on indicators of unemployment and dependency on social security — women in Northern Ireland find they have the highest ratings. It is against such a background that the term 'feminisation' of poverty takes its meaning. It is women who experience poverty as prisoners' wives, as widows, as single parents, divorced, separated or unmarried, as part of a long-term unemployed family, as single and elderly women living alone, or as low-wage earners (McWilliams, 1987). For the majority, it is both humiliating and degrading. In attempting to combat this many local community/women's groups have now started offering advice and information to women. Women's centres have produced thousands of simple self-explanatory leaflets enabling this process to take place and helping to empower women in the face of overwhelming bureaucracy. Existing from day-to-day can often become an intolerable strain for women who have to provide a reasonable standard of living for their children, as well as having the additional anxiety in Northern Ireland of worrying about husbands and children when they are out of the home. The years of 'the troubles' have added to their pressures and many respond by using tranquillisers or smoking excessively (McGivern and Ward, 1982).[15]

It is women who have led the anti-poverty campaigns

— a politically significant role which is often ignored by the media, by church leaders and by politicians. Kate Kelly argues that the Women's Information Day group was conscious of the way it organised on these issues and therefore refused to let single individuals (or political parties) become solely identified with their campaigns (Kelly, 1985). Their non-hierarchical structure proved time and again to be the kind of supportive political environment the women required. Each became knowledgeable about the issue. Confidence and experience were gathered together and often the women maintained links even after the campaign had been dissolved.

Like women everywhere, women in Northern Ireland have developed interests and confidence through traditional groups such as mother and toddler groups, and budgeting and benefit classes. Although initially daubed as 'family feminists' (because of their altruistic concern with husbands and sons) the Women's Information Group, with many other community groups, has avoided the risk of containment of women. These women's groups have provided a necessary plank in gathering support for women's issues and have initiated campaigns of community validity which have united women across the sectarian divide.

Political divisions and the way forward

It is important finally to examine some of the issues which divide feminists in the women's movement. They are mostly related to the 'national question' — a question which still haunts many women in Northern Ireland. Whether they are single-issue women's groups such as Women's Aid or the Rape and Incest Line or generic groups such as Derry, Belfast or the Falls Road Women's Centres, the political affiliations of the members may be surreptitiously guessed at in order to clarify the line they might take on the national question. The latter might never be discussed in the day-to-day running of the organisation, or if known, may be deliberately ignored to avoid confrontation. Rather than interpreting this as an attempt to silence republicans (or indeed loyalists), what this does mean is that different women's groups adopt different tactics when raising the issue of partition. In Northern Ireland, it would be difficult for any women's group to assume the exclusive prerogative to speak on the national question. Disputes occurred in the late 1970s and early 1980s between the Relatives Action Committee, and Women Against Imperialism, predominantly supporting Sinn Féin, and other women's groups such as the Belfast Women's Collective and the Northern Ireland Women's Rights Movement. The Belfast Women's Collective, formed in 1977, argued that it was 'vital to work in as wide a range of ways as possible, including those which may not initially meet with a large response because they challenge traditional political and religious beliefs' (*Women's Action* May/June, 1978). The Relatives Action Committee, organising around the withdrawal of political status from the H Block Maze Prison, took the view that the campaign around the prisons and particularly that for women, Armagh Prison, should be central. They argued that imperialism was the major dominating force in the lives of women throughout Ireland and specifically the women in West Belfast. (*Women's Action* June, 1978)[16] Whether or not the national question is the *dominant* feature in working-class women's lives remains the subject of much controversy.

Christina Loughran argues that those feminists who gave up their autonomy to go into Sinn Féin have made real gains in terms of the policies adopted. One of the gains to which she refers is 'women's right to choose' which Sinn Féin as a party had opposed until 1985. It does appear that its position on these issues has become more progressive when compared to its earlier castigation of the Northern Ireland Women's Rights Movement for seeking extensions to British legislation on divorce and abortion on the grounds that they were imperialistic reforms and diluted the women's struggle.[17] It has taken a major effort by feminists to challenge the often patriarchal and reactionary attitudes to women which have characterised the nationalist movement. Marie Mulholland argues that this has been the case because much of the experience of women in anti-imperialist and republican organisations is one of having to subjugate their needs as women for the good of the greater cause (Mulholland, 1989).

Despite these divisions in the women's movement which are not uncommon in other organisations in Northern Ireland, it remains the case that the oppression caused by the present political impasse is deeply destructive to all women. Some are psychologically scarred by the deaths of, or injuries to, loved ones, whilst others are emotionally drained trying to cope with the daily tensions of living in the midst of such intense political conflict. Women on both the nationalist and loyalist sides have faced the destruction of family life when husbands, brothers or sons have been arrested under the emergency Prevention of Terrorism Act, tried by Diplock (non-jury) courts and held for long periods without trial on remand. Women have also been subjected to the humiliating and degrading treatment of strip-searching, and women, like Emma Groves, have been blinded by plastic bullets. Two hundred women have been killed since 'the troubles' began and more recently women have become the direct targets of sectarian assassinations (*Belfast Telegraph* February 10, 1993). Women live in fear for their children. Fear that they will be caught in crossfire, shot or injured in a riot or be blown up in an explosion. Eighty children have died in this way and their deaths have pointed to the enormous personal tragedies which some families have had to endure. For others, simply living in the insidious atmosphere of sectarianism and violence can cause increased anxiety in itself whilst other women on a daily basis have to endure the incessant barking of patrol and guard dogs and the continuous noise of army helicopters. These multiple layers of oppression affect the psychological and physical well-being of women in Northern Ireland; some affect women living in nationalist areas more, while others affect Catholics and Protestants equally. These are some of the major issues which feminists have had to tackle, alongside their struggle against economic exploitation and sexual oppression.

The women's movement in Northern Ireland has a daunting task, particularly in the aftermath of the Anglo-Irish Agreement and the recent display of conservative sexism in both Britain and Ireland. In the process many Catholic as well as Protestant women have been further alienated but the women's movement in general is actively striving to create a politics which challenges the conservativism of the northern state, as well as the southern, and the male-dominated ideas of the governing churches. Some progress has been made on the question of equal opportunity. Legislation has been introduced which will monitor workforces for religion (and sex) in order to prevent job discrimination. Interestingly the Equal Opportunities Commission (EOC), which is known to play a much more active role in women's lives than its British counterpart, was almost relegated in Northern Ireland.[18] As a consequence of lobbying and submissions from trade union and community women, the EOC continues to function and provide support for a wide variety of women's groups in the province. Twenty years on and the questions of religious and sex discrimination remain just as pertinent. In their efforts to allay USA fears about Catholic male unemployment, the Northern Ireland Office needs constant reminding that women face the double exploitation of both their sex and their religion. In an attempt to raise women's issues beyond the backyard conservativism of Northern Ireland, women are now organising into a network to directly lobby the European Commission. Some answers have to be found as to why Northern Ireland does not move nearer to the position of European countries on issues involving sexual morality and women's rights. The lack of any liberal democratic representation does make the task more politically difficult for the women's movement. Amidst these difficulties, however, there is a feeling that the ground is being laid for political and social change to take place and that there is a new generation of younger women who are prepared to take up the mantle and speak for themselves. It is their view that women's lives cannot be controlled to the extent that they once were or that women's rights cannot be so blatantly obstructed as they were in the past. In the trade union movement, in students' unions, the Women's Support Network and the wider community, women are negotiating a new agenda. The question of partition will undoubtedly continue to create internal and external divisions amongst women's groups. It is too much to expect that there will not be these differences, or that they will always be healthy. Learning to respect each other, and to prioritise differently has long been a feature of the women's movement. It is to the credit of women's groups that they have 'stayed the course' against all odds. They have recognised that mobilisation around issues of social emancipation and economic advancement can in turn lead to movement on issues of democratic rights. Moreover, they have crossed over traditional boundaries and drawn women from all sections of the working class into such struggles. Any categorisation of such a strategy as 'reformist' invariably attempts to dismiss the progressive advances that they have made.[19] It will be the case though, that when the alternative ways forward in Northern Ireland are being debated, the mainstream politicians will still need reminding that the women's movement should be included in such discussions. Women have ensured their right to be involved and now need to be central and not marginal in the social, economic and political decisions which affect their lives. They have endured too much for that to happen again.

Notes

1 Gemma Hussey used this phrase frequently during speeches as a minister in the coalition government in the Irish Republic in the late 1970s.

2 This was later amended in 1984, due mainly to demand and the backlog of cases awaiting hearing at the Belfast High Court.

3 Interview with J. McGettrick, Belfast solicitor, speaking about his first case under the new legislation.

4 Interview with Madge Davidson, barrister, recalling her work in magistrates' courts.

5 Derry Film and Video Workshop, 'Mother Ireland', (1988-89) researched and directed by A Crilly, scheduled to be televised on Channel 4 but not shown, following the death of Mairéad Farrell in Gibraltar. An edited version was eventually broadcast in 1991.

6 Nóirín Ní Cléirigh, Nuala Ní Dhómhnaill and others involved in 'Women in Irish Culture' workshop, Conway Mill, March 1989.

7 *Regional Trends 1992*. In 1985 the figure for Britain was 52 per cent and that for Northern Ireland was 45 per cent.

8 1.9 children is the equivalent British figure.

9 75 per cent of births outside marriage are to women under 20 years (HMSO *Social Trends*, 1992). For earlier debates see J. Ditch, *Social Policy In Northern Ireland 1939-50*, Avebury 1988.

10 Phrase coined by Charles Haughey, Taoiseach, to describe Irish family planning.

11 Board of Guardians in P. Devlin. 1984. *Yes, We Have No Bananas*, Farset Press, Belfast. Eddie McAteer, nationalist MP in Stormont in the 1950s, responded to this by suggesting that Catholics in turn should take all the benefits to which they were entitled and not concern themselves with any allegiance to the British Welfare State as a consequence of claiming. J. Biggs Davison also reports that Catholics were prepared to accept the half crown but not the Crown.

12 ICTU Women's Conference, Malahide 1986. In April 1986 representatives of the Northern Ireland Committee (ICTU) met with Nicholas Scott and the Northern Ireland Office at Stormont Castle to negotiate over the issue of strip-searching when the women were being changed from Armagh Jail to the new prison at Maghaberry. The female prisoners were not stripsearched when the move took place.

13 Women's Information Day meets on the first Tuesday of each month in alternative Catholic and Protestant (or neutral) venues. Between 70 and 100 women attend these meetings.

14 This lobby was organised by the Northern Ireland Women's Rights Movement as part of the protests against the White Paper on Social Security, November 1986.

15 McGivern and Ward (1982) claim that 35 million tranquillisers are used in Northern Ireland each year and that twice as many women as men are dependent.

16 *Women's Action* was the newsletter of the Belfast Women's Collective. It is now defunct. A different newsletter, *Women's News*, began in 1985 in Belfast and is still in operation.

17 Minutes of the Northern Ireland Women's Rights Movement, 1976.

18 The question of religious discrimination was to dominate the legislation, with issues of sex discrimination and in turn equal opportunities taking a secondary role.

19 Christina Loughran has used the term 'reformist' in her analysis of feminism in Northern Ireland in *Trouble And Strife*, No. 11 (1988).

References and further reading
Harkin, C. and Kilmurray, A. 1985. In Abbott, M. and Frazer, H. (eds), *Women In Community Work*. Farset Press, Belfast,

Healey, S. and Reynolds, B. 1987. 'The Christian Churches and the Poor'. In E. Hanna (ed.), *Poverty In Ireland*, Social Study Conference.

Holland, M. 1988. *The Irish Times*, February 20.

Inglis, T. 1987. *Moral Monopoly*. Gill and Macmillan, Dublin.

Irish Catholic Bishops' Pastoral Letter. 1985. *Love Is For Life*. April.

Kelly, K. 'Women's Information Day' In *Women In Community Work*, Farset Press, Belfast.

McCafferty, N. 1989. In Mulholland M. (ed.), *Unfinished Revolution*,

McDonagh, R. 1989. Review of *Unfinished Revolution* in *Women's News*, Belfast. April.

McGivern, M. T. and Ward, M. 1982. 'Images Of Women In Northern Ireland'. In *The Crane Bag*, Vol. 4, No. 1.

McShane, L. 1987. 'Day Nurseries in Northern Ireland 1941 — 1955'. In Curtin, C. et al, (eds.), *Gender In Irish Society*. Galway University Press, Galway.

McWilliams, M. 1987. 'Poverty in N Ireland'. In Hanna, E. (ed.), *Poverty In Ireland*. Social Study Conference.

McWilliams, M. 1991. 'Women's Paid Work and the Sexual Division Of Labour'. In Davies C. and McLaughlin E. (eds.), *Women, Employment and Social Policy in Northern Ireland*. Policy Research Institute, Queen's University, Belfast.

Morrissey, H. 1980. *Unemployment, The Other Crisis*. Ulster Polytechnic, Occasional Papers.

Mulholland, M. (ed.). 1989. *Unfinished Revolution*. Maedbh Publishing, Belfast.

NI Abortion Law Reform Association. 1989. *Abortion in Northern Ireland, The Report of an International Tribunal*. Pale Publications, Belfast.

O'Dowd, L. 1987. 'Church, State and Women'. In Curtin, C. et al (eds.). *Gender in Irish Society*. Galway University Press, Galway.

Rowland, B. 1985. In Abbott, M. and Frazer, H. *Women in Community Work*. Farset Press, Belfast.

Warner, M. 1985. *Alone Of All Her Sex*. Quartet, London.

Discussion Topics

1 Discuss the impact of church and state on women's lives in Northern Ireland.

2 Discuss the impact of the political situation on the women's movement in Northern Ireland.

3 Analyse the interaction of nationalism and feminism in Northern Ireland.

4 What effective political, legislative and social changes have women been responsible for initiating in Northern Ireland?

5 Ways forward for the women's movement and the creation of safe spaces for women to organise.

Women and the Law in Ireland

Senator Mary Robinson

An examination of the laws of a country, including its Constitution, gives important insights into the approach of that country to women and to issues of importance to women. A Constitution which recognises 'that by her life within the home, woman gives to the State a support without which the common good cannot be achieved,' and which both prohibits divorce and equates the right to life of the mother with the right to life of the unborn child sets defined limits on the role of women in that society.

Law is a hidden infrastructure which conditions our society and pervades almost every aspect of our lives. People have different perceptions of law, but on the whole tend to underestimate its scope and influence. However, if we run through a quick checklist — the Constitution, the courts, the government, the Oireachtas, legislation, the common law, the civil service, the gardaí, the prison system and the legal profession — it becomes obvious how significant law is and how deeply it penetrates into every aspect of our lives.

Since law has such a significant and far-reaching role in our society, this gives rise to the next set of questions. Who has been making the law? Who has been interpreting the law? Who has been administering the law? Who has been enforcing the law? Who has been providing legal services? The answer is the same in each case: either exclusively or predominantly, men. No woman had a hand in drafting the Constitution. The vast majority of TDs and senators have been, and continue to be, male. In recent times there has been one woman in government, a ratio of 1:15. Ireland inherited the common law system which had been compiled by male judges, and most of the judges who interpret our Constitution and laws are men. Men are dominant at the senior levels of the civil service, in the gardaí, in the legal profession and even among trade union officials.

The extent to which this matters can best be illustrated by looking at how law has affected women in an historic perspective. At the beginning of the nineteenth century, when Britain and Ireland were joined in the Act of Union, women had virtually no rights at all. They were chattels of their fathers and subsequently of their husbands. They could not vote. They could not sign contracts. When married, they could not own property. They had no rights over their children and no control over their own bodies. Their husbands could rape and beat them without any interference from the law. Those women who worked were forced to join the lowest levels of the labour force for unequal wages. From that grim starting point considerable progress has been made in eliminating the obvious areas of sex discrimination and victimisation. Indeed, during the 1980s Ireland ratified the UN Convention for the Elimination of all Forms of Discrimination against Women and had to implement a series of EC directives ensuring equality in the work force and in social welfare.

Law can be an important instrument of social change. This has been recognised by those individual women who were prepared to use the courts to challenge the existing system. Their names have entered legal history: Mrs Magee on the contraceptive issue; Máirín de Burca on jury selection, Mrs Airey on legal aid, the Murphys on married taxation, and later the Johnstons on the rights of a family outside marriage. Of course, there have been set-backs as well, as evidenced by the Hamilton judgement,[1] but the potential of test cases has been realised.

It is hardly surprising that women in Northern Ireland who have examined the laws in this part of the country have been less than enthusiastic. But we do not like or appreciate their critical appraisal of our laws. An example of this was provided by the New Ireland Forum. There were two public sessions in which issues of equality and the position of women were raised. At the first, the Women's Law and Research Group from Northern Ireland compared in detail the social legislation affecting women in both parts of Ireland and were very critical of the south. Although this session was filmed by RTE there were objections by certain Forum members to it being broadcast — an interesting example of Forum censorship. At the second, the chairperson of the Employment Equality Agency, Sylvia Meehan, urged that in the context of a new Ireland what was needed was an integrated economic and social approach to the achievement of equality. Despite the fact that there was a full discussion of the values and issues which arose during each of these sessions, when it came to writing the final report on a new Ireland all reference to this dimension of equality was omitted. The subject had been dealt with, but it did not really impinge on the political realities with which the forum members were preoccupied.

Another revealing aspect of a country is its approach to law reform, particularly in the social and family area. Ireland's record has been poor, as is shown in the Report of the Joint Committee on Marriage Breakdown. However, a significant impact on the approach to law reform has been achieved by women's organisations which focussed their energies in this area: Cherish, in securing the abolition of the concept of illegitimacy; AIM in securing reform of maintenance and barring orders; the Rape Crisis Centre in urging reform of our rape law, etc.

However, whilst acknowledging the importance of the progress which has been made, it is necessary to pose the further question: Is it significant for women in Ireland in 1986 that men are still dominant as lawmakers, as members of the government, as judges, as senior civil servants, as law enforcers and as legal practitioners?

I believe the answer is Yes, and that the significance is greater than many women appreciate. It is not simply a question of wanting more women *per se* involved in the various bodies. It is because the male domination at all levels affects the very ethos and culture of our society. It reinforces sex stereotyping and role conditioning. Those with control over the levers of power have little reason to want to change the establishment. At the moment it is male perceptions and male priorities that dominate. Are they necessarily the same as the perceptions and the priorities of women?

One way of testing that is to imagine an Ireland where women shared equally in the government and administration of the state. If half the Oireachtas and half the members of the government were women, would the priorities remain the same? Most men would probably doubt whether it would make a significant difference, whereas most women would see immediately that there would be a different order of priorities. Social legislation and family law reform would have a much higher rating. Unemployment and under-employment would be looked at from a different perspective and lead to more imaginative solutions. Business lunches and expense accounts might come under a colder scrutiny as would the whole ordering of the working week. It is hard to believe that childcare facilities and crèches would remain such a neglected area.

Another way of putting it to the test is to examine the approach adopted to the scope and interpretation of the two basic concepts in the Constitution: the protection of the family and the guarantee of equality under the law. Articles 41 and 42 recognise the family as the fundamental unit group of society and guarantee it special protection. However, the family in question is the family based on a valid subsisting marriage. These provisions have been interpreted to exclude from the definition of family the single mother and her child or children. A whole jurisprudence has been built up on this concept of the constitutional family.

The child of a constitutional family has more rights under the Constitution than a child who was not fortunate enough to be born into a constitutional family, and so on. The constitutional family is the traditional model family: husband, wife, and children. The Constitution recognises that the wife in this model family 'by her life within the home . . . gives to the State a support without which the common good cannot be achieved'. But what kind of limbo does this create for the other families of the state? What about the large number of single mothers and their children? What about couples who live together without marrying, either by choice or because one or the other is already married? This approach of confining family rights only to the family based on a valid subsisting marriage is contrary to the European Convention for the Protection of Human Rights and Fundamental Freedoms, and it is contrary to the interests of a significant number of women and their children.

The second concept, equality before the law (Article 40.1) has been characterised by one High Court judge as 'probably the most difficult and illusive concept contained in the Constitution.' Equality was interpreted as being confined to equality as a human person, and equality in relation to being involved in a trade or profession. As a consequence, it was not the guarantee of equality under the Constitution, but rather the obligations on Ireland of membership of the EC which led to the enactment of equality legalisation in the mid-1970s.

Devising an effective strategy
Given that the numerical situation is unlikely to change in the short term, in that men will probably be dominant in the power structures for the foreseeable future, can an effective strategy be devised to redress this imbalance? The answer is Yes, but the approach must be strategic and effective. The following factors are relevant to the formulation of such a strategy.
- It is vital that a sufficient number of women recognise that the domination by men in the power structures of our society *does* matter.
- That it is an imbalance which affects the ethos and priorities of that society, and that it must be altered in a concerted manner.
- That knowledge is power. Unless women's groups and women more generally have access to knowledge of the laws and institutions which affect them, they cannot seek to exert effective influence.
- Because women are outnumbered in the various power structures, it is all the more important that they develop skills of effective lobbying in order to influence priorities and bring about change.

- Consideration should be given in appropriate circumstances to the use of the test case to accelerate legal change. Women's organisations could consider establishing a legal fund to help support test cases in appropriate areas.
- Women activists in the trade union movement should examine their ambivalence towards lawyers and the courts. However understandable their reservations in that regard, equality law cannot be fully effective until there is a healthy jurisprudence developed in the Labour Court and on appeal on a point of law to the High Court.
- In recent years there has been a welcome development of Women's Studies in third level colleges and extra-curricular courses throughout Ireland. An important component in such courses should be a basic grounding in law.
- Women judges and lawyers could be more active in challenging any traditions of their profession which are blatantly sexist.

Conclusion
Until now the broad approach of the women's movement has been to seek the removal of existing discrimination against women or victimisation of women. From now on the strategy must become more positive. Women must learn to harness the existing resources in an effective and strategic manner in order to compensate for their lack of numbers in the power structures themselves. For centuries women were the victims under discriminatory laws. Now that same instrument of law can be invoked by women as a powerful ally in seeking social change.

Note
1 This refers to the High Court case taken by the Society for the Protection of the Unborn Child (SPUC) in 1984, against the Dublin Well Woman Centre and Open Line Counselling. Justice Liam Hamilton ruled that it is against the Constitution to discuss the option of abortion with another person, or to give any information which might facilitate her to obtain an abortion. As a consequence, both counselling services have had to cease functioning. *Editor's note.*

Further reading *Suggested by the Editor*

Buckley, M. and Anderson, M. 1988. *Women, Equality and Europe.* Macmillan, London.

Connelly, A. (ed.). 1993. *Gender and the Law in Ireland.* Oak Tree Press, Dublin.

Curtin, D. 1989. *Irish Employment Equality Law.* Round Hall Press, Dublin.

Irish Council for Civil Liberties. 1990. *Equality Now.* ICCL, Dublin

O'Connor, P. 1989. *Key Issues in Irish Family Law.* Round Hall Press, Dublin.

Reid, M. 1990. *The Impact of Community Law on the Irish Constitution.* Irish Centre for European Law, Dublin.

Reid, M. 1992 'Abortion and the Law in Ireland after the Maastricht Referendum'. In Smyth, Ailbhe, (ed.), *The Abortion Papers: Ireland.* Attic Press, Dublin.

Report of the Second Commission on the Status of Women. 1993. Stationery Office, Dublin.

Robinson, M. 1978. 'Women and the New Irish State'. In MacCurtain M. and O Corráin D. (eds.), *Women in Irish Society: The Historical Dimension.* Arlen House, Dublin.

Scannell, Y. 1988. 'The Constitution and the Role of Women'. In Farrell, B. (ed.). *De Valera's Constitution and Ours.* Gill and Macmillan Dublin.

Shanahan, K. 1992. *Crimes Worse than Death.* Attic Press, Dublin.

Shatter, A. 1986. (3rd ed.) *Family Law in the Republic of Ireland.* Wolfhound, Dublin.

Whyte, G. 1988. *Sex Equality, Community Rights and Irish Social Welfare Law.* Irish Centre for European Law, Dublin.

Discussion topics *Suggested by the Editor*

1 Discuss the ways in which law marks our everyday lives. Choose one aspect of the scope of the law (eg government, legislation, the civil service, the prison system) and examine its particular impact on women's lives.

2 Discuss the principal ways in which the 1937 Constitution limits the role of women in Irish society.

3 Do you agree that law can be an important instrument of social change? To what degree has it been used as such by women in contemporary Ireland?

4 Choose one area in which you consider law reform to be urgently needed and discuss the reforms you would like to see introduced and why.

5 What kinds of strategies do you think have been — or will be — most effective in seeking to change the gender imbalance within Irish power structures?

6 Discuss the ways in which gender and class combine to produce particular forms of discrimination against women in Ireland.

Rape: Myths and Reality

Madeleine Leonard

Introduction

The fourteen-year-old girl who travelled to England for an abortion in February 1992 catapulted the issue of rape into the centre of public consciousness in Ireland. The incident simultaneously challenged and reinforced myths regarding rape in modern society. One of the most frequent assumptions about rape is that it is a rare and random act committed by strangers usually in dark, deserted streets and alleyways. The girl in this case not only knew her attacker but he was a trusted family acquaintance and the father of one of her school friends. Mr Justice Costello, in his judgement granting an application for an injunction restraining the girl from travelling to England for an abortion, described the girl's abuser as 'depraved and evil'. In doing so, Costello strengthened the myth that rape is committed by a small lunatic fringe of the male population. While such a view may indeed explain why some males rape, a closer look at the facts of rape reveals a much more systematic occurrence of the phenomenon. Feminist researchers link rape to the structural conditions of inequality between males and females in patriarchal societies. Interacting with other patriarchal social structures, rape functions as a mechanism of social control to keep women in their place. Through rape myths, the state and male ideologies legitimate and conceal male violence against women. This chapter elaborates on the issue by demystifying some of the most prevalent rape myths. By drawing mainly on the cases reported to the Belfast Rape Crisis Centre, it will illustrate how rape and the fear of rape produce and reproduce patriarchal social structures sustaining female subordination to males.

Psychological approaches to rape

Up until the 1970s, most of the research on rape was psychological rather than sociological. Rather than look for cultural and social explanations of rape as an act, researchers looked at rapists as individuals. Hence the research focused on convicted offenders. Such a focus failed to acknowledge the widespread under-reporting of rape to the police. The convicted rapist's problems were found to lie in early childhood with the rape being viewed as an attempt to overcome castration fears, fears of sexual inadequacy or latent homosexuality (Wilson, 1983: 63). The rapist was portrayed as a sexual psychopath unable to contain or control his sexual urges. Media coverage of a few notorious rapists served to reinforce this stereotype of the typical rapist. However, studies of known rapists have undermined this notion. In fact, less than 5 per cent of convicted rapists have been diagnosed as clinically psychotic during the time of a rape assault (Scully, 1990; Walby, 1990). Indeed a number of recent psychological studies indicate the normativeness of rape (Matoesian, 1993: 6-10). Wilson points out that most rapists are 'quintessentially ordinary'. It is not so much that they are rapists rather they have simply 'as normal men raped someone' (1983: 60). This view is backed up by Mackinnon (1989) who argues that the propensity to rape is not only widespread but also normative sexual behaviour or an extension of normal sexual behaviour in the male population. If this is the case, then we need to focus on the structures and myths through which rape and sexual violence against women are reproduced and legitimated.

Rape myths
Radical feminists suggest that while patriarchal ideology overtly condemns rape, it covertly legitimates it by upholding various myths regarding male and female sexuality. One of the most prevalent cultural stereotypes of rape is that it is an act between strangers carried out in a dark deserted place. However, rape is not, for the most part, committed by strangers in lonely places. Amir (1971) found that just 50 per cent of victims and offenders in rape cases were known to each other. Moreover most rapes occurred in the home of either the victim or offender. Russell's data revealed that a staggering 83 per

cent of rapes she studied took place among people known to each other (1984). Similarly in Belfast, the cases dealt by the Rape Crisis Centre indicated that 71.5 per cent of women were raped by someone they knew (Belfast rape Crisis Centre, 1991). The Belfast Rape Crisis Centre also found that the most dangerous place for women is their own home. Thirty-one per cent of the women they dealt with were raped in the one place where they should feel most safe and secure, their own home.

Wilson (1983: 65) argues that planned rape dismantles the myth of rape as the expression of explosive, urgent, uncontrollable sexual urge. This myth also transfers the blame to the woman as it was her body that engendered the desire which was then enacted upon it (Smart, 1991: 164). In fact, rape is often a carefully planned act rather than the outcome of uncontrollable sexual desire and provocation. Sixty-three per cent of cases dealt with by the Belfast Rape Crisis Centre in the first six months of its existence were planned rapes.

Sexual gratification is rarely the basis for rape. Smart and Smart (1978) argue that rape is an act of violence and domination in which the sexual act becomes the mechanism to totally debase and dehumanise the victim. Hence the rape is usually unrelated to the physical characteristics or behaviour of the specific rape victim. Yet, common-sense understandings of rape continue to focus on the attributes of the individual rape victim. Hence 'nice girls don't get raped', 'women enjoy or want sex', 'they ask for it', 'women lie/exaggerate about rape incidents' 'a woman can't be raped against her will' (Matoesian, 1993: 13). These myths serve to underline the impression that rape is an isolated act having no structural relationship to other social practices and phenomena, or to the unequal and exploitative nature of the relationships between men and women in general (Smart and Smart, 1978).

The legal system upholds these myths and in the process decriminalises and legitimates the act of rape. According to Smart (1989), rape cases illuminate the operation of the law not as a gender-neutral institution but as a socially structured and gendered component of patriarchal domination. In Britain and Northern Ireland, rape is solely defined as a crime in which a man through the threat or actual use of force penetrates a woman`s vagina with his penis. The Belfast Rape Crisis Centre argues that this definition is inadequate. It needs to be extended to include oral and anal rape as well as rape with inanimate objects. Many women who consulted the Belfast Rape Crisis Centre were raped with items such as pokers, bottles, umbrellas and knives (Belfast Rape Crisis Centre, 1991: 8). To date, none of these are classified as rape but diminished to sexual assault.

Rape within marriage
One recent feminist victory was having the issue of rape extended to forced sex within marriage. Up until 1991, marital rape was non-existent within British law. Drawing on the writings of Sir Matthew Hale, an eighteenth-century legal commentator, there could be no such thing as rape within marriage (Kennedy, 1992: 130). This was because marriage was viewed as a contract between husband and wife, one of the terms of which was that the wife would consent to sexual intercourse at any time. It also lent weight to archaic assumptions that the wife was the husband's property. Indeed, the original meaning of the Latin word from which rape derives was 'to seize or carry off' (Wilson 1983: 60). In ancient times, warring tribes commonly raided one another and women as well as cattle and goods were abducted. Hence, women were considered as one component of the man's property. In January 1992, the Law Commission stated that rape within marriage should be recognised as a crime and added to the statute books on the same basis as any other rape. In his ruling, Lord Lane stated: 'A rapist remains a rapist irrespective of his relationship with the victim' (Belfast Rape Crisis Centre, 1991: 7). This ruling has met with strong opposition from some quarters of the legal profession. In two articles of the *New Law Journal* in 1992, Professor Williams, an academic authority on clinical law, has scolded feminists for this reform. He argues that husbands who enforce intercourse on their wives should

at most be charged with common assault and tried in the Magistrates' Court. Alternatively, a new, less serious offence should be introduced, called 'marital abuse' which would not carry the threat of imprisonment. As Williams puts it:

> Occasionally some husband continues to exercise what he regards as his right when his wife refuses him, the refusal most probably resulting from the fact that the pair have had a tiff. What is wrong with this demand is not so much the act requested but its timing . . . The fearsome stigma of rape is too great a punishment for husbands who use their strength in these circumstances. (Cited in Kennedy, 1992: 134).

However the occasional nature of this offence is not backed up by the research in this area. Recent surveys in countries where rape within marriage has been illegal for a number of years have shown that at least one in seven wives suffer rape within marriage. Statistics for the Rape Crisis Centre in Belfast show that almost ten per cent of the women who contacted the Centre had been raped by their husbands or boyfriends (Belfast Rape Crisis Centre 1991: 7). Moreover when married women involved the police, the rape has usually taken place against a background of domestic violence and is often the culmination of beatings and other indignities (Kennedy, 1992: 133).

Rape and the Legal System

One crucial problem regarding rape within marriage and indeed rape in general concerns the issue of consent. The word 'No' is at the centre of a rape trial. A 'No' may be unproblematic when a 'respectable woman' is attacked by a total stranger in a dimly lit street, but since the majority of rapes are committed by men known to the victim, consent in rape trials has always been a problematic issue. As Kennedy puts it 'where does seduction end and rape begin' (1992: 111). Stanko argues that the perception of 'force' and 'consent' are constructed through the use of male definitions of these terms (1985: 38). These understandings are generally perceived in terms of women's sexuality rather than men's coercion. So, to fully understand women's experiences of rape then we need to reconstruct these concepts. When looking at the concept of force, for example, we must recognise the relatively smaller size and strength of women compared to men. Women are often surrounded by experts who suggest ways about how to say 'No' to a rapist and survive. Yet when women adopt a passive role in order to minimise the potential physical violence accompanying the rape, then they are accused of co-operating with being raped. According to Stanko, the notion of consent is also wrapped within the blanket of male presumptions about women's behaviour (1985: 39). Getting a woman to submit is part of the sexual game enhanced by the notion that once pressed into submission, the woman will melt into the experience and find pleasure in it. Such a view erases the responsibility for the violence, fear and humiliation involved (Kennedy, 1992: 111). These male prejudices are often reflected in the comments of judges at rape trials. Judge Wild stated in 1982:

> Women who say No do not always mean No. It is not just a question of how she says it, how she shows and makes it clear. If she doesn't want it she only has to keep her legs shut and she would not get it without force and then there would be the marks of force being used

Kennedy cites another example from a trial at the Old Bailey in 1989:

> *Prosecuting Counsel:* And you say she consented?
> *Defendant:* I didn't say she consented.
> *Prosecuting Counsel:* Did she agree?
> *Defendant:* She didn't agree.
> *Prosecuting Counsel:* Having said No at first, she just gave in?
> *Defendant:* She enjoyed it.

Here the judge offered some judical assistance:

> *Judge:* The enjoyment wiped out her initial resistance — is that what you are saying?
> *Defendant:* Yes.
> (Kennedy, 1992: 112).

Kennedy's book is full of other examples which illustrate male assumptions regarding female sexuality. She argues that in court, the woman's 'No' is covered in ambiguity and not taken seriously if she is vivacious and friendly, if she dresses provocatively, if she goes out late at night or has had sex with others before. Smart argues that rape trials illustrate the 'maleness of the law' and often this maleness is reflected in the contentious prejudicial statements of judges involved in rape cases (1991). In rape trials, the woman's experience of rape is transformed into consensual sex through the social organisation of courtroom talk (Matoesian, 1993: 8). Wilson suggests that this denies women the reality of their experience, account and memory (1983: 61). The result of this is to make women non-persons in rape trials.

Judges also disclose their biases in passing sentences. Rape still has a lower conviction rate than any other crime. The maximum penalty for attempted rape has increased from seven years to carry a life sentence. However, in practice sentences rarely reflect the gravity of the crime. In the experience of the Belfast Rape Crisis Centre, judges often give lighter sentences when the rapist pleads guilty using the reason that he wanted to spare the woman the trauma of having to give evidence. While this may well be commendable, the Rape Crisis Centre believe that such remorse is merely a ploy to obtain a reduced sentence and is an insult to the survivors of sexual violence. The Belfast Rape Crisis Centre cites the following examples of convictions in rape trials.

> In September 1986, a fifty-year-old man admitted in Belfast Crown Court to raping and indecently assaulting a ten-year-old girl. Judge Gibson accepted that the man had been under severe emotional difficulties and had shown 'great remorse' for what he had done. He was sentenced to five years imprisonment.
>
> In 1986, a forty-one-year old man was convicted for six years in Armagh Crown Court for raping his sixteen-year-old daughter.
>
> In 1987, Judge John McKee gave thirty-five-year old Philip McCann a one-year sentence for attempted rape of a five-year-old girl.
>
> (Belfast Rape Crisis Centre, 1991: 9-10).

Until judges and other men in the legal system look seriously at their attitudes to women we will have to continue to deal with a legal system which can get away with making such statements in rape cases as:

> Judge Gibbens in 1983 told a man accused of raping a seven-year-old girl that he had 'considerable sympathy' with the case which struck him as 'one of the kind of accidents which happen in life to almost anyone' (Belfast Rape Crisis Centre, 1991: 9).

> Mr Justice Alliot in July 1991 gave a rapist a three-year jail sentence (although the recommended minimum was five years) because his victim was a 'common prostitute' and a 'whore'. In passing sentence he explained 'while everyone is entitled to complain about being violated, someone who for years has flaunted their body and sold it cannot complain as loudly as someone who has not' (Kennedy, 1992: 121).

> Judge John Prosser in 1993 ordered a fifteen-year-old rapist who had raped a fifteen-year-old girl to pay her £500 to 'give this girl a chance to have a good holiday to help her get over her trauma, and went on to describe the rapist as 'one of the most popular boys in the school' (*Daily Telegraph*, 20 February, 1993).

In the light of these lenient sentences and the judges' patriarchal attitudes, many women are unwilling to report rape to the police. The Belfast Rape Crisis Centre estimate that only about 21 per cent of the cases they deal with are reported to the police.

Another problem involves the distinction between rape and incest. If forced intercourse takes place between father and daughter, it is classified as incest rather than rape. In the Republic of Ireland, the maximum sentence for incest is seven years whereas the maximum sentence for rape is life imprisonment. This disparity in sentencing was clearly evident in a case that came before the Central Criminal Court in Dublin in March 1993. A man received a seven-year jail sentence for subjecting his daughter to a sixteen-year nightmare of unrelenting sexual and physical attacks. The woman had a son by her father and in one particularly savage attack was blinded in one eye.

Her father also smashed her fingers with a lump hammer and broke her ribs with a steel bar. The director of the Rape Crisis Centre in Dublin described the sentence as 'appalling' and pointed out 'if the man had raped a woman outside the family, he could have been given life imprisonment, but the maximum sentence for incest is seven years'. Clearly, a change in the law is needed. In general, sentencing in rape and incest cases remains too lenient.

Pornography and rape
Over recent years there has been a growing awareness of the links between pornography and rape. Feminists argue that pornography reinforces rape myths. This is because most rape stories in pornography end with the woman changing her mind and having orgasms and being represented as enjoying rape. Such a representation enables rapists to justify and legitimate what they do (Wyre, 1992: 236). According to Wyre, the rape myths that are promoted in pornography also influence the attitudes of the police and the courts. In February 1993, anti-pornography campaigners, including the MP for South Belfast, staged a two-day exhibition of obscene material at the House of Commons. Concern in Northern Ireland focuses on the alleged links between paramilitaries and the pornography trade. Unclassified explicit videos are available on the black market in Northern Ireland and it is alleged that most of these videos are supplied by paramilitaries. During November 1991, police seized 750 pornographic tapes in raids across the province. A 1990 Home Office Report concluded that 'existing evidence did not point to pornography as a cause of sexual deviation in offenders.'

However some groups in Northern Ireland are convinced that such links exist. In 1989, the Christian Action Research and Education Group (CARE) launched a campaign against pornography called 'Picking up the Pieces'. They visited newsagents and encouraged them to stop stocking 'soft' porn magazines. A spokesperson for the organisation stated 'pornography ruins relationships, degrades and exploits women and in our opinion is related to sexual crime' (*Belfast Telegraph*, 16 February, 1993). From their research, both Wyre and Russell believe that pornography trivialises the trauma of rape and encourages audiences to believe that only certain types of women are likely to be raped (Wyre, 1992; Byrne, 1992). Russell argues that pornography undermines some men's internal inhibitions and social inhibitions against acting out their desire to rape (1992: 321). The belief that women secretly like to be raped diminishes men's internal inhibitions against acting out this desire. The most obvious social inhibition against acting out a desire to rape is getting caught and convicted for the crime. Pornography dilutes this threat. Russell argues that viewing violent pornography leads males to believe that rape is a much easier crime to commit than they had previously assumed. Pornography viewers are less likely to believe that rape victims would report their rapes to the police and are more likely to believe that rapists would not be prosecuted or convicted in those cases that are reported.

Strip-searching, sectarianism and rape

Two other issues peculiar to Northern Ireland are worth mentioning here. The first concerns strip-searching in Maghaberry prison and the second concerns the link between sectarianism and rape. As regards the first issue, since April 1991 the prison administration at Maghaberry have stated that anyone refusing to comply with a strip-search can have their clothes forcibly removed by prison officers. This threat was carried out on 2 March 1992 when twenty-one women refused to comply with a strip-search. These women were forcibly strip-searched in their cells. This was achieved by four female officers holding the woman down while others tore her clothes from her body. In some cases this was in view of male prison officers. The Committee Against Strip-Searching regard forcible strip-searching as sexual assault. They see this process as legalised rape. A case brought against the prison administration by the women was unsuccessful and is being appealed. It is worth noting that strip-searching in general has only uncovered some perfume and a five pound note. However, many women's groups in Northern Ireland are unwilling to become involved in this issue. Rather than see strip-searching as a violation against women in general, they see the issue as a political one and feel that backing this campaign is also backing the republican movement in Northern Ireland. This is despite the fact that women other than 'republicans' were involved in the strip-searches. Moreover, many women's groups obtain government funding for their work and feel this source of income could be withdrawn if they become too critical of aspects of the state in Northern Ireland.

McVeigh, in his analysis of sectarianism in West Belfast, found a link between sectarianism and rape. Catholic women in particular seemed to feel threatened by sectarian harassment in Belfast city centre. While initially McVeigh believed that this was simply due to the possibility of any woman feeling unsafe in the city centre at night, the explicitly sectarian aspect was pointed out by a spokesperson from a women's group located in West Belfast:

> As a woman you are always aware that violence is always there because men have that power. In a sectarian society you are aware that that power can be directed in a sectarian way. It is a status symbol among loyalist skinheads to rape a Catholic woman. There's a parallel there with black women — the idea of using sexual violence to defile a woman . . . I know of three (Catholic) women who have been raped in that way in the last year (McVeigh, 1990: 193).

However, while this may account for a small percentage of rapes in Northern Ireland, it neglects the fact that most rapists are known to their victims and most rapes are carried out in the home of the attacker or victim. The correlation that the respondent makes with the race aspect of rape reinforces the archetypal mythic rape of a white woman by a black man. Again this myth does not correspond to the reality (Wilson, 1983: 66). One is left wondering whether the political situation in Nothern Ireland is simply utilised by some rapists to provide them with an excuse and a reason for doing what they do. A parallel can be drawn here between political rape and the 'deviance disavowal' techniques outlined by McCaghy in his study of drinking and deviance (1968). McCaghy was looking at a group of men who were all pleading guilty to the sexual abuse of minors. They admitted that they did the deed but tried to excuse and justify their behaviour by arguing that it wasn't they who did the molesting but the alcohol. When they were sober they were decent people who would never hurt a fly but when they drank this horrible beast came out. In relation to rape and sectarianism, we need to ask if these political beliefs preceded the behaviour or if they merely constitute a later attempt to rationalise the behaviour. Doing it 'for God and Ulster' allows some rapists to explain, excuse, minimise, justify and legitimate their sex crime.

Rape and social control

According to Brownmiller, rape is neither more nor less than a conscious process of intimidation by which all men keep all women in a state of fear (1975: 15). She goes on to outline elaborate safety procedures which women should implement to safeguard against rape. The Belfast Rape Crisis Centre outlines strategies women should follow to lessen the possibility of rape — in the home, on the street and in the car. Hence the fear of rape constitutes an effective form of social control. Giffin states:

> The fear of rape keeps women off the streets at night. Keeps women at home. Keeps women passive and modest for fear that they be thought provocative (Wilson, 1983: 100).

As Wilson points out, it is not the rape itself which constitutes a form of social control but the internalisation by women of the possibility of rape. In this sense then, all women are victims of rape. As Clarke and Lewis conclude:

> The fear of rape affects all women. It inhibits their actions and limits their freedom, influencing the way they dress, the hours they keep, the routes they walk. The fear is well founded, because no woman is immune from rape (1977:23).

This fear of rape produces and reproduces patriarchal social structures and institutions which sustain and justify female subordination to males (Walby, 1990). Differential sex-role socialisation plays an important role here. Male violence against women is normalised and legitimised in sexual practices through the assumption that when it comes to sex, men are by nature aggressive and dominant whereas women are by nature passive and submissive. Males express their superiority over women and express their manhood through sexual violence. Tong argues that because male dominance and female submission are the norm in something as fundamental as sexuality, they become the norm in other contexts as well (1989). Hence women will never be men's full political, social and economic equals until heterosexual relations become egalitarian. Tong concludes that such a state of affairs remains unlikely to be achieved so long as sexuality is interpreted in terms of men's sexuality.

The state through its legal apparatus ideologically condones rape as it continues to reflect patriarchal standards and beliefs about sexual access. Failing to take into account the female's experience of violation, the legal system institutionalises a decriminalised position on rape (Matoesian, 1993). As a result, women who have been sexually assaulted frequently end up feeling that they themselves are to blame. Rape stereotypes and myths allow women to take the blame and rapists to excuse their behaviour. The media, the police and the judiciary reinforce these myths by implying that only certain women are likely to be raped. Yet the social facts of rape outlined in this paper do not back up this argument. Since rape victims are chosen indiscriminately, no woman is immune from rape. The fear of rape reminds all women that they are subordinate to men and keeps them in a conscious or sub-conscious state of fear. It thus functions as an effective means of controlling women and restricting their actual and potential freedom.

Conclusion
In this chapter, I have shown many common beliefs about rape to be false. Far from being an isolated act committed

by a few deranged men, rape is a culturally conditioned and ideologically supported social fact (Matoesian, 1992). It is not for the most part the result of overwhelming sexual desire but due to the ties between sexuality and feelings of power and superiority. This power is sanctioned by the state and institutionalised into the legal system. The legal system enshrines male predatory sexual activity as the normal mode of sexuality while simultaneously denying the female's individual experience of rape. The law shapes the social order to legitimate and conceal male domination in society, making that order appear normal and natural (Smart, 1989). Through the legal system and media reporting of rape cases, rape myths are upheld, namely that women who get raped are in some sense responsible for their own fate or could have avoided their ordeal by not putting themselves at risk by entering the specific social space within which the rape occurred (Smart and Smart, 1978). This in turn ensures an effective, subtle form of social control aimed at keeping women in 'their place'.

References and further reading

Amir, M. 1971. *Patterns in Forcible Rape*. University of Chicago Press, Chicago.

Belfast Rape Crisis Centre Report. 1991-1992. Rape Crisis Centre, Belfast.

Brownmiller, S. 1975. *Against Our Will*. Simon and Schuster, New York.

Clark, L. and Lewis, D. 1977. *Rape: the Price of Coercive Sexuality*. The Women's Press, Toronto.

Kennedy, H. 1992. *Eve Was Framed*. Chatto and Windus Ltd., London.

Mackinnon, C. 1989. *Towards A Feminist Theory of the State*. Harvard University Press, Cambridge.

McCaghy, C. 1968. 'Drinking and Deviance Avowal'. In *Social Problems*, No. 16.

McVeigh, R. K. 1990. *Racism and Sectarianism: A Comparison of Tottenham and West Belfast*. Unpublished PhD Thesis. Queen's University, Belfast.

Matoesian, G. 1993. *Reproducing Rape: Domination Through Talk in the Courtroom*. Polity Press, Cambridge.

Russell, D. 1992. 'Pornography and Rape: A Causal Model'. In Itzin, C. (ed.), *Pornography: Women, Violence and Civil Liberties*. Oxford University Press, Oxford.

Russell, D. 1984. *Sexual Exploitation*. Sage, Beverly Hills.

Scully, D. 1990. *Understanding Sexual Violence*. Unwin Hyman, Boston.

Smart, C. 1991. 'Penetrating Women's Bodies: The Problem of Law and Medical Technology'. In Abbott, P. and Wallace, C. (eds.), *Gender,*

Power and Sexuality. Macmillan, London.

Smart, C. 1989. *Feminism and the Power of Law*. Routledge, London.

Smart, C. and Smart, B. 1978. 'Accounting for Rape: Reality and Myth in Press Reporting'. In *Women, Sexuality and Social Control*. Routledge and Kegan Paul, London.

Stanko, E. 1985. *Intimate Intrusions: Women's Experience of Male Violence*. Routledge and Kegan Paul, London.

Tong, R. 1989. *Feminist Thought*. Unwin Hyman, London.

Walby, S. 1990. *Theorising Patriarchy*. Blackwell, Oxford

Wilson, E. 1983. *What is to be Done about Violence Against Women?*. Penguin, Harmondsworth.

Wyre, R. 1992. 'Pornography and Sexual Violence: Working with Sex Offenders'. In Itzin, C. (ed.), *Pornography: Women, Violence and Civil Liberties*. Oxford University Press, Oxford.

Discussion topics

1 Outline the most prevalent rape myths and supply evidence to support or refute them.

2 Media reporting of rape cases serves to confirm and perpetuate specific widely held cultural values concerning the general character of rape. Discuss and illustrate.

3 To what extent does the legal system decriminalise and legitimate the act of rape?

4 Do rape convictions reflect the seriousness of the crime?

5 Is there a link between pornography and rape?

6 Rape constitutes a form of social control in so far as it represents a means of keeping women in their place. Discuss and illustrate.

The Relationship Between Women's Work and Poverty

Mary Daly

. . . the contradiction between waged labour and domestic labour has not necessarily been resolved to women's benefit. In most cases where women go out to work, there is still housework to be done, and in most cases it is still left to women (Novak, 1984: 61).

All women work and always have done. Yet most of their work is unpaid which makes them financially dependent — mainly on men or the state. The right to an independent income secured through paid work was one of the founding principles of the women's liberation movement. Feminists wanted women to be free to work outside the home or, in some cases, to be paid for their labour within it. A job is the single most effective escape route from poverty — it is through employment that most people get an adequate income as well as access to other resources. There are two main ways in which work is connected with women's poverty:

- The majority of women are without an earned income of their own since they are involved fulltime in home work which is unpaid work.
- When women are employed they usually earn less money than men, they work in lower level jobs and they may experience discrimination because they are women.

Women working for no pay
Most Irish women work for no pay — 53 per cent of all women over the age of fifteen are working fulltime in the home (see Table 1). Nearly 700,000 women, then, spend long hours caring for their families, and quite often for an elderly or ill relative as well, for no pay. The remaining women are either in the labour force (32 per cent), in education (10 per cent), retired or ill or disabled. Paid work, is therefore, secondary for Irish women.

122

Contrast women's situation with that of men, over 70 per cent of whom are in the labour force (see Table 1). For every individual employed woman there are more than two men earning an income of their own. Only in their early twenties are women's and men's employment situations similar. After this, they diverge: women mainly to marry and/or to have children and remain within the home; men to continue in the labour force, either employed or seeking work, until retirement. Women's employment pattern is changing, slowly. More Irish women are working outside the home than ever before: the numbers grew by over 40 per cent between 1971 and 1987. Most of this increase is due to greater participation by married women in paid work — growing by nearly 500 per cent over the last fifteen years. Yet, in percentage terms, the proportion of women working outside the home is practically the same as it was at the foundation of the state: 32 per cent. Today, about one in every five married women is in the labour force.

Table 1:
Women's and Men's Principal Economic Status in 1987

	Women		Men	
	000s	%	000s	%
In employment	252.5	28	735.1	59
Unemployed/seeking work	55.2	4	176.3	14
Home duties	669.8	53	5.5	0
Students	130.6	10	132.3	11
Retired	44.6	3	149.1	12
Ill/disabled	19.6	2	47.7	4
Others	7.9		4.8	
Total	1,280.2	100	1,250.8	100

Source: Labour Force Survey, 1987, Table 7.

Women based fulltime in the home do far more than domestic work. In the farming community, for instance, women make an enormous contribution (one of the main farming organisations produced evidence to show that a woman married to a farmer puts in between fifty and sixty hours a week on the family farm (*The Irish Times*, 3 February, 1989). Add this to the secretarial and administrative back-up that women provide for most family-run businesses, including farms. Research into entrepreneurship, for instance, proves that most new businesses rely very heavily on the unpaid support and assistance of women (O'Connor and Lyons, 1983). We should remember also the contribution women make to the local community, providing, among other things, a network of care for the elderly, the ill and disabled and children that saves the state a lot of money.

Agriculture more than any other sector shows the grey area between household work and market or paid work: women's contribution to the farm household is impossible to distinguish from the farm as a productive unit. So, there is undercounting of women's contribution to agriculture. National accounts statistics undervalue or give no economic value to a lot of women's labour. When domestic labour is costed, the result is astonishing. A very conservative estimate, based on a thirty-seven and a half hour week, in 1984, valued work in the home at nearly £3 billion (equivalent to about 18 per cent of Gross Domestic Product) (*Irish Women*, 1985: 41). It is not that women do not work, rather that much of their work is unpaid, which is a very different thing.

Consequences for women

While not forgetting that many women choose or prefer to be based fulltime in the home, such high levels of non-employment have serious consequences for women, not all of whom may be aware of them. For a start, it means that most women do not have an independent income of their own: two-thirds of Irish women are financially dependent either on men or on the state. While not all of these are in the same situation, the incomes of a substantial minority are low and may also be insecure. Because of the way poverty has been measured, we do not know precisely how many men fail to hand over sufficient money in the home. Not earning increases women's risk of poverty in another way as well: two-earner households have a much better chance of avoiding poverty than households with only one income. Consider what a woman gives up by remaining in the home. To begin with, just think about the earnings she forgoes:

British women are estimated to lose a minimum of £135,000 in earnings over their lifetime because of their family responsibilities (Joshi, 1987: 114). This would actually be a conservative estimate for Irish women who are far more likely to permanently give up fulltime employment to care for their families. An Irish woman working in industry at 1987 pay levels who leaves her job at the age of twenty-seven and never returns to paid work will forego at least £200,000 in earning over her lifetime. and this takes no account of the extra time (above the forty hours working week norm) a woman will put into her caring role. It takes mothers about fifty hours a week just to feed, wash, change nappies and perform other services for pre-school children (Joshi, 1987: 114).

Spending a considerable part of her life in the home significantly disadvantages a women in other ways as well in our society: it does not confer any qualifications, it does not count as work experience and the skills developed are not perceived as employable skills. Yet they are used all the time in jobs, eg managing money and other resources. Women working long-term in the home are also excluded from social welfare benefits in their own right (ie payments made on social insurance contributions) like contributory pensions or disability benefit. One of the worst catastrophes that can befall a family is when the mother becomes ill — social insurance does not cover this and there is no compensation for families who have to employ somebody to carry out the mother's work

As well as these drawbacks, joblessness leads to exclusion from rewards such as status, from opportunities for self-fulfilment and self-development, from social contacts and networks. Powerlessness and joblessness often go hand in hand because it is through their jobs that most people get a chance to influence decisions. Obviously, it is not only women who are jobless, but more women than men are systematically excluded from the labour market, from access to an independent income and from being considered as workers, even though they work very hard. Even the terms used to describe and classify work — job, employment — refer only to paid work, which automatically excludes the majority of women's labour.

One way of reducing women's poverty would be for women to be paid fully for their work. Women should have the choice of working outside the home and being paid an adequate wage, or receiving an independent income while working fulltime in the home. Employment by itself is not the solution — for many women it is too poorly paid and they prefer to be fulltime mothers. An adequate, independent income is what women need.

Among the reasons why more married women are now employed is because they are having fewer children and also because of the removal of obstacles like the marriage bar in the public service. However, Ireland still lags significantly behind other countries: an average of 40 per cent of EC women were in the labour force in 1986, compared with our 32 per cent.

Why don't more Irish women work outside the home?

As we have seen, being married still makes a big difference to Irish women's employment situation, while it makes no difference to men's work patterns. However, when we ask women themselves we find that it is not so much marriage as childcare which determines whether they are in a job or not. 74 per cent of married women (and 44 per cent of women generally) say that they are not in a job because of their children or more precisely because of their childcare responsibilities (Fine-Davis, 1988). Only 2 per cent of men give this reason: education, learning new skills and widening their opportunities, along with unemployment, are the main factors that take men out of the labour force. Some women leave the workforce to rear their children and then find it difficult to get back in. Working in the home is not always a choice for women — as many as a third of married women say that they regret not having a job. Economic factors are not the only concern: 'housework is basically dull and boring' and 'being at home with the children all day can very often be boring for a woman' were views shared by 68 per cent and 76 per cent of a sample of Dublin women and men in 1986 (Fine-Davis, 1988: 41). Housework is likely to be even more boring and certainly more arduous for women who live in poor conditions: old and shabby rooms are much harder to keep clean, as are cheap clothes for children and adults. Inexpensive goods break down more often and wear out faster than costly items.

The barriers that prevent women or make it difficult for them to take up a job are crucial to any discussion of women's poverty. While they apply to women in other circumstances as well, women on low incomes have fewer resources to enable them to overcome these barriers and at the same time a greater need of additional income. Three main barriers make it difficult for women to work outside the home:

- Absence of childcare facilities and other support services for working parents.
- Negative attitudes towards working mothers.
- Lack of encouragement and support for women returning to the workforce.

Support services for working parents

On the face of it, there is no reason why having children should stop women from getting a job — it doesn't in other countries to the same extent. But in Ireland little attempt is made to make it easier for mothers to work outside the home. For a start, childcare facilities, important for all employed mothers but crucial for lone parents, are limited. Only 35 per cent of all children under the age of six are provided for in services outside the home, and three-quarters of these are in primary school (McKenna, 1988). In all, only 35,000 children or 9 per cent of all the under-sixes are in a service other than school, mainly in private play groups. State provision is virtually non-existent — less than 2 per cent of children under the age of six are in state-funded nursery activity (funded mainly through the health boards). So childcare is almost entirely in the private sector, much of it black market. Charges are uncontrolled and are likely to be beyond the budget of women on low incomes. We know virtually nothing about the numbers of children being cared for in private homes or the quality of the care they are receiving, since there is no official registration of child-minding facilities.

Workplace crèches are a rarity — in 1988 only nine were known to exist in the whole country. There are five in the the third-level education sector and four in large service companies. Only a few hundred Irish children are known to be cared for in workplace crèches. A further barrier to women's employment is in the tax system. There is no tax relief for childcare expenses — an additional incentive for a woman to give up her job, especially if she has a second child. This is a serious gap given the high cost of childcare. With high costs and generally low wages, many women find that it is not worth their while financially to work outside the home. Other supports for mothers are also necessary, maternity leave for instance. While Irish women were given a statutory right in 1981 to pregnancy leave and job security in becoming mothers, the financial compensation (70 per cent of earnings) is among the lowest in Europe: most European women receive their full wages while on maternity leave. An additional aid to working parents is parental leave — Ireland, Britain and Holland are the only three EC countries with no provision for parental leave. Among other helpful supports for employed mothers are flexible hours of work, job sharing, career breaks — all still scarce in Ireland.

Attitudes to employed mothers
Although there is more support now for a broader role for women, the motherhood role is still highly valued here. The Constitution, for instance, places the family as the 'natural primary and fundamental unit group of Society' and pledges that the state will try to ensure that women will not be forced by economic necessity to take up paid work. Some public attitudes still reflect such a traditional view of women: almost half of the people surveyed in Dublin and some rural areas in 1986 believed that women who did not want at least one child were selfish (Fine-Davis, 1988: 48). Men's attitudes are more traditional but the most conservative attitudes of all are held by people from low-income backgrounds. This means that mothers from poor communities are likely to

have to face many negative attitudes, along with other difficulties, should they try to get a job.

The idea of mothers working outside the home is still not universally supported here: 46 per cent of Irish people believe that it is bad for young children if their mother goes out to work and over a third are of the view that women should be more concerned with house-keeping and bringing up their children than with a career. This same report comments:

> Men are still more traditional than women in their perceptions about appropriate gender role behaviour, ie, they are more likely to see a women's role as in the home and the man's outside the home. They are also more likely to see women as dependent and to believe that the wife and mother role is the most fulfiling one women could want (Fine-Davis, 1988: 48).

However, women themselves, also in quite large numbers, believe that mothers should not be employed while their children are young. This can lead to guilt among employed mothers and heightens ambivalence about taking up a job among others who are not employed.

Supports for women coming back into the workplace
Working long-term in the home isolates women from the job market. Skills become redundant, it is difficult to find potential areas of work, confidence in seeking work drops. This happens to the unemployed generally as well as women in particular but working in the home is especially isolating and often lessens women's self-esteem. Women returning to work may encounter age discrimination as well. So one of women's greatest needs is for training and development if they are to re-enter employment. FÁS, the national training agency, runs a small number of courses for women returning to the workforce. However, these courses are just a fraction of total FÁS training activity. Since they were not widely advertised in the past, women on low incomes were less likely to hear of them. Apart from this, women may experience difficulty in getting involved in other work-related activities. The Social Employment Scheme (SES),

for instance, which provides work on a half-time basis for social welfare claimants, requires that people be registered for at least a year at the employment exchange. Women have less chance of getting on these or other schemes because they tend not to register themselves as unemployed. And those on the 'women's schemes' ('deserted wife's', 'unmarried mother's' and so on) are totally excluded from these activities.

Clearly then, the fact that so much of women's work is unpaid contributes in a major way to keeping women poor. But this is not the only link between women's work and poverty: when they do work outside the home women earn less and do not fare as well as men.

Paid work: creating poverty for some women

Apart from the 53 per cent of Irish women who have no income of their own, many women who do have a job are badly paid. Men still earn more than women. At the end of 1987, the average gross weekly pay of women in industry was 40 per cent below the average male wage: £139.89 as compared with £232.45 a week. This means that a woman in an industrial job would have to work a further twenty-five hours a week to earn the equivalent of a man's wage. Women's hourly earnings are a bit closer to those of men: 67.9 per cent in 1988. Twenty years ago, in 1968, women's earnings were roughly half of men's. So the equal pay legislation has had a limited effect, showing that legislation is only one way of dealing with the problem of sex segregation of work. Unless women can take up different types of jobs, their earnings, relative to those of men, will not significantly improve.

Irish women's earnings compare badly with those of women elsewhere. In 1986, of all EC countries, Ireland had the biggest gap between the earnings of women and men industrial manual workers, apart from Luxembourg and Britain. Danish and Italian women were at the top of the league earning 85.9 per cent and 84.4 per cent of men's hourly earnings respectively.

Women start their work careers being paid similarly even slightly more than men. In 1987 the average weekly earnings of girls who had left school a year earlier were

£71.80 compared with £69.30 for men (Blackwell, 1989). This is due in part to the low wages paid to apprentices, most of whom are men. However, women soon lose their early advantage since their earnings do not increase with age as much as those of men. Women's earnings peak earlier — between twenty-five and thirty-four years of age, whereas men in industrial jobs earn their highest wages between the ages of thirty-five and fifty-four. So, over the life cycle, women do not do as well from employment as men which increases their risk of poverty.

Why is it that women are paid less than men? There is no one reason for this, although the following five factors are all very significant:

- Women work in very different kinds of jobs to men, often those that are low-paying.
- Women do not advance up the hierarchy as quickly as men.
- Women's family responsibilities may hold back their careers.
- Women work for fewer hours than men.
- Women still suffer discrimination.

Women are in different jobs to men
In 1987 just about a third of women were in the labour force (ie in employment or seeking work). Most women are in service jobs: nearly four-fifths of women were employed to provide services for other people in 1987. The proportion was two-thirds in 1971. Meanwhile, the numbers of women in both agriculture and industry are dropping: just 3 per cent of women work in the agricultural sector while 19 per cent are in industry. The contrast with men is stark: services — 48 per cent; agriculture — 21 per cent; industry — 32 per cent. Men's work situation has also changed over the last sixteen years: the numbers in agriculture continued to decline while those in service-type jobs increased. Also, of course, there has been a big rise in unemployment — for both women and men.

Women dominate the sectors where wages are lowest. Service jobs among women are distinguished by their lower pay and poorer working conditions. There is more than this to sex segregation, however: within each sector women do only certain types of jobs — mainly profess- ional jobs (teaching, nursing), commercial-type work and jobs which involve providing personal services for other people. In all, 60 per cent of women work in these three general types of job. To put names on some of the jobs women do: they are shop assistants and bar staff (31,800); professional and technical workers (89,700); clerical workers (96,200); service workers (54,000). When in industry, women work mainly in textiles, clothing and footwear: areas traditionally associated with women.

Nearly half of all women working in both industry and distribution were on low pay (ie earning less than £65 a week) in 1979, compared with 13 per cent and 18.5 per cent of male workers in industry and distribution.[1] Those in industry are the worst paid of all: over 70 per cent of all low paid women workers in 1979 were working in industrial jobs. The earnings gap is largest at the lower levels.

In truth then, there has been no revolution in women's employment, apart from the fact that married women are working outside the home in larger numbers than before. The jobs they do are generally low-level and low-paying. Because there is very little movement of women into new areas of work, the sex structure of employment has remained largely unchanged. 'Women's jobs' and 'men's jobs' still exist and women work mainly with other women. In textiles, clothing and footwear for instance, 58 per cent of the workers are female; in professional services nearly 60 per cent of the workers are women; and in personal services women make up 63 per cent of all workers. Because of this segregation, women may not always recognise discrimination — when they compare themselves with their colleagues (mostly women) they may appear to be doing well but they cannot know how they compare!with men. Apart from the pay, there is another strong connection between women's employment and domestic work: the type of work involved in 'women's jobs' is often 'caring' in nature (nursing, teaching) or providing for people's personal needs (hairdressing, catering).

Women are not advancing up the jobs hierarchy

Usually the more senior the job the more it pays. The labour market is segregated vertically as well as horizontally and men dominate the top positions. Although more women are employed now, they are not making their way to the top jobs. Women professionals, for instance, are mainly in the so-called lower professions such as teachers and nurses, whereas men dominate the better-paying professions such as accountancy, medicine, dentistry. Generally, whatever hierarchy we examine, women are likely to be at the bottom with men at the top. Take the health services for example. Over 70 per cent of the workers are women but men hold 70 per cent of the top positions (Blackwell, 1986). Such low level 'crowding' of women is clearly a major reason for the poverty of households headed by a women.

It is not only Irish women who have difficulty improving their employment positions. Sex segregation in work applies with 'amazing uniformity' in the industrialised world (Scott, 1984: 25-28). In each of the twenty-four most developed western countries in 1980, for example, women were concentrated in clerical and service jobs. Even in Sweden, which has very strong commitment to women's equality, the workforce remains very segregated, with 80 per cent of women in just thirty types of jobs (Scott, 1982: 21-22).

Women's family responsibilities

Women enter and participate in the labour market as existing or future wives and mothers, unlike men who are workers first and last. This difference is crucial, both on the part of workers themselves and for the way they are treated. Women's family responsibilities impinge on their work in many ways. First, employed mothers can have less time available for the job — to do overtime, to participate in educational courses outside of work, even to devote the time necessary to develop social contacts and networks — so important in many jobs today. Work in the home is still mainly a woman's responsibility whether she is employed or not. Husbands of employed women spend only about four more hours a week on housework than men whose wives are fulltime in the home — sixteen against twelve hours a week (Fine-Davis, 1988). So, if a woman goes out to work, she usually still retains the responsibility for home and family and the very heavy workloads associated with both. The average employed married woman in Ireland puts in a seventy hour week between home and job, compared with a sixty hour week on average for men (Fine-Davis, 1988: 70-71) The typical working week for the woman in the home is about sixty-eight hours.

Women's employment careers are also interrupted for child-bearing and child-rearing. At best, they are out of their jobs for a few years. This may not seem a lot but women are often away from their jobs during the time that is most important for career advancement, the late twenties, early thirties. So, their family responsibilities are a major source of disadvantage to women in the workplace, given the present structure of work in our society.

Women are employed for fewer hours than men
According to the 1987 Labour Force Survey, women spend an average of thirty-eight hours a week on the job while the average man works a forty-seven hour week. This explains some of the difference in earnings. Another factor is women's fairly high involvement in part-time work. Almost one in five women workers work part-time, usually paid less and in poorer conditions than fulltime jobs. Women held 78 per cent of the 96,800 part-time jobs in Ireland in 1987. In fact, this kind of work is becoming more and more important for women. In contrast, just 2 per cent of men work in a part-time capacity, usually young and single men. Two industries predominate for part-time work: professional services (ie education, health, legal services, etc); and a group consisting of distributive trades, insurance, finance and business services (Blackwell, 1986: 5). Most (63 per cent) part time women workers are married, so it is mainly women involved in rearing families, or those who have already done so, who work on a part-time basis. Whether

women work part-time by choice or not is far from certain. One thing we can be sure of: part-time work has many disadvantages that may heighten women's risk of poverty in the long run.

Part-time jobs are paid at a lower rate. Part-time workers are among the worst paid in the labour force and women part-timers earn least of all. This stems from a number of facts such as: many part-timers work in industries which are traditionally poorly paid; part-timers are mainly concentrated in manual occupations which are not defined as skilled, and they are in the lower grades; part-timers do not as a rule receive overtime payments; their hours are often limited and rates of pay are not covered by legislation (Daly, 1985: 9).

As well as the low earnings, the expansion of part-time work has other negative consequences. The low number of hours worked excludes many workers from legislative protection. Employers' costs are substantially reduced when workers are not covered by legislative protection: their PRSI contribution is lower, among other things. So, there is an incentive for employers to push their workers' hours below the statutory minimum: small wonder, then, that the hours worked by part-timers are decreasing.

Another disadvantage of part-time work is that it rarely offers any opportunities for career advancement and promotion, developing new skills or training. In addition, working conditions are often very poor in part-time jobs: cleaning work, for instance, involves very heavy workloads, unsocial hours and little work satisfaction (Daly 1985). Most part-time workers are excluded from pension schemes and they will receive sick pay only if they work more than eighteen hours a week.

Discriminatory attitudes and practices still exist in Ireland

Women themselves judge the extent of sex discrimination at work to have increased over the last ten years. Substantial numbers of women say they are being discriminated against in relation to recruitment, promotion and pay (Fine-Davis, 1988: 5-15). Married women particularly report more discrimination, and women on low incomes feel especially discriminated against in the quality and type of work they are asked to do. Other groups in the population, especially married men, identify far more widespread barriers to women's advancement than do women themselves. Men also identify different barriers: particularly the attitudes of management to women, lack of flexible hours and the lack of social supports for employed women.

What about the future?

Women's disadvantages at work cannot be seen in isolation from developments in the rest of the economy. The structure of the labour force itself is changing in the search for greater profits. Employers increasingly want a more flexible and cheaper labour force. Women, as the weaker sector of the employed, are very vulnerable to higher unemployment and other changes such as increasing technology and job deskilling.

Today almost a quarter of a million people are unemployed in the Republic, although the rate of increase has slowed down, mainly because so many people are emigrating. Usually thought of as a man's problem, women are increasingly affected by unemployment — 70,424 women were registered as unemployed in November 1988 (ie signing on the Live Register as available for work). At this time, some 163,896 men were on the Live Register. According to the 1987 Labour Force Survey, 14 per cent of women in the labour force were unemployed or seeking their first regular job in mid-1987, over a quarter of whom were under twenty-five years of age. Both the absolute numbers of women and the rate of women's unemployment are increasing all the time. In fact, women's rate of unemployment has almost tripled since 1971: from 5 to 14 per cent.

Unemployment among Irish women differs in a number of ways from that of men. The official rate of female unemployment is lower than the rate for men: 14 per cent as against 19 per cent, but this difference may be more apparent than real, since unemployment statistics need to be treated cautiously, especially those for women. The Live Register (compiled at the employment exchanges) underestimates the 'true' rate of women's unemployment because many women do not bother to sign on as they are not eligible for benefit (mainly because their husbands are claiming means-tested unemployment assistance for the family). Also, women cannot sign on if they are available only for part-time work (Blackwell, 1989: 63-64). In addition, women may be more likely than men to become discouraged and to withdraw from the search for work, giving in to pressure to remain in their traditional roles. While the social welfare changes introduced for the implementation of the EC Equality Directive in 1986 have reduced the extent to which the Live Register undercounts women, an unknown number of unemployed women still go unnoticed and unrecorded.

A lower rate of women's unemployment makes us very unusual internationally. Among our EC neighbours we share this only with Britain and Holland. In other countries, women have been more affected than men by unemployment: in 1982 the *OECD Observer* reported 'those people hardest hit are those whose supply has expanded most rapidly — youth and women' (Scott, 1984: 30; see also Oakley, 1976: 6).

Women are disadvantaged in the new and developing industries as well. Take electronics, for instance, a particularly dynamic sector. A survey of the electronics industry found that only 3 per cent of all managers and 15 per cent of all professionals were women, while they comprised over 70 per cent of all assembly workers (Wickham and Murray, 1987). This is very entrenched segregation in such a young industry. Women were disadvantaged because they did not have the right (technical) qualifications to begin with, and once in the firm they received only a very limited type of training and were not promoted as readily as men. Developments like the increased computerisation of white collar occupations do not bode well for women's employment. Women will probably face greater competition for the jobs that they have traditionally done from redundant and unemployed male workers and young men seeking their first job.

What are the chances of breaking down segregation? There is certainly cause for pessimism, given that the equality legislation appears to have reached the limits of its effectiveness. And of course, legislation alone cannot end segregation. Positive action programmes are also needed to encourage and train women to enter new spheres of activity, while at the same time attacking the negative attitudes and prejudices that exist about women working. It must also be made easier for women to work outside the home, if that is their wish. Vital support services for working parents, like crechès and other childcare arrangements, flexible working times and parental leave, are not widely available in Ireland. Childcare especially can be expensive.

Low pay continues to be a major problem: significant numbers of women are in low paying, low level jobs and this means that work can contribute to women's poverty rather than end it. So, unless something is done about the wage rates paid by employers to employees, and especially women employees, women will continue to be poor as workers.

Note
1 Blackwell, J. *Low Pay and Women:* 12-15. The source for these data is the 1979 Structure of Earnings Survey which examined earnings in industry, wholesale and retail distribution and certain financial services.

References and further reading

Blackwell, J. 1986. *Women in the Labour Force.* Employment Equality Agency, Dublin.

Blackwell, J. 1987. *Low Pay and Women.* REPC, University College Dublin

Daly, M. 1985. *The Hidden Workers.* Employment Equality Agency, Dublin.

Drew, E. 1990a. 'Part-time Working in Ireland'. *Equal Opportunities International.* Vol. 9, No. 3/4/5.

Drew, E. 1990b 'Women and low Pay'. In *Low Pay: The Irish Experience.* Combat Poverty Agency, Dublin.

Jackson. P. and Barry U. 1989. 'Women's Employment and Multinationals in the Republic of Ireland: The Creation of a New Female Labour Force'. In Elson, D. and Pearson, R. (eds.), *Women's Employment and Multinationals in Europe.* Macmillan, London.

Jackson. P. and Barry U. 1988. 'Women on the Edge of Time: Part-time women workers in Ireland, North and South'. In Buckley, M. and Anderson, M. (eds.), *Women and Equality in Europe*. Macmillan, London.

Irish Women: Agenda for Practical Action. 1985. Stationery Office, Dublin.

Fine-Davis, M. *Changing Gender Role Attitudes in Ireland: 1975-1986*. Vol. I. First report of the Second Joint Committee on Women's Rights, 1988.

Joshi, H. 1987. 'The Cost of Caring'. In Glendinning, C. and Millar, J. (eds.), *Women and Poverty in Britain*. Wheatsheaf, Brighton.

McKenna, A. 1988. *Childcare and Equal Opportunities*. Employment Equality Agency, Dublin.

Novak, T. 1984. *Poverty and Social Security*, Pluto Press, London.

Oakley, A. 1976. *Housewife*. Penguin, Harmondsworth.

O'Connor, J. and Lyons, M. 1983. *Enterprise — The Irish Approach*. Industrial Development Authority, Dublin.

Scott, H. 1984. *Working your Way to the Bottom: The Feminisation of Poverty*. Pandora Press, London.

Scott, H. 1982. 'Equality Swedish style', *Working Woman*, June.

Wickham, J. and Murray, P. 1987. *Women in the Irish Electronics Industry*. Employment Equality Agency, Dublin.

Discussion topics

1 What are the major factors which explain Irish women's relatively low participation in the workforce?

2 In what ways does the state — or Irish society generally — provide support services for women who work outside the home? Are these services satisfactory or unsatisfactory? In what ways do you think the problem could be resolved?

3 Has employment equality legislation been effective in overcoming discrimination against women and in genuinely equalising the relative position of women and men in paid work? What further actions and/or changes in legislation do you think are necessary?

4 Select a workplace that you know or have access to (a business, a school) and list the various types of jobs, and who does them, female and male. Are there particular jobs done mainly by women or mainly by men? Are women, or men, more numerous at some levels of the job hierarchy than at others?

5 To what extent do you think that the trades unions are responsive to the needs of women at work? In what further ways could trades unions be working on behalf of their women members?

6 'Wages for housework': to what extent would this be a solution to the economic oppression of women?

Revealing Figures?
Official Statistics and Rural Irish Women

Anne Byrne

Introduction

There are many annual published statistical sources of information which are used by a variety of agencies, organisations, community groups and individuals in the course of their work. Reflecting the growing interest in gender issues, these statistics have been much criticised for the lack of attention to the particular position of women (Blackwell, 1987). Other problems arise in relation to how statistics are generally read and regarded — from irrelevant, to boring, to complex, to meaningless — so that information contained in statistical tables is often dismissed by the reader. A feminist approach to statistics is being advocated by researchers (Ayers-Nachamkin, 1992). This approach challenges the intimidatory power of numbers and works to understand the practical application of statistics. Women's organisations have gradually taken up this approach and recognised the power of numbers when lobbying for resources. For example, look at the many reports, surveys and statistical accounts published by rape crisis centres, family planning clinics, Women's Aid, the Federation for Services of Unmarried Parents and their Children and by groups such as the Irish Association for the Improvement of Maternity Services. Much of this work is carried out on a voluntary basis, with poor resources — yet the value and power of numbers is inherent in the activity. A feminist approach also teaches us to be critical of numbers and to understand when statistics are being misused and used against women's interests. As Ayers-Nachamkin states, 'Statistics imposes structure on the natural universe. One of the functions of statistics is to give shape to our messy world, by classifying, dichotomising and rank-ordering it.' (Ayers-Nachamkin, 1992: 91). Sometimes we need to ask who is imposing the order, and why?

It has been stated by many commentators that women

are undercounted in the official statistics so, for example, we have no clear idea how many women are unemployed, as many working in the home are not eligible to 'sign on' the official unemployment register (Daly, 1989 and in the present collection). But what do the statistics tell us? If we direct our attention to women in the countryside, what type of picture emerges from the published sources?

Women in the countryside

There is a large proportion of the population whose opinions are rarely heard, whose labour is neither valued nor recognised, whose problems and needs are not responded to and whose existence is further marginalised through living on a low income in rural Ireland. The term 'rural' can be defined on the basis of numbers of people living in an area so that 'city' is differentiated from 'town', 'village', 'townland' and the 'country'. 'Rural' and 'urban' are terms used to illustrate different styles of living but in many ways the definitions create false dichotomies.

But there is a difference between living in the town and living in the country when you are living on a low income. There are marked differences when you are a poor woman who requires the same essential services as your urban sisters but they are not provided in the local community. Rural women do have opinions and their contribution to the rural economy both on and off the farm is vast and they do have the same problems and needs of essential education, health, welfare, communication and childcare services as all women. Rural women who are living on a low income or who are dependent on social welfare are a distinct group who lead a deprived and marginal existence. What we know about women's lives in the countryside is limited.

While it may be a misconception to examine the position of women in rural Ireland in isolation from the total population of women, there are particular disadvantages that are part of being a woman in the countryside that are not shared with women living in urban areas. These disadvantages prevent rural women from participating fully in community life and benefiting from some of the changes in attitudes and improvements in services for women that have been achieved within the

141

past ten years. The principal disadvantage experienced by rural women is the lack of access to resources and facilities which are more often available in large urban areas. Women who have a secure financial income can travel to the nearest family planning clinic and pay the required fee for a medical examination or for contraceptive devices. But what about the woman on a small farm, whose income is limited and whose medical card does not entitle her to the full range of family planning facilities? What about the women who have to travel an additional forty miles because the local maternity unit has been closed? What about the woman who has to travel to a clinic to have a smear test in the nearest urban centre because her local clinic has been closed? What about the woman who would like to attend adult education classes but cannot afford the transport to the nearest centre or cannot pay for child care? What about the woman whose child is a victim of sexual abuse and does not know where to turn? What about the woman who is a single parent living in a rural community? Who provides social support for her? Do the local media represent the issues that are relevant to rural women? Do the local newspapers advertise the 'alternative' health services such as rape crisis centres, refuges for women who are victims of family violence or training courses which might contribute to the alleviation of some of the isolation that rural women experience?

Young women reared in rural areas tend to leave in the search for work, once their secondary education is complete. Only a few remain behind to raise families and care for elderly parents or relatives (Byrne, 1991). Women work on farms, in part-time employment, doing seasonal work, and a few hold professional jobs in rural areas. Most women however are engaged in child rearing, though there is a significant number of elderly women living alone in the countryside. Labour force data on farm women indicates that women are leaving rural areas at a rate which ought to give rise to considerable concern, indicated in the decreasing numbers of women working in agriculture, from 42,000 in 1961 to 12,300 in 1991 for the country as a whole (Labour Force Survey, 1991). This points to a fundamental problem for the regeneration of families in rural areas.

There are many more questions to be asked on the issues of health, education, social welfare, employment, childcare and on the media in relation to women who are poor both in financial terms and in terms of their lack of access to resources. There has been little or no research carried out which can answer some of the questions posed above. It is difficult to assess and evaluate the current provision of services for rural Ireland in any coherent manner, because of the lack of research or statistics which might provide some valuable insights into the lives and living conditions of rural women who are poor. This paper examines some of the published statistics to highlight rural women's marginalisation and reduced access to essential services and resources. This reduced access affects the quality of life for many women and their dependents in the countryside.

Demographic information

The population of the Republic is 3,523,401 according to preliminary results from the 1991 Census of the Population, a 0.5 per cent increase on the 1986 Census. The 1986 Census showed for the first time in census history since the foundation of the state, that the number of females (1,759,700) exceeded the number of males (1,755,500). This trend continues with 1,771,012 females to 1,752,389 males being recorded for the 1991 Census. Perhaps no significance can be attached to this new development, beyond pointing to possible explanations concerning increased male emigration in the search for work or decreased female emigration. Recent National Economic and Social Council (NESC) research has shown that over time equal numbers of men and women have emigrated, but in particular eras sometimes more women emigrate and other times more men emigrate. During the Second World War, men left either to fight or to work in wartime industry, while after the war, we had a higher incidence of women leaving the country. This is explained as a 'delayed action' by women who were prevented by wartime conditions from emigrating, but who then left either to marry returning soldiers, to join husbands who had settled in England or to join the UK labour force (NESC, 1991: 68). Current emigration trends show that more men are emigrating than women as male unemployment grows at a faster rate than female unemployment. Other explanations for the higher incidence of females over males, may be found in greater opportunities for female employment. This is reflected in labour force trends which show that women's participation rate in the Irish labour force has remained fairly constant in the past thirty years compared to a decreasing participation rate for men (see Table 1).

Table 1: % Female labour force participation rates, 1961-1991

	1961	1971	1977	1981	1987	1989	1991
All women	29.7	28.2	28.2	29.7	31.9	30.9	32.9
All men	85.0	82.0	76.8	76.4	72.9	71.4	70.9

Sources: Callan, T. and Farrell, B. (1991), Table 3.1; Labour Force Survey, 1991.

While a large proportion of the population is concentrated in the three major cities of Dublin, Cork and Limerick and along the eastern sea-board in general, a significant proportion make up the 'rural' population. The 1986 Census of Population indicated that more than half a million women were living in rural areas — places in which less than 1,500 people reside. Table 2 compares rural and urban women by marital status, showing a higher proportion of married, widowed and older women in rural Ireland.

Table 2: Demographic indicators for rural and urban female population, 1986

	Rural	Urban	Ireland
Females per 1,000 males	928	1,061	1,001
% Single	30.3	38.5	35.2
% Married	55.3	48.7	51.4
% Widowed	13.4	10.4	11.7
% Separated	0.9	2.4	1.8
% 65 Years +	13.5	11.2	12.2

Source: CSO, 1986.

An analysis of the population by health board region shows that 35 per cent of the population are concentrated in the Eastern Health Board area with the remaining 65 per cent in all other regions. The Eastern Health Board area is also distinguished by the fact that it is the only region in which the number of females is greater than the number of males. Table 3 gives a description of the main characteristics of the population by health board region. A number of urban-rural differences emerge from this description, such as the higher number of elderly and widowed persons in the rural west and north-west compared to the greater Dublin area. Trends such as these would indicate that the demand for support services for the elderly and those living alone will be greater in the countryside but this may not match provision (Byrne, 1991). The dependency ratio also tends to be much higher in rural areas.

There are over one million women living outside the Eastern Health Board area, and while some of these women are living in the larger cities and towns such as Cork, Limerick, Galway and Sligo — more than half a million are the women of rural Ireland. But in terms of access to services, information, education and training facilities, childcare services and support groups rural women are severely disadvantaged compared to women living in towns and cities. Some of the trends discernible in the published statistics focus our attention on the lives of rural women and on how little we know about the impact of reduced access to services on the quality of life for women in the countryside. The recently published report of the Second Commission on the Status of Women (1993), pays much attention to rural women and makes many recommendations for change, including improved transport plans for rural areas, the introduction of mobile health centres, that the work of women on farms be categorised and counted for statistical and policy purposes and that training and education needs of rural women be met.

Table 3: Population of each health board area: Main characteristics for census year 1991.

	East	Midland	Mid-West	North East	North West	South East	South	West	Ireland
Pop	1,244,238	202,948	310,511	300,265	208,027	383,003	531,533	342,876	3,523,401
Female	641,910	99,621	153,760	148,484	102,873	189,656	265,401	169,307	1,771,012
Male	602,328	103,327	156,751	151,781	105,154	193,347	266,132	173,569	1,752,389
Age Groups %									
0-14 yrs	26.0	39.2	27.8	29.5	28.2	28.4	26.9	27.6	27.3
15-44 yrs	47.5	41.6	42.8	42.4	39.8	42.4	43.1	40.5	43.9
45-64 yrs	17.3	17.4	17.9	17.1	17.6	17.8	18.0	17.7	17.5
65+ yrs	9.2	11.8	11.6	11.1	14.3	11.4	12.1	14.3	11.2
Dependency Ratio %	54.5	69.5	64.8	68.2	74.0	66.3	63.8	72.0	62.7
Marital Status (15 yrs+) %									
Single	40.3	38.5	38.6	37.2	39.5	38.0	39.1	40.1	39.3
Married	53.3	53.7	53.8	55.3	51.9	54.3	53.0	51.4	53.3
Widowed	6.5	7.8	7.7	7.5	8.6	7.6	7.9	8.5	7.4

Source: CSO, 1991.

Demographic trends are usually measured by the number of births and deaths, marriage rates and information on infant mortality. Women live longer than men, female life expectancy at birth being seventy-seven years compared to the lower rate for males at seventy-one years in 1989. But the principal causes of death, for both females and males are heart disease (25.8 per cent), cancer (23.2 per cent), cardiovascular disease (9.5 per cent), other circulatory diseases (10.3 per cent), pneumonia (6.6 per cent), other respiratory disease (7.5 per cent), injury and poisoning (4.3 per cent) and all 'other' causes account for 12.9 per cent of deaths (Department of Health, 1991). Social class, poverty and gender are good predictors of women's health status, so that, for example, women in lower socio-economic groups have higher rates of maternal nutritional deficiency and infant mortality than other socio-economic groups (Cullen and Morrissey, 1982). Recent research on the 'feminisation of poverty' shows quite clearly that women living on low incomes are more likely to die younger than other women, have increased rates of depression, are exposed to a greater risk of illness, are more likely to smoke, are less aware of preventative health measures and have restricted choices in relation to access to health services (Daly, 1989).

The high death rates amongst Irish women from heart disease have been associated with high animal fat intake and smoking. For 1986/1987, 34 per cent of men smoked compared to 31 per cent of women. The lowest socio-economic group has a higher rate of smoking which is currently 41 per cent, compared to the rate for the highest socio-economic group which is 26 per cent. Table 4 gives information on the death rate by health board area.

For 1991, the death rate was lowest in the Eastern Health Board area and highest in the North-Western Health Board area. The Eastern Health Board area also had the lowest death rate from circulatory diseases while the North-Western Health Board area had the highest. What do these different rates tell us? Can these trends be taken as an indication that urban-based populations have a better quality of life than rural-based populations?

Table 4: Death rates by selected causes and by health board area, 1991.

Health Board	Death rate per 1,000 pop.	Circulatory Disease	Cancer*	Motor Accidents*
Eastern	7.3	310.3	196.5	7.6
Midland	9.6	459.7	217.3	14.8
Mid-Western	9.5	441.2	204.5	11.2
North-Eastern	8.8	412.3	203.8	19.3
North-Western	11.3	529.3	207.2	12.5
Southern	9.4	418.8	207.8	15.7
South-Eastern	10.1	494.8	224.3	10.7
Western	10.4	471.9	221.7	13.1
Ireland	8.9	407.4	207.5	11.5

*Per 100,000 population.
Source: CSO.

Table 5: Crude death rates by sex, per 100,000 population, 1991.

	Females	Males
Death rate	833.0	955.0
Cancer	191.0	225.0
Circulatory diseases	381.0	434.0

Source: CSO, Health Statistics

For 1991, the infant mortality rate was lowest in the midland and western areas at 5.6 per 1,000 live births. But according to this latest data, the highest infant mortality rates are in the mid-western and north-western regions (see Table 6). If infant mortality rates are compiled over a number of years, it becomes evident that the rates vary both over time and between regions. For example in 1988, the highest infant mortality rates were in the southern region at twelve deaths per 1,000 live births. Maternity units have been closed in Manorhamilton, Donegal, Dungloe, Gorey, Athy, Ballyshannon, Carndonagh and Lifford and in many other rural areas since 1986. What effects have these closures had on women in the countryside? The variation over time and region in infant mortality rates needs to be investigated further. While there may be economic and technical benefits in closing small maternity units and directing women to larger, better equipped hospitals in urban centres, the Second Commission on the Status of Women recommends that maternity services, post-natal clinics and screening services should be as locally based as possible.

The crude birth rate per 1,000 population for 1991 was 15. The birth rate has been decreasing since 1980, from 21.8, to 14.7 in 1989. Table 7 gives some information on births inside and outside marriage. The statistics for each set of figures are not calculated on the same basis and therefore are not strictly comparable.

Table 6: Infant deaths by health board area, per 1,000 live births, 1991.

Eastern	8.9
Midland	5.6
Mid-Western	9.6
North-Eastern	9.2
North-Western	1.3
Southern	7.7
South-Eastern	6.8
Western	5.6
Ireland	8.2

Source: CSO, Health Statistics

Table 7: Births by health board area, 1988/1991.

Health Board	Birth inside marriage per 1,000 married women		Births ourside marriage as % of total births	
	1988	1991	1988	1991
Eastern	107.3	88.3	15.0	22.4
Midland	135.6	117.0	5.5	11.5
Mid-Western	121.7	103.6	7.4	14.4
North-Eastern	121.9	100.5	5.6	13.3
North-Western	134.0	107.8	6.6	12.0
Southern	121.5	97.4	7.2	17.1
South-Eastern	123.6	101.2	9.4	13.2
Western	138.8	116.4	4.7	9.2
Ireland	119.6	96.7	10.7	16.6

Source: CSO.

While a large proportion of births outside marriage take place in the Eastern Health Board area, there are significant numbers of women who give birth outside marriage in rural areas. This can be a lonely and isolating experience, particularly if there are few support services available or facilities for women in this situation. It would be interesting to examine the outcome of extra-marital pregnancies by area of residence. The assumption that can be made is that women who have access to support services for single parents are more likely to keep their children than women who do not have access to such facilities. In addition, there are a number of religious and social control factors which may have a greater degree of influence on a woman living in a small rural community than on a woman who has chosen to live in the anonymity of the greater Dublin area. The number of births outside marriage is on the increase for all regions. Women who are living in rural areas and who cannot afford to travel to urban areas to avail of facilities or services for single parents remain isolated and excluded.

Combat Poverty Agency research on lone parents estimates that there are over 40,000 lone parent families in Ireland, which amounts to 10 per cent of all families with children less than fifteen years of age (Millar, 1992).

Marriage rates began to fall in 1984, and were the second lowest in the EC in 1989, Germany being the lowest. Table 8 describes marriage rates by health board area and includes data on age of marriage for both bride and groom. With the decreasing rate of marriage we need to predict the likely consequences for populations in rural Ireland. Emigration from rural areas has reduced the opportunity to marry and leads to an increase in the number of single person households. This is particularly evident in the West of Ireland (Byrne et al, 1991). In the West there is a lower rate of marriage and people tend to be older than average in 'tying the knot'. Other possible explanations of falling marriage rates compared to the rest of the EC may be the consequences of the absence of divorce in Ireland compared to the opportunity to remarry in other countries. The absence of census categories to count the number of people cohabiting prevents an accurate count of these households in Ireland, but more and more people choose to cohabit rather than marry or have to cohabit in cases where one partner is already married because of the absence of divorce.

Table 8: Marriage rates (1991) and average age of marriage (1988) by health board area, per 1,000 of population.

Health Board	Marriage rate	Age of bride	Age of groom
Eastern	4.7	26.1	28.2
Midland	5.0	25.7	27.7
Mid-Western	4.9	26.3	28.3
North-Eastern	4.8	26.0	28.2
North-Western	5.1	26.6	28.8
Southern	4.6	25.4	27.6
South-Eastern	4.8	26.5	28.3
Western	4.7	26.7	28.7
Ireland	4.8	26.1	28.2

Source: CSO, Health Statistics.

Labour force trends

Labour force statistics also highlight the differential trends among the regions. While Dublin and the eastern region have the largest proportion of the population in the labour force, the statistics for the other regions are worth examining. Table 9 provides information on the proportion of women in the labour force by region. For the Republic in 1991, women represented 32 per cent of the labour force and 33.5 per cent of employed persons. Dublin and the east had a higher proportion of women at work than the country as a whole, while the south-east and the midlands had the lowest proportions. An examination of the numbers of women who are excluded from labour force statistics reveals some interesting patterns which are of particular relevance to the position of rural women. There are more women classified as being 'at work' in the Dublin area and the eastern region than elsewhere in the country, while more rural women are counted being engaged in 'home duties' rather than in the labour force.

Table 9: Women in the labour force aged 15+ years, 1991

Region	Women as % of those at work (females/males)	Women as % of those unemployed (females/males)	Total labour force (000s)
Dublin	38.8	28.0	415.7
Rest of East	31.4	28.6	123.0
East	37.0	28.1	538.8
South-West	31.9	24.9	200.3
South-East	29.6	24.5	141.4
North-East	29.9	21.6	73.6
Mid-West	32.5	19.6	112.2
Midlands	28.4	23.3	92.4
West	32.1	22.2	101.7
North-West & Donegal	33.6	19.4	73.1
Ireland	33.5	25.0	1,333.51

Source: Labour Force Survey, 1991.

While there are 429,100 women (32 per cent) and 904,400 men (68 per cent) in the labour force, there are 876,300 women (70 per cent) and 370,800 (30 per cent) men not in the labour force. Of those engaged in 'home duties', 99 per cent of them are women. While it is claimed that more women and men in the home are sharing housework and childcare, the published statistics continue to describe very separate roles. Either the statistics are inadequate or they reflect the chosen 'occupations' of women and men in Ireland today. The 1992 MRBI poll claims that the most important perceived role for modern Irish women is motherhood and providing for the family, with fulltime wives and mothers being held in the highest esteem by 70 per cent of respondents, compared to 5 per cent who felt that a career was the most important role for women today (MRBI, 1992).

Table 10 gives a regional breakdown of the proportion of women who are classified as 'not in the labour force'.

**Table 10: Women not in the labour force as % of total female pop.
15+ yrs, 1991**

Dublin	61.4
Rest of East	67.3
East	62.8
South-West	69.0
South-East	70.4
North-East	70.8
Mid-West	69.3
Midlands	72.4
West	69.5
North-West & Donegal	69.6
Ireland	67.1

Source: Labour Force Survey, 1991.

Of these 876,300 women, 640,600 are engaged in 'home duties', 151,100 are 'students', 54,600 are 'retired', 19,000 are 'unable to work due to permanent sickness or disability' and 11,100 are classified as 'other'. The midlands and north-east have the highest proportion of women who are not in the labour force, compared to Dublin which has the lowest proportion. Opportunities for employment and support services are obviously greater in urban areas, while women in rural Ireland who may want to work are hampered by few employment opportunities, transport difficulties and lack of childcare facilities. The differences in the proportion of women and the proportion of men in the labour force and not in the labour force emphasises the differences between male and female roles in Ireland. Traditional role models are still strong, with 71 per cent of the total male population aged fifteen years or more in the labour force, compared to the 73 per cent of the females population aged fifteen years or more engaged in 'home duties'. The male provides cash income, the female cares for the family. Tables 9 and 10 provide information on females in each region 'in' and 'not' in the labour force for 1991.

Women in paid employment

Even when women are at work we find that they are concentrated in certain sectors of the labour force and at the lower end of the status hierarchy. Women are the workers and not the decision makers in the jobs game. While we know that women's unpaid domestic labour is undervalued, there is much evidence to indicate that women's paid labour is also undervalued. Free labour and cheap labour are beneficial to the economy, but not to the individual who is doing the work. Women constitute a 'secondary' labour market that is characterised by low status, low pay, poor working conditions, high job turnover, few career prospects, little trade union protection and little or no further training and education. Woman's work is service-oriented mirroring the work that she does in the home. Irish women's hourly earnings are still 68 per cent of men's hourly earnings (CSO, 1992). These differences which are reflected right across the EC are due to many factors including fewer hours worked by women, poor career advancement, interruption of career due to family responsibilities and attitudes which sustain the view that 'women's work' deserves 'women's pay' — that is, low pay.

Table 11: Women at work as % of all workers by occupational group and region, 1991.

Region	Agriculture	Industry	Services
Dublin	9.7	23.3	44.3
Rest of East	11.7	18.2	42.4
East	11.3	21.8	44.0
South-Eest	6.2	19.1	46.6
South-East	7.6	18.3	47.4
North-East	6.7	24.1	44.4
Mid-West	14.2	19.8	48.7
Midlands	6.6	20.0	46.2
West	4.2	24.0	48.5
North West & Donegal	6.8	29.4	47.9
Ireland	7.9	21.4	45.6

Source: Labour Force Survey, 1991.

The raw figures show that employment opportunities for women are concentrated in urban areas and particularly in the eastern regions. Table 11 illustrates the 'crowding of women' into the service sector which is associated with the secondary labour market. Women's decreasing involvement in farm labour is evident from the 1989 Labour Force Survey which shows that 11,900 women are classified as being involved in agriculture, forestry and fishing. But a closer examination of these statistics shows that only 5,600 women are classified as farmers in their own right. Eighty per cent of these are widows or single women. The married woman who works on the farm is not counted as a distinct labour unit in her own right. Her labour is subsumed and hidden within the category 'household'. The true extent of the number of women who work on farms is unknown. Whether or not they have enough money to live on from week to week is an even greater unknown, as many are dependent on their spouses for cash income. From the 1990 Farm Structures Survey it can be estimated that there are 111,000 farm wives in the farm labour force which amounts to less than 30 per cent of the total family labour force on farms. This is an underestimate and the truer proportion is more likely to be 50 per cent. But because of the categorisation of women within the official statistics as dependents or part of the household unit, their farm work is not 'statistically' recognised. Rural women are doubly excluded from the statistics on work as both their farm work and their housework are classified as 'non-work'. In making census returns, many women will classify themselves as being engaged in 'home duties' when in fact they also contribute to farm work.

The term 'farmer' refers to the person who owns the farm and infers that this person is also the head of household and decision-maker. By definition the 'farmer's wife' occupies a secondary and subservient position in relation to the 'farmer'. The farmer's wife is not entitled to maternity benefit, retirement pension, sickness or disability benefit in her own right. There is no social security protection for women on family farms in spite of EC directives which advise that spouses should have independent entitlement to social security.

While there has been a fairly constant level of female participation in the Irish labour force (33 per cent), we still have the lowest level of women working compared to our EC sisters (42 per cent). Though single women are still a strong presence in the labour force, more single women are choosing to stay on in fulltime education and more married women continue to work and rear children at the same time. In 1991 42 per cent of the female labour force were married, while 53 per cent were single (see Table 12).

Table 12: Marital status and participation rates of women in the labour force, 1991.

Marital Status

% Single	% Married	% Separated	% Widowed	Total
52.9	41.8	2.7	2.7	429,100

Participation rates*

% Single	% Married	% Separated	% Widowed	Total
50.0	26.9	38.8	7.4	32.9

* Participation rate is the ratio of persons in the labour force to the total population in the relevant category.

Source: Labour Force Survey, 1991.

Social welfare statistics

In 1987, the Combat Poverty Agency estimated that more than 274,000 women lived in low-income households — that is, households in which each adult was trying to survive on £48 each per week (Combat Poverty Agency, 1990). The categorisation of women within the social welfare statistics is similar to the statistics on employment. Women are categorised largely as adult dependents within a household or they are categorised in terms of their relationship with a man. An adult dependant receives 60 per cent of the amount that is paid to the main recipient. Most adult dependents are women. Many women do not receive the 60 per cent equivalent from their spouses and are forced to budget on low and erratic incomes. We have little or no information on how income is distributed within households, and even less on rural households. A woman who provides evidence of need through a letter from a doctor, social worker or priest can apply for 'separate payments'. But though the income received under this arrangement is paid to the woman on a weekly basis, the amount is totally inadequate. The woman only receives 60 per cent of the main payment and the allowances for any dependent children that she may have. Women who are trying to maintain families on separate payments are particularly poor.

Women who receive income maintenance in their own right are those women whose spouses have died, deserted them or have been jailed, or women who are single parents or single women aged between fifty-eight and sixty-four years who require income maintenance. Most of these 'women only' schemes are means-tested. Each woman has to undergo a face-to-face interview with an official from the Department of Social Welfare, in which she is obliged to reveal details of her family life and living conditions in order to be assessed for eligibility. Many women find these interviews gruelling as they are being asked all the questions and they are not provided with information on the basis of the assessment. These interviews have been described as 'humiliating', 'painful' and 'distressing'.

The Family Income Support Schemes include many of the 'women only' payments. They are the widow's contributory and non-contributory pension, deserted wife's benefit and allowance, prisoner's wife's allowance, single parent's allowance, the maternity benefit and the supplementary welfare allowance. Table 13 provides information on these schemes for select counties. This is one of the few published statistics available which provide some estimate of the number of women in rural Ireland who are living on the poverty line. The isolation and exclusion experienced by women in these situations is difficult to combat because of lack of money and lack of support services that are rural based. According to the Second Commission on the Status of Women, the group most likely to be poor are rural women.

Table 13: **Family Income Support — payments by county, December 1990.**

Schemes	Clare	Galway	Mayo	Dublin
Widow's Pension	2240	4720	3752	5,400
Lone Parent's	400	950	460	11,280
Deserted Wife's	190	350	170	5,680
Prisoner's Wife's	-	-	-	5
Carer's Allowance	60	100	110	110

Source: Statistical Information on Social Welfare Services, 1990.

The 'missing' statistics on family planning facilities

How do women in the countryside control their fertility, limit family size or consider the question of reproductive 'rights'? Statistics on the use of birth control devices can only be gleaned from the published reports from family planning clinics, which are private commercial enterprises. For example, a brief look at the data from one Dublin-based clinic shows that 13 per cent of clients were not from Dublin city or county (Irish Family Planning Association, 1991). Does this imply that local facilities were either not available or insufficient? Research in this area is much needed. Many clinics have indicated that the number of patients who do not have the money to pay for contraceptives is on the increase. Medical card holders are not entitled to free family planning services beyond what they can obtain from their local GP. This places the burden of provision of facilities for low income patients on the clinics rather than on the public health service. Women who are living in rural communities have a social relationship with the local GP. In some instances this may deter women from seeking information about family planning or other services which they may require. However, research carried out by O'Hare on depression amongst women has shown that rural women who experience depression are more likely to go to a GP than to a hospital (O'Hare, 1987). The GP acts as a filtering agent and will decide whether the woman ought to be hospitalised or provided with a course of medication. It is assumed that female rates of depression are under-reported. O'Hare suggests that pressure of housework and childcare, low visibility of rural women in the wider community and difficulties in expressing feelings of emotional distress and receiving support for them are all factors for the under-reporting of the 'woman's disease'.

Alternative models of care have been created on a voluntary and self-financing basis by women's groups to provide services for women who require refuge for themselves and their children from a violent partner, or who require counselling about parenthood, marriage, contraception, sexually transmitted diseases or child abuse. These alternative models of health care do not receive any substantial state funding and are staffed largely on a voluntary basis. But they do provide a responsive service. However because the services are urban-based, many women in rural Ireland are not aware of these services nor do they have the money to pay for transport or for service fees. For example, a brief look at the statistics from the Galway Rape Crisis Centre shows that rural women do use these services and are demanding better access to essential services for women (see Table 14). Cork, Limerick, and Clonmel Rape Crisis Centres also provide counselling and support for women who have been subjected to sexual violence. For all the centres, the numbers of cases increase steadily year by year and yet in three health board areas there are no rape crisis centres.

Table 14: Number of cases reported to Galway Rape Crisis Centre, 1991/1992.

Category	1991	1992
Rape	45	51
Sexual assault	7	10
Incest	33	53
Child sexual abuse	8	29
Sexual violence*	43	48
Total number	136	191

*Note: Denotes a report of sexual violence for which no further categorical details were collected.

Source: Galway Rape Crisis Centre Annual Reports, 1991/1992

Summary

So what do the published statistics tell us? Perhaps they confirm what we already know. Because of the inadequacy of the statistics it is very difficult to evaluate the position of women in the countryside. But there is no doubt that rural women are deprived in relation to essential services and employment opportunities. The lack of support services such as marriage counselling and family planning services for women on low incomes living within the traditional family unit have consequences for rural women who want to make changes and benefit from the services that are available to urban-based women.

But the consequences for rural women who are living outside the norm and on the poverty line, such as single parents or women who have been deserted are even greater. Lack of childcare facilities, expensive public transport, few employment opportunities or educational facilities contribute to maintaining the silence and invisibility of women who are poor in rural Ireland. This lack of access to resources needs to be documented and enumerated to a far greater extent than is currently provided by research or by the official statistics, so that the female voices in rural Ireland can be heard

References and further reading

Ayers-Nachamkin, B. 1992. 'A Feminist Approach to the Introductory Statistics Course'. In *Women's Studies Quarterly*, Vol XX, Nos. 1 and 2.

Blackwell, J. 1987. 'Gender and Statistics'. In Curtin, C. et al *Gender in Irish Society*.

Byrne, A. et al. 1991. *North-West Connemara - A Baseline Study of Poverty*. FORUM, Connemara West, Galway.

Callan, T. and Farrell, B. 1991. *Women's Participation in the Irish Labour Market*. NESC Report No 91. National Economic and Social Council, Dublin.

Combat Poverty Agency. 1990. *Towards a Policy of Combating Poverty Among Women*. Combat Poverty Agency, Dublin.

Cullen, M. and Morrissey, T. 1982. *Women and Health: Some Current Issues*. Health Education Bureau, Dublin.

Curtin, C., Jackson, P. and O'Connor, B. (eds.). 1987. *Gender in Irish Society*. Galway University Press, Galway.

Daly, M. 1989. *Women and Poverty*. Attic Press, Dublin.

Galway Rape Crisis Centre. 1991, 1992. *Annual Reports*.

Irish Family Planning Association. 1991. *Annual Report*. IFPA, Dublin.

Market Research Bureau of Ireland. 1992. *Mná Na hEireann Inniú. An MRBI Perspective on Women in Irish Society Today*. MRBI, Dublin.

Millar, J., Leeper, S. and Davies, C. 1992. *Lone Parents, Poverty and Public Policy In Ireland*. Combat Poverty Agency, Dublin.

NESC. 1991. *The Economic and Social Implications of Emigration*, Report No. 90, National Economic and Social Council, Dublin.

O'Hare, A. 1987. 'Gender Differences in Treated Mental Illness in the Republic of Ireland'. In Curtin C. et al., *Gender in Irish Society*.

Owens, M. 'Women in Rural Development: A Hit or Miss Affair?' In *UCG Women's Studies Centre Review*, Vol. 1. Galway.

Second Commission on the Status of Women. January 1993. *Report to Government*. Stationery Office, Dublin.

Discussion topics

1 How do you feel about reading material that contains tables, statistics and figures? Why do you think you have this response? What suggestions do you have to make quantitative material more open to Women's Studies students?

2 How do you explain the fairly constant rate of labour force participation of Irish women since the 1960s? Do you think women

are taking jobs away from men?

3 Which health board area do you live in? What do the published statistics tell you about your area? Which health board area has more women than men? Why is this so? What areas have the highest and lowest percentage of older people? Can you think of reasons why women live longer than men? What does the dependency ratio tell you? How does it affect women's position and roles?

4 How do you explain the increasing number of babies born to either women living alone, with a partner or with someone to whom she is not married? What do you think of this trend? What does parenting mean to you? Is parenting any different for a woman rearing children alone, compared to a woman rearing children with a partner?

5 What factors do you think are the most convincing in explaining the decreasing rate of marriage in Ireland? Does the absence of divorce encourage people to live together before marriage or if one partner is already married? What is the legal status of children in households where parents are not married to each other? To whom does it matter if people cohabit rather than marry?

Women and Poverty

Eileen Evason

Introduction

Women and poverty is a deceptively simple title for an area of discussion that stretches across complex theoretical issues, main areas for research and difficult tactical problems. Accordingly this discussion begins by first reviewing definitions and measurement of poverty in general and the specific issue of integrating women into this theoretical context; it then focuses on the concept of independent access and the causes of poverty among women; and finally looks at relevant policy changes focusing particularly on income maintenance policy in the Northern Ireland context.

Defining poverty

The problem of defining and measuring poverty has been a central strand in the study of social policy for decades. In the 1960s, Townsend proposed a complete shift away from a minimum, physical efficiency, subsistence approach to a relative perspective and sought to develop methods of measurement based on this in his massive survey published at the end of the following decade (Townsend, 1979). We may call this approach scientific objective relativism. It was criticised on a number of grounds: that it failed to allow for taste or individual preference; that the data did not clearly demonstrate the existence of a threshold dividing the poor from everybody else (Piachaud, 1981); that it may not be possible to define poverty objectively (Orshansky, 1969); and that the concept of relative poverty is not 'sellable' politically or socially. New ground was broken by the development of the social consensus approach in the survey by London Weekend Television (LWT) (Mack and Lansley, 1985). In essence this approach argued that what constituted necessities of life should be defined by reference to the views of the general population. In fact, the gap between Townsend and the consensus approach turned out to be more apparent than real in as much as the LWT survey (and subsequent similar data) suggested that the majority of the population perceives poverty as a relative state; and the threshold, or poverty line (established by the two sets of work respectively at 133 per cent and 150 per cent of supplementary benefit rates) were also fairly close. This came as something of a relief to those who for years had used a 140 per cent cut-off point. One outstanding difficulty with the consensus approach, however, is that people may lack some items considered generally to be necessities but enjoy others which are not. For this reason, Bradshaw's efforts to revive interest in 'budget standards', that is, what can be purchased with set amounts of money — basing these on a relative approach — are of value (1987).

I would draw two conclusions from these and allied developments. The first is that, as a pragmatist, I am concerned that emphasising differences rather than the degree of consensus which has emerged has political consequences for which the poor may bear the costs. Piachaud has warned of the possibility of the debate on definitions becoming 'a semantic and statistical squabble . . . a discussion that is part of the problem rather than part of the solution' (Piachaud, 1987). We should note that these theoretical divisions were indeed seized on by government in 1985 in order to validate cuts and a restructuring of the benefits system based on concepts such as 'targeting' and 'efficiency' rather than 'need' and 'adequacy' (DHSS, 1985). As a feminist, however, I draw a second conclusion: I am equally concerned that women have been largely invisible in an academic debate that has gone on for nearly a century and the task of painting women into the picture, so to speak, poses formidable problems. It is, in fact, difficult to think of a task which more clearly exemplifies Pascall's proposition that:

> Feminist analysis is most obviously about putting women in where they have been left out, about keeping women on the stage rather than relegating them to the wings. But to do this suggests questions about the structures that have left women out; about the way academic disciplines work; about language, concepts, methods, approaches, and subject areas. Such a quest leads to a profound rethinking (Pascall, 1986: 1).

Moreover, bearing in mind my first conclusion and Desai's warning that 'only those definitions of poverty which appeal to the widest possible audience will stick', the tactical problems appear as substantial as the conceptual ones (1986: 1). Nevertheless, this task, I believe, is an essential one, as failure to build women into the debates on the definition, measurement and, to a lesser extent, the causes of poverty, has meant hardship for women; it has further meant policies which seem incapable of grappling directly with the problems they are supposed to address, and a lack of fit between our concepts and methods on the one hand and the world that women and men recognise themselves as inhabiting on the other.

Defining poverty: whose poverty?

With regard to definition, statements such as 'their resources are so seriously below those commanded by the average' (Townsend, 1979: 4) beg the crucially important question, 'whose resources'? For women who are heads of household, this is not a problem but Continuous House-hold Survey (CHS) data show that at least half of all married women in Northern Ireland are not in paid employment, and as Pahl (1989) has noted, British law eschews the concept of community property and there is no legal requirement for a primary wage earner to share his/her earnings with the other spouse. Thus effective rights to maintenance only exist when the marriage has ceased. Family law is not, therefore, founded on an assumption that resources are pooled, commonly controlled and enjoyed, and the work of Wilson demonstrates that women — and men — are acutely aware of to whom the financial resources in a marriage really belong. Wilson noted that:

> For most of the women interviewed, men had the money and they had a share of it — how much or how that share was arrived at was something they preferred not to think about (Wilson, 1987: 141).

Failure to take account of this fundamental question means that current definitions of poverty wrap up together persons whose experiences, perceptions, entitlements and circumstances may vary enormously. As Glendinning and Millar have noted:

> Surprisingly, the incorporation into relative definitions of poverty of important social dimensions such as powerlessness have not been extended to any examination of the position of women and men (1987: 11).

At a minimum, definitions need, therefore, to distinguish between those whose access to resources is direct, formal and legal and those, principally non-earning married women, who may manage some or all of a household's income but whose access to resources is actually indirect and at the discretion of another person. The two experiences are clearly very different and the latter contains risks of poverty which have only recently begun to be examined. Research on single parents has long suggested a problem of hidden poverty amongst women and children in two parent families. Pahl, when interviewing women in a refuge, found that:

> many of them claimed to be financially better off since leaving their husbands. All were living on supplementary benefit (now income support) receiving sums of money which represented the minimum amount on which anyone in Britain was expected to live. Yet on these meagre amounts they felt 'better off'. As I became sensitive to the implicat-ions of what the women were saying I started to ask about financial arrangements in the households from which they had come. It was clear that some of the husbands had had substantial incomes, but had kept so much for their own use that their wives and children lived in grim poverty (Pahl, 1989: 1).

A survey of single parents in Northern Ireland noted that:

> For many of these women single parenthood represented a movement from poverty, as a result of the inequitable division of resources between husband and wife, to poverty, as a result of the lowness of benefits — not automatically, as is popularly supposed, from adequacy to penury (Evason, 1980: 22).

Measuring poverty

With regard to the measurement of poverty, the focus on the family, household, or tax/benefit unit, has meant that our methods assume, or at least imply, an equitable division of resources amongst family members and hence an equality of living standards between family members. However, Charles and Kerr's work, for example, on the allocation of something as basic and essential as food (which was the bedrock of early poverty research) suggests considerable inequality of living standards (1987). At a minimum, we need more work of this kind looking at outputs in the form of aspects of living standards for different family members to complement the extensive data on inputs in the form of income. At the same time, we need to be aware that this more accurate focus is itself being overtaken by events. On the basis of British data, and looking at the position of all women, Glendinning and Millar have argued:

> The traditional position of the financially dependent woman now applies only to a very small minority — about 18 per cent — of all women . . . It can hardly be realistic, therefore, to ignore any longer the issue of women's independent access to resources (as conventional studies of poverty have done) on the grounds that this does not reflect their real total access (1987: 19).

Independent access
The concept of independent access has a number of advantages. It offers an alternative for those of us who are as uneasy about classifying women on the basis of resources owned and controlled by others as we are about allocating women to this or that social class on the basis of their husbands' occupation. In my experience of working with women married to violent men of all social classes, I have been struck by the fact that dependence is dependence is dependence. Statistics relating to income to which a person has independent access may thus come closer to conveying the reality of women's material position. For example, if we calculate the proportion of women living around the poverty line by reference to receipt of specific means-tested benefits (family credit, income support), we find that approximately 54 per cent of the adult female population and 50 per cent of men are

living around the poverty line. But such an exercise obscures the experience of those women who do not have a right to 'their' share of benefit payable or wages received. It also ignores the circumstances of women in households where income levels are above those giving entitlement.

Turning to income to which women have independent access, the picture is much clearer. We can quickly establish that the majority of women have no income or low incomes and are, I would argue, poor. On this basis, the female population divides up into three main groups. Firstly, non-working married women — some of whom are of working age and some of whom are retired. In Northern Ireland few women of retirement age are in receipt of pensions based on their own contributions, while most of those of working age will have no entitlement to any benefit in their own right (other than child benefit where there are dependent children). These women account for one-third of Northern Ireland's total adult female population. Secondly, there are roughly 230,000 married and single women in employment in Northern Ireland. One-third of these women are employed part-time. Using CHS data, we can classify 60 per cent of these as low-paid (that is, earning under £100 gross a week) workers. These women account for nearly one-quarter of the total adult female population. The third group of women are non-employed single women receiving benefits in their own right. Receipt of means-tested benefits (income support and housing benefit) by such women adds a further 17 per cent of the female population to our total. Note that no account is taken in this overview of women receiving national insurance benefits without means-tested additions, even though there will be many of these whose incomes are little above those on means-tested benefits. Nevertheless, the total amounts to three-quarters of all women in Northern Ireland. That is, three-quarters of adult women in Northern Ireland do not have access in their own right to income above the level of means-tested benefits. The concept of independent access clearly, therefore, demonstrates the limited reward that women receive for their work: a consideration that leads us to the issue of explanations of poverty.

Explaining poverty

Fortunately, there is now a substantial body of theoretical material on the construction of female poverty. Most of this material falls easily into the now dominant structural explanation of poverty. Interestingly, however, as late as 1978, Holman's apparently exhaustive analysis of the ways in which poverty may be explained contained not one reference to women's poverty as such (Holman, 1978). Theory has thus developed very rapidly in the 1980s and essentially locates the roots of female poverty in the general socio-economic position of women — namely in the division of labour between the sexes and the assumption that women are or should be dependent on and supported by men. This assumption dictates the rights and possibilities of all women, even though, as noted earlier, at any point in time only a minority of the female population may conform to this stereotype. Thus as Glendinning and Millar have noted:

> Far from protecting women from poverty . . . women's
> assumed and actual dependence on men is in fact the
> major cause of poverty (1987: 26).

The assumption and, indeed, prescription of dependence has four main consequences. Firstly, it legitimates the channelling of resources from the state to the household via the male. The debates which have surrounded the two exceptions to this rule — child benefit and family credit — suggest that policy-makers are aware of the problem of the hidden poverty of women inside the household but only feel comfortable curtailing masculine control over resources when the issue can be overtly and emotively linked to child welfare. Apart from hidden poverty and the refusal of the state to build into its own structures the concept of marriage as a partnership, the resultant dependency for women can be offensive and damaging. The woman who is caring for a disabled husband may be astounded to learn that she is actually the dependant person; widows are exasperated that their benefits depend on their husbands' contributions and their own count for nothing. In addition, data indicating that the wives of unemployed males are likely to withdraw from employment come as little surprise to those of us who have observed the reactions of unemployed husbands, for example, when the impact of wives' earnings on their benefits is explained.

Secondly, the assumption of dependence legitimates a benefit system which fails to deal with the full range of contingencies which may produce poverty, and is limited in its capacity to deal effectively with those risks which are recognised. I shall look more closely at this later. Thirdly, as many have observed, the assumption of dependence legitimates the low wages paid to women as such, the treatment of women as a reserve army of labour, and was, of course, a major obstacle for decades in the way of equal pay legislation. Fourthly, it legitimates the assumption that women are and should be available to work on an unpaid basis in a wide variety of settings and, of course, this has a severe impact on opportunities with regard to paid employment.

The issue of unpaid labour deserves special attention in Northern Ireland, though of course this is a worldwide issue. Within Northern Ireland a number of factors suggest that the volume of unpaid work here deserves special priority in future research: larger families, for example, the higher incidence of disability and the significance of agriculture. Women's unpaid work falls under a number of headings. Husband/children and home care, and the care of the disabled and elderly, are the two areas most commonly focused on. We have little data on the first, though on the second a number of studies has demonstrated that informal welfare networks, held out by some as the lynchpin of community care policy, are very limited. In a small study of 100 mentally handicapped persons and their families a few years ago, for example, shared care even within the immediate family was a rarity, with the bulk of the burden of care in almost all cases falling on a woman (Evason, 1984). The area where we have least knowledge, however, relates to the unpaid work women do in small enterprises and on farms. The inadequacy of official statistics showing that only 0.2 per cent of women in Northern Ireland work in agriculture is indicated by a number of sources including the Northern Ireland Rural Action Project (see, for example, Kilmurray, 1991). Reflection on this total volume of unpaid work suggests to me that if we cannot all agree that most women are poor, there can be little doubt that many are shortchanged.

Future policy
Measures to resolve these inequalities are easily delineated but will be implemented only with great difficulty. The need is not simply to address the amendment of the social security system, but to resolve the problems of low pay and unpaid work and to consider the broader implications of current trends in social policy. These matters are now considered in turn.

With regard to low pay, the obvious options are minimum wages legislation, vigorous application of the principle of equal value and the expansion of day-care provision. All of these proposals have run into difficulty and are counter to the current philosophy of the UK government. Wages councils are being dismantled and the United Kingdom equal value provisions, are deliberately tortuous and unhelpful (Maxwell, 1991). In addition, whilst it was hoped that a government caught between neo-conservative family policies on the one hand and a growing shortage of labour on the other might change course on childcare, Bronagh Hinds shows how, to date, ministers have placed responsibility for making such provision firmly on the shoulders of women and employers — despite the emphatic view of the latter that there is no prospect of industry making a substantial contribution (Hinds, 1991).

With regard to unpaid work, the obvious options are an end to social policies which assume women will fill the gaps as the state withdraws from a variety of areas of care and a fairer division of labour within the home. On the question of women filling the gaps in welfare, whilst we tend to focus on the specific policy of community care there is a need for a broader analysis examining the ways in which the concepts now dominating social policy — the new macho managerialism in health and welfare — exploit and penalise women. So often policies concerned with value for money, increases in productivity — by reference to debatable performance indicators — and efficiency savings, result in a transfer of labour from poorly paid to unpaid women. The majority of those affected by competitive tendering for catering, laundry and cleaning services in the health service, for example, have been women who have lost their jobs or voluntarily accepted cuts in wages. Increasing productivity by raising throughput in hospital care means, in plain English, discharging people as soon as possible. Often we are not in practice treating people more rapidly but simply offloading part of the total care formerly provided in hospital onto the community, that is, women. The end of the traditional school meal also means that women must spend time (and money) compensating for the fact, for example, that their children now eat junk food in school cash cafeterias, or elsewhere, at lunchtime (Evason and Woods, 1989).

On the second question, that of achieving a fairer division of labour within the home, the problems here appear formidable and have been compounded by economic trends of the past ten years. Across the UK, rather than increasing production and pro-ductivity through investment, the trend has been to rely on fewer workers, with male employees doing more overtime and thus having less capacity to share in home and childcare.

With regard to broader trends in social policy, the consequences of moving towards the assumption that the state should have a residual role, and as far as possible there should be reliance on the private sector, deepen dependence and narrow the options of the poor generally and of women in particular. State provision has been crucial in providing women and children with access to services which relate to needs rather than to what wage earners can, or choose to, pay, and private market welfare theorists have never addressed the gender of the sturdy individuals they envisage buying whatever quantities of welfare they wish in the market place. In housing, the drive towards owner occupation and the end of the concept of the state as a general provider of housing — as opposed to a provider for special groups — has narrowed drastically the chances of women securing good accommodation in their own right. In education, as state schools decline and students in higher education receive less and less state support, how soon will it be before the issue of gender surfaces as parents make 'choices' about the education of their children? In health care, in the move towards a two-tiered structure, with a thriving private sector for some and a poor quality National Health Service (NHS) for the rest, women will figure disproportionately in 'the rest'.

Turning specifically to social security, the problem of poverty amongst women has to be addressed at three levels: amendment or abolition of the insurance principle, a restructuring of pensions policy and a new approach to reduce women's disporportionate dependence on the means test.

The current operation in the UK of the concept of insurance in the benefit system is based on, and deepens, the dependence of, married women. Insurance benefits are provided for a range of contingencies (sickness, disability, unemployment) with entitlement depending on the fulfilment of complex contribution conditions. The insurance principle can be seen as indirectly discriminatory as women, with their lower wages, broken career patterns and greater involvement in part-time work, are less likely to qualify for such benefits. In Northern Ireland, this problem is of particular concern since, as McWilliams (1991) has shown, women are less likely to be in employment than women in Britain, and increasing numbers of those who are in work are in part-time employment. It can, moreover, be noted that recent legislation has introduced stricter contribution conditions with regard to short-term benefits, hence current policy serves to exacerbate existing difficulties.

One obvious solution would be to simply abolish the contributory principle. My own view, however, is that the problems relate not to the principle itself but to the manipulation of contribution conditions to ration and limit access to benefits. If we assume claimants prefer entitlement based on the concept of contribution, then we could simply widen this so that contributions — obviously more progressively structured than at present — were paid by all employees (full- and part-time) and, extending the home responsibilities protection provisions, credit women with real contributions acceptable for all benefits for all periods spent caring for children or the disabled or elderly. This, along with an increase in child benefit and a more generous, accessible invalid care allowance, would build into our social security system real recognition of unpaid work.

For pensions, women outside the labour force could be credited with earnings. However, the problems here go much deeper. Pensions policies in the post-war period have been remarkable inasmuch as every White Paper has focused on the implications of this or that policy for the average male wage earner when, of course, the majority of pensioners are women. The problem of poverty amongst the elderly cannot be resolved until policies focus squarely on women. Worse still, recent policy developments indicate that the government's general strategy is to limit state provision in order to provide room for company and personal pensions schemes. Women will, by virtue of their poorer employment opportunities, do particularly badly out of this trend towards privatisation and the consequences are likely to be particularly serious in Northern Ireland. Pensioners in Northern Ireland are already less likely to have occupational pensions than pensioners in Britain and those who do so are generally male. As a result, elderly women in Northern Ireland are much more likely than women elsewhere to be in poverty and claiming means-tested help. Thus, for example, in 1985, 80 per cent of elderly persons on supplementary benefit in Northern Ireland with no entitlement at all to a pension under the insurance scheme were women (PPRU, 1987). Moreover, even of those women entitled to a state insurance pension in their own right, 62 per cent still had incomes so low they had to claim means-tested help, compared with 19 per cent of single unmarried male claimants. For the UK as a whole and Northern Ireland in particular, there must be a reversion to the principle that provision for the elderly is primarily a state responsibility, that pensions should be adequate and that further provision is a matter for the individual. This means a reversion to the State Earnings Related Pension Scheme (SERPS) in its original form with an increase in the proportion of earnings replaced and the assumption that all women will receive a pension based on their own actual or credited earnings.

Finally, there is the question of removing women from the means-test. In all EC countries it is noticeable that women have to resort to such aid to a greater extent than men. This issue can be addressed directly by extending the insurance structure through the adoption of what may be called the 'principle of equal concern'. There is an analogy here with the evolution of equal pay legislation. Equal pay for women doing the same work as men had little impact because women normally do women's work. The concept of equal value was a means of trying to correct this distortion. Similarly, in social security, giving women access to benefits on the same terms as men has little impact, partly because, as has already been noted, women are less able to meet the qualifying conditions attached to benefits. Often, however, the problem is that the benefits system is geared to those 'risks' likely to be experienced by men. The risks to which women are subject have been discounted and hence women in poverty as a result of risks in women's lives, tend to be left to the least eligible part of the benefit system — means-tested assistance. The most obvious examples of this process are women who cannot work because they are caring fulltime for the disabled and elderly, and single parents, apart from widows. The principle of equal concern would mean a reform of the benefit system so that within a new approach to insurance all risks were covered.

Conclusion
This chapter has sought to build women into the debates about the definition, measurement and causes of poverty.

It has been suggested that the concept of independent access is an important step forward both in terms of research and in terms of future policy development. Using this concept it is clear that the vast majority of women are poor in Northern Ireland. A range of possible strategies for the future has been reviewed, but perhaps the most important of these is a change in the way we think about women in our theoretical discussions. The assumption of dependence, acknowledged or not, has had advantages for researchers and policy-makers. Life is easier when large numbers of people (women) can be bundled into larger units (households) and what actually happens within these units can be disregarded. The result of this strategy, however, is poverty for women and policies which fail directly to address need.

References and further reading

Bradshaw, J. et al. 1987. 'Evaluating Adequacy: The Potential of Budget Standards'. In *Journal of Social Policy*. Vol. 16, Part 2.

Charles, N. and Kerr, M. 1987. 'Just the Way It Is: Gender and Age Differences in Family Food Consumption'. In Brannen, J. and Wilson, G. (eds.), *Give and Take in Families*. Allen and Unwin, London.

Department of Health and Social Security. 1985. *Reform of Social Security*, Vol. 1. HMSO, London.

Desai, M. 1986. 'Drawing the Line in Defining the Poverty Threshold'. In Golding, P. (ed.), *Excluding the Poor*. CPAG, London.

Evason, E. 1980. *Just Me and the Kids*. Equal Opportunities Commission, Northern Ireland, Belfast.

Evason, E. 1984. *Who Cares: A Study of Mentally Handicapped Persons and their Families*. Triangle Housing Association, Northern Ireland.

Evason, E. and Woods, R. 1989. 'Poor Children, Poor Diet'. In *Health Education Journal*, 48 (1).

Glendinning, C. and Millar, J. 1987. *Women and Poverty in Britain*. Wheatsheaf, Brighton.

Hinds, B. 1991. 'Childcare Provision and Policy'. In Davies, C. and McLaughlin, E. (eds.), *Women, Employment and Social Policy in Northern Ireland: A Problem Postponed?* Policy Research Institute, Queen's University, Belfast.

Holman, R. 1978. *Poverty: Explorations of Social Deprivation*. Martin Robertson, London.

Kilmurray, A. 1991. 'Rural Women and Socio-economic Development Policies: The Case of South Armagh'. In Davies, C. and McLaughlin, E. (eds.), *Women, Employment and Social Policy in Northern Ireland: A Problem Postponed?* Policy Research Institute, Queen's University, Belfast.

McWilliams, M. 1991. 'Women's Paid Work and the Sexual Division of

Labour'. In Davies C. and McLaughlin E. (eds.), *Women, Employment and Social Policy in Northern Ireland: A Problem Postponed?* Policy research Institute, Queen's University, Belfast.

Mack J. and Lansley, S. 1985. *Poor Britain.* Allen and Unwin, London.

Maxwell, P. 1991. 'Equal Pay Legislation: Problems and Prospects'. In Davies, C. and McLoughlin, E. (eds.), *Women, Employment and Social Policy in Northern Ireland: A Problem Postponed?* Policy Research Institute, Queen's University, Belfast.

Orshansky, M. 1969. 'How Poverty is Measured'. In *Monthly Labor Review,* February.

Pahl, J. 1989. *Money and Marriage.* Macmillan, London.

Pascall, G. 1986. *Social Policy: A Feminist Analysis.* Tavistock, London.

Piachaud, D. 1981. 'Peter Townsend and the Holy Grail'. In *New Society,* 10 September.

Piachaud, D. 1987. 'Problems in the Definition and Measurement of Poverty'. In *Journal of Social Policy,* Vol. 16, Part 2.

Policy, Planning and Research Unit. 1987. *Northern Ireland Annual Abstract of Statistics.* PPRU, Belfast.

Townsend, P. 1979. *Poverty in the United Kingdom: A Survey of Household Resources and Standards of Living.* Penguin, Harmondsworth.

Wilson, G. 1987. 'Money and Marriage'. In Brannen, J. and Wilson G. (eds.), *Give and Take in Families.* Allen and Unwin, London.

Discussion Topics

1 Discuss the ways in which poverty has traditionally been defined. How do these fail to address the needs of women?

2 How useful is the concept of independent access in measuring the extent of poverty amongst women?

3 Why are women prone to poverty?

4 Discuss the changes which need to be made in benefits systems to deal with poverty.

5 Apart from the benefits system, which other areas of social policy need reform to prevent poverty amongst women?

6 How can women get their poverty on to the agenda?

Bringing the Margins into the Centre: A Review of Aspects of Irish Women's Emigration from a British Perspective

Ann Rossiter

In consigning the Irish and their contribution to the success of the British industrial revolution to the end of his book, *Industry and Empire* (1968), in a chapter headed, 'The other Britain', the economic historian E. J. Hobsbawm (1968) was merely reflecting the level of importance ascribed to the Irish in Britain, up to the late 1960s when the book was published, and indeed, until quite recently. Hobsbawm was probably the first writer to employ the term 'the invisible Irish' which is now widely used to describe the low profile of Irish immigrants. Though increased academic interest in the USA, Britain, Australia and elsewhere over the past decade or so means that the notion of invisibility is now less apt where males are concerned, sadly, it remains an accurate description of the treatment of female migrants. As Bronwen Walter points out, 'Irish women have been hidden behind Irish men in academic studies . . . accounts of emigration from Ireland ignore gender but deal implicitly with men's moves' (1989a). This should come as something of a surprise, since as early as 1983, Robert Kennedy in his path-breaking work, *The Irish: Emigration, Marriage and Fertility*, (1983) stressed the fact that women have dominated the outflow of Irish migration in most periods of the nineteenth and twentieth centuries and that their reasons for emigrating did not mirror those of their male counterparts. However, the importance of these distinguishing features seems to have had little impact, for in more recent works such as *The Irish in the Victorian City*, (Swift and Gilley, 1985) *The Irish in Britain, 1815-1939* (Swift and Gilley, 1989) and *The Irish in Britain, 1815-1914*, (Davis, 1991) women, if they appear at all, do so merely on the margins. Puzzling over the marginal-isation of women in Irish historiography, Margaret Ward, in a thought-provoking essay, suggests that the extent of sexism in academic circles is such that even in an area so vastly under-researched as gender in Irish history (and, as such, ripe for a male takeover), male historians are in the contradictory position of damaging not only their credibility, but also their careers (1991: 14-15). Her viewpoint is endorsed by two other Irish women historians, Maria Luddy and Cliona Murphy, who suggest that the discipline has been reduced to 'a narrative account of the doings of men, largely carried out by men, written by men and taught by men' (1990: 7). Surveying the literature on Irish emigration and observing 'the collective amnesia' of its authors on the question of gender, it is difficult not to draw the same conclusions about this field of study.

A serious departure from the status quo could well have been expected in a new series of five volumes on Irish migration launched in 1992, since the editor, Patrick O'Sullivan, freely acknowledges his debt in devising his methodology to the American feminist historian, Gerder Lerner (O'Sullivan, 1992). Having pioneered a number of new approaches to the study of women's past, not least a challenge to traditional sources and the way they are used by historians, Lerner insists that gender must be integrated as an analytical category in the study and writing of history. 'When gender is considered with race, class, ethnicity, and religious affiliation in analysing any given period or event,' she says, 'an entirely new dimension is added to social history.' (Lerner, 1979: 172). Lerner is therefore not just a feminist historian who has happened to present the world of historiography with an interesting methodology, but a scholar who suggests that history can no longer be regarded as such if it omits more than half the human race. Unfortunately, the two volumes to have appeared in O'Sullivan's Irish migration series at the time of writing, *Patterns of Migration* and *The Irish in the New Communities*, fail to reflect Lerner's approach, with the majority of the contributions clearly located in a male-centred view of the Irish universe, even on subjects where source materials on women are available. The promise of a volume on female migration in the series will hardly break the mould, and is more likely to have the effect of tagging women on, hardly what Lerner had in mind.

The marginalisation of women in history has been a major preoccupation of the current wave of British feminism and Anna Davin spoke for many when, in 1972, she wrote: 'Women's history and therefore people's history — has yet to be written, and to write it is part of our present struggle. We are formed by the past, and yet we know nothing about it.' (Davin, 1972: 215) Twenty years on, and a great deal of feminist research later, we have learned much about women's lives in past generations. We are now more knowledgeable about British women in the family and work place, and about the political and ideological forces that have shaped their destiny. However, British feminist scholarship has tended to concentrate on gender and class to the exclusion of all other factors such as nationality, race and ethnicity. This means that the presence in Britain of Afro-Caribbean, Asian, Irish and other ethnic minority women, as well as their contribution to the building of their adopted land, has been ignored, as have women generally in male scholarship (Rossiter, forthcoming).

Acutely conscious of their 'invisibility', Irish women immigrants have begun to record their presence and their achievements. In 1988, *Across the Water: Irish Women's Lives in Britain,* an oral history and the first book dealing exclusively with Irish women's emigration to Britain, appeared (Lennon et al, 1988). (This has recently been joined by an oral history of Irish women in the USA by Ide O'Carroll (1990).) Together with a novel by Maude Casey (1987), charting the painful journey of a young second-generation Irish girl in coming to terms with her Irish identity, and a collection of short stories by Moy McCrory (1985) about growing up Irish and female in Liverpool, these works have sparked a great deal of interest and opened the way for future research and writing. A number of articles have also been published in British feminist journals such as *Spare Rib* and *Trouble and Strife,* as well as reports of the London Irish Women's Conferences, published by the London Irish Women's Centre during the 1980s.

A further report, *Irish Women in London: The Ealing Dimension*, by the British geographer, Bronwen Walter (1989b), provides valuable insights into the numbers of Irish women in London in the contemporary period, their geographic distribution, demographic characteristics, employment and housing. Two scholarly works, *Erin's Daughters in America: Irish Immigrant Women in the Nineteenth Century* by Hasia Diner (1983) and *Ourselves Alone: Women's Emigration from Ireland 1885-1920* by Janet Nolan, (1989), both concerning the exodus to the USA, have appeared in the 1980s. Lynn Hollen Lees' *Exiles of Erin, Irish Migrants in Victorian London*, (1979), while not exclusively a study of women, is the only academic work on the Irish in nineteenth-century Britain to give serious treatment to women, albeit as a separate category.

Irish women's emigration in the nineteenth century

As a result of British colonial intervention, economic distress and religious persecution, emigration had become a fact of Irish life long before the nineteenth century. In the thirty years between the end of the Napoleonic wars and the eve of the great famine of 1845-9, an estimated 800,000—1,000,000 Irish people had crossed the Atlantic to North America. (Miller, 1985: 193). In 1841 there were 419,256 Irish-born residents in Britain; a decade later the figure had climbed to 727,326 as a result of the famine influx. (O'Tuathaigh, 1985: 14). Between 1845 and 1870 at least three million people left Ireland as a whole and 1.1 million emigrated between 1871 and 1891 (Kennedy, 1983: 27). Added to these were large numbers of seasonal migrants, both male and female, who travelled to England, Scotland and Wales on a yearly basis. (Fitzpatrick, 1989a: 16-19).

During the famine period and immediately after it, whole families emigrated, but subsequently the migrations were largely made up of young, single people. Precise figures for the sex ratios of emigrants first became available in the late 1800s, and consequently we know that of the 1,357,831 who left between 1885 and 1920, 684,159 were female; of these, 89 per cent were single and most were under the age of twenty-four. (Nolan, 1989:

100). Diner remarks that this constituted a mass female movement without parallel in the history of European emigration and a 'defeminisation' of the Irish country-side. Both Diner and Nolan inform us, as did the work of Maxine Seller (1975) and Kristian Hvidt (1975) almost a decade earlier, that the extent of this emigration of single Irish women, travelling alone and independently of parents or husbands, was an anomaly in the history of overall European emigration to the United States. It stood in marked contrast to the custom among other European groups, such as Danes, Italians or Jews, where women's emigration was generally led and financed by male relatives. In the case of Ireland, annual remittance from America amounted on average to five million dollars between 1848 and 1900 and financed the emigration of at least three-quarters of all those who went to the United States in that period (Kennedy, 1983: 22). Much of the passage money came from women anxious to secure an independent livelihood for their female siblings and relatives and to help them regain the respect and status that wages brought.

While work on women migrants is still in its infancy, the social processes which propelled this unique exodus of women out of Ireland in the nineteenth century are now better understood. Although there were significant differences in the economic roles of women according to class, research on the role of rural women in the eighteenth and early nineteenth centuries shows that they played a significant part in the type of mixed agriculture prevalent at the time. Lynn Hollen Lees quotes contemporary reports, such as Edward Wakefield's of 1812: 'They [women] are subjected to all the drudgery generally performed by men: setting potatoes, digging turf, and the performance of the most laborious occupations.' (1976: 26). Other observers reported that women were engaged in binding corn, harvesting flax, digging potatoes, saving hay and looking after fowl. The dependence of the family economy on women's labour was crucial, especially on those activities which could be converted into cash. Arthur Young, in the 1770s, had found that 'they make their rents by a little butter, a little

wool, a little corn, and a few young cattle and lambs'
(quoted in Hollen Lees, 1976: 27). Women's role in this
process was crucial, says Hollen Lees, 'for they made the
butter, spun the wool, cared for the pigs and poultry, and
sold the eggs, diverting food away from the family' (1976:
27). On the western seaboard, knitting was an important
cottage industry, and in the towns the wives of craftsmen
shared some of the tasks of the workshop and supervised
the welfare of apprentices and servants. Widows continued to manage businesses until children were sufficiently
grown to take over responsibility (O'Tuathaigh, 1978: 28-
9). This is not to suggest that women enjoyed equality
with men in the patriarchal society that was Ireland in the
eighteenth and nineteenth centuries, but their status was
undoubtedly enhanced by their ability to contribute to
the family economy, and this was reflected in their
freedom to marry more or less at will and at a relatively
early age.

By mid-nineteenth century this situation had dramatically altered. The market for homespun thread virtually
disappeared as the British industrial revolution began to
make itself felt in Ireland with the dumping of factory-
made goods. The Act of Union of 1800 had created a free-
trade zone between the two countries, and, given
Britain's position as the world's leading industrial nation,
especially in textiles, it is not surprising that Ireland's
more primitive wool and cotton industries were quickly
undermined. It was only in areas of Ulster that any
significant native industry developed and provided
women with paid work. Mary E. Daly (1981a) points out
that manufacturing industry employed a mere 17 per cent
of the Irish work force in 1891 as compared with 27 per
cent in 1841, the brunt of the decline being borne by
women workers. The proportion of women recorded in
the census as occupied fell steadily from 29 per cent in
1861 to 19.5 per cent in 1911, the 1861 level never being
regained. Women's employment was further affected by
the shift away from tillage caused by falling prices and
the repeal of the Corn Laws in Britain in 1846. The
flooding of the British market with cheap foreign grain

was a devastating blow for Irish producers, not least for women, whose role was even further marginalised, with the switch to less labour-intensive and male-dominated activities, such as the keeping of livestock. The lack of any significant industrial infrastructure outside Ulster meant that few opportunities for paid employment occurred for women over the next century, the only significant exception being domestic service. The pattern was repeated in the farmyard. J. J. Lee (1978) draws our attention to the mechanization of dairying, previously a female domain, but one which had become exclusively male by the end of the nineteenth century as creameries took over from domestic production.

In 1884, Frederick Engels (1970) noted that as the household economy dwindled in importance, so did the role of women. Having been pushed out of participation in social production, their oppression then became fixed through confinement in the household, and although there were variations according to class and to financial need, the domesticated wife became the ideal to which all classes aspired. In the case of Irish women, this development is striking and the link between economic status and social position seems inescapable. Large numbers of women who could no longer find independent employment or supplement family income, now became vulnerable as the dependants of fathers and husbands. Marriage and motherhood increasingly came to be the only occupation available to them, but this avenue was reserved for those who could secure a dowry. The custom of dowering daughters had previously been confined to the larger farmers and gentry. Amongst the lesser peasantry, land was continually subdivided to provide for children once they married. This arrangement was favoured by absentee landlords primarily concerned to secure the high income such an arrangement brought. The system of sub-division came to an end by the mid-nineteenth century for several reasons, not least the successive failure of the potato crop, the staple food of those who tilled the dwindling, dwarf-sized plots.

The post-famine restructuring of the economy favoured larger farms for cattle grazing and, although there was a significant drop in the population, land became scarce and the earlier, more spontaneous attitude to marriage was soon a thing of the past. Only one son now inherited the farm and his bride was required to provide a substantial dowry. Marriage in this context, writes Hugh Brody, 'was fundamentally unromantic; arranged by a matchmaker, attended by endless negotiations and wrangling over dowry and worth, the wedding eventually paired a girl of twenty with a man often well over forty' (1973: 111-12).

Even in the areas of Ulster (South Antrim, North Down, Armagh and Belfast) where domestic textile employment was transformed into factory-based employment for women, the cataclysmic social and demographic effects of the great famine and structural adjustment of economy and society generally which followed in the wake of the industrial revolution had considerable fall-out. Peter Gibbon notes that religious revivalism was widespread throughout the area in the period, attracting large numbers of young, unmarried women who frequently displayed 'manic behaviour' patterns. Protestant, especially Presbyterian, fundamentalist enthusiasm, says Gibbon, 'provided a means by which personal and collective fears, frustrations and expectations could be handled' (1975: 60).

Although there is a certain amount of controversy over when precisely the new social order took root, writers are in agreement that the great famine period was a watershed in Irish life. Following the famine, people were subordinated to the land in a manner that was unique in Europe. Between 1845 and 1914 the age of the average male at marriage rose from about twenty-five to thirty-three, and the age of the average female from about twenty-one to twenty-eight. Husbands were generally older than their wives as a result of the reluctance of the man's parents to relinquish the farm and allow a new family to be formed. Large numbers did not marry at all and celibacy became increasingly common. By the turn of the century 88 per cent of women between the ages of twenty and twenty-four were unmarried, as were 53 per cent of those between the ages of twenty-five and thirty-four (Commission on Emigration, 1954: 72). By postponement and reducing the rate of marriage, the Irish peasantry attempted to curb population and ensure that the trauma of famine would not be repeated. They were aided in this enterprise by a restructured and revitalised Catholic Church in the latter half of the nineteenth century. A huge church building programme was put in motion, the number of clergy increased dramatically and the population underwent what has been described as a 'devotional revolution'. A strongly puritanical attitude to all matters concerning sex became widespread, and a rigid moral code was enforced which heavily punished all those who deviated. Opinion has differed on how instrumental religion was in the forging of this new morality, but there now appears to be general agreement with Eugene Hynes's assessment:

> They [the Irish peasantry] accepted puritanical teaching because, from their own experience, they knew that illegitimacy would threaten the foundations of the stemfamily system and increase the number of mouths dependent on a given farm. But, and this is the important point, the people were discriminating in regard to what teaching they accepted from the church, and the church was a follower of the people, not vice versa. Officially, Catholicism favoured early marriage, but the people did not marry early. The priests were 'ineffectual champions of marriage'. . . because, for very good reasons, people did not believe in early marriage. Early marriage would virtually have made impossible what they wanted — a higher standard of living (Hynes, 1978: 147-8).

This uncompromising order was accepted by successive generations of men and women who remained in Ireland, although Pauline Jackson found that folk poetry of the time reflected a certain rebelliousness concerning the arranged marriage and dowry system (1984: 1011-12). Those who chafed at the idea of loveless marriages determined by matchmakers, and the many who failed to secure a dowry, emigrated to find a freer and more independent existence. For those women who left Ireland, suggests David Fitzpatrick, the nineteenth century was often a period of triumph rather than subjection (1989b: 217-18).

The search for work

The large numbers of single women, surplus to the needs of nineteenth-century Irish society, who crossed the Atlantic, and the smaller number who made their way to Britain, Australia and New Zealand, were primarily employed as domestic servants. They entered the labour force at the very bottom of the hierarchy and in the USA occupied a position possibly as low as that of black women. However, such work was favoured, as it not only solved accommodation problems, but made saving money and the sending of remittances to Ireland much easier. Many women were also occupied as seamstresses, milliners, factory and mill workers. Although the vast majority were unskilled workers, there is ample evidence to show that some became successful. Diner refers to community histories and parish and charity records in various parts of the USA which testify to the impressive sums of money accrued by numbers of unmarried Irish women, which they sent back to Ireland, gave to their parish church or invested in property. She also considers that the tradition of late marriage or non-marriage, which had sprung up in post-Famine Ireland, remained strong among Irish immigrant women, even when marriage opportunities existed. The importance attached to family and the farm in Ireland may have accounted for this, since marriage would have signalled a drying up of vital financial aid (1983: 52). Rita M. Rhodes (1986), researching letters from Irish women in America, concludes that female emigrants were a more reliable and constant source of remittance, since sons would be more tempted to spend the money on themselves. One of the letters she quotes is especially poignant:

> I am sending you two pounds. Annie is sending you one pound and Liz is sending you ten shillings so you see you are not forgotten here although Liz is a great many years here don't think I would forget you either if I was away so long. Indeed I never could forget my darling

mother. (Cited in Rhodes, 1986)

Unlike the tendency in America for Irish women to remain unmarried, their sisters in Britain seem to have returned to the pre-Famine practice of universal and early marriage (Hollen Lees, 1976: 38).

The pattern of work for single women migrants in Britain was broadly similar. Domestic service headed the list, but Irish women faced considerable competition from their English counterparts in this line of work. Catholic priests frequently issued warnings of the dangers facing girls in London, seeing that it was not uncommon for them to quit work or be fired, their only recourse then being begging or prostitution. The long tradition of seasonal agricultural work involved women travelling to Britain, especially at harvest time, to participate in reaping, turnip singling and potato-lifting, the latter being immortalised in *Children of the Dead End*, Patrick MacGill's semi-autobiographical novel (1982: 74-5). Irish women also worked seasonally in the iron furnaces of South Wales and in mining, both on a temporary and long-term basis (Fitzpatrick, 1989: 18). With the exception of their involvement in the jute industry of Dundee and the muslin, silk and cotton manufacturers of Paisley (Collins, 1981), we know little or nothing of those Irish women who found employment in the textile areas of Britain generally. For instance, in 1851, the census figures show that 13.1 per cent of the population of Manchester and Salford was Irish-born (this figure does not include their descendants) (O'Tuathaigh, 1985: 15). We learn from a feminist study of Lancashire women textile workers, *One Hand Tied Behind Us* (Liddington and Norris, 1978), that not only had the industry a predominantly female work force, but a tradition of women continuing to work after marriage. Because the study makes no mention of ethnic origins, we do not know if this tradition existed among Irish women.

In Britain, as in the USA, there was a strong tendency for Irish women to retire from work outside the home once married. To supplement family income, many took in piecework of different types — sewing, embroidery, the making of artificial flowers, lint scraping, fur-pulling and, of course, laundry. The practice of taking in lodgers was also widespread. Among the poorest, women with their small children hawking in the streets and markets were a common sight (Hollen Lees, 1976: 96-7).

As the nineteenth century closed, Irish women in the USA moved in significant numbers into nursing, clerical, secretarial, sales work and teaching. Upward mobility was more delayed in Britain due to widespread anti-Irish and anti-Catholic feeling, but the emergence of a small proportion of Irish women in lower-middle-class jobs, such as clerical work, and in the professional occupations of nursing and teaching, is apparent in a survey of Irish-born workers in Scotland in 1911 (Fitzpatrick, 1989a: 16-19). The struggle to gain professional status in the face of widespread discrimination emerges even in the religious orders, re-established in mid-nineteenth-century England after a break of over two hundred years. Susan O'Brien notes that 'although all English congregations readily accepted Irish-born women as laysisters [their function essentially being that of domestic servants], the brogue was not always felt to be suitable in a choir nun [the more middle-class sister occupied as a teacher, nurse or social worker].' (1990: 455).

In both Britain and the USA women climbed the social ladder more quickly than men. The reasons for the disparity are examined by David Fitzpatrick, who argues that this was due in no small measure to the higher literacy and numeracy rates amongst women. These he ascribes to declining work opportunities for women and children as Irish domestic industry collapsed, the greater diligence of girls in the schoolroom, and the culture of emigration which recognised the merits of education, built into the life-cycle of women (1989b: 218-20).

Women emigrants in the twentieth century

Between 1901 and 1921, a total of 510,400 men and women left the thirty-two counties of Ireland and from 1926 to 1961, the net figure for those leaving the twenty-six county independent state was 882,149 (Commission on Emigration, 1954). The Free State (later to become the Republic of Ireland) was bequeathed the legacy of a backward rural economy, with a minute, unsophisticated industrial sector still vulnerable to the dumping of British goods, despite independence. Between 1949 and 1956, a period when many European countries were experiencing a major economic boom, national income in the independent state rose by a mere 8 per cent and emigration averaged about 40,000 a year (Daly, 1981b: 163). The severe depopulation of the Irish countryside evoked memories of the great famine diaspora, and the consequences of this new outflow again permeated national life to a major degree. Demographically, it produced an unbalanced population structure and a high dependency rate. Socially, by draining the country of its youth, energy and discontent, it removed an important source of change.

Unlike nineteenth-century emigration, the destination of most emigrants was Britain, as a result of the quota system operated by the authorities in the USA and the contraction of the labour market there. The composition of the emigrant flow was broadly similar to that of the latter part of the nineteenth century, as far as age structure and sex balance were concerned. The majority of emigrants were under the age of twenty-five, but women tended to be younger than men. The rate of male to female emigration varied, with women outnumbering men at various stages.

Although valuable insights into the lives of Irish women in contemporary Britain and the USA have been provided by two oral history works recently published (Lennon et al, 1988; O'Carroll, 1990), the lacunae in our knowledge of Irish female emigrants in the twentieth century are vast. From existing information we know that, as in the nineteenth century, women's reasons for emigrating were primarily economic, and that there was also a strong desire to improve status. Clearly, the long struggle for an independent Ireland, in which women had participated, failed to deliver them from their marginalised position, both economically and legally. Female suffrage was achieved, it is true, but Irish women paid the price of a partitioned Ireland, where two mutually antagonistic states adopted ideologies which were religiously orthodox and patriarchal. Protectionist measures to help the ailing southern economy were introduced in 1924 and lasted until the end of the Second World War. In this period women's share of the industrial work force increased from 20 per cent to 22.4 per cent, but by 1961 this share had only risen to 23 per cent (Barry and Jackson, 1988).

The majority of those employed were unmarried women under the age of twenty-five. In 1935, the Conditions of Employment Act provided powers to bar or restrict the numbers of women working in a host of industrial occupations. In keeping with the tenets of orthodox catholicism and right-wing ideology prevalent in Europe at the time, marriage bars were introduced in the civil service, local authorities and health boards, obliging women to leave work as soon as they married. This misogynist attitude received its fullest expression in Article 41 of the southern state's 1937 Constitution, which defined the role of mothers as properly belonging in the home. The same constitutional article introduced for the first time a prohibition on divorce. Given this combination of economic and social factors, it is hardly surprising that so many young women repeated the nineteenth-century pattern of seeking economic opportunities, independence and social status elsewhere.

Despite women's (including married women's) higher participation rate in the labour force in Northern Ireland emigration for economic purposes has also been high (*Fortnight*, 1991). Figures giving a gender breakdown appear to be unavailable, and are not stated in a report of a seminar, held in Belfast in 1991, on aspects of emigration from the area (Daly, 1981a: 77).

Employment opportunities for Irish women in Britain
The outbreak of the Second World War provided Irish women immigrants in Britain with their first significant opportunity to break out of the traditional mould of domestic service. The Republic had declared its neutrality at the outset of the war and severe restrictions were imposed on travel between the Republic and Britain. However, the demands of war created labour shortages in the public services and certain sections of British

industry, which resulted in an agreement being reached early in 1941 between the British Ministry of Labour and the Republic's Ministry of Industry and Commerce. In all, approximately 100,000 Irish workers arrived in Britain during the war years and a substantial number of them stayed. Female recruits were employed as teachers, nurses, midwives and domestics in hospitals and hotels, while others were directed into the munitions factories, the cotton mills and transportation, particularly bus-conducting (Jackson, 1963: 102, 103). After the war, when travel restrictions between the two countries were lifted, the Irish contribution to the reconstruction of the British economy was highly significant. In 1947 alone, 1,176 Irish women travelled on assisted passage and went into nursing (Jackson, 1963: 104). With the creation of the National Health Service, the demand for health personnel was high and British hospitals regularly advertised for staff in the Irish national and local press. By 1951, 22.4 per cent of Irish-born women were engaged in professional occupations, mainly nursing and midwifery. The rest were to be found in domestic, clerical and general manufacturing (Jackson, 1963: 106). Interestingly, the occupational patterns of Irish female immigrants, as revealed by the 1966 census, continued to show a generally higher socio-economic status than their male counterparts in Britain. Rose's study categorises 48 per cent of Irish women as middle class, compared with 19.7 per cent of Irish men (1969). The Limerick Rural Survey, published in 1962, confirmed the continuation of the nineteenth-century practice of girls receiving some post-primary education where non-agricultural jobs were limited, thus enabling a greater proportion of them to take up more attractive and socially desirable jobs after leaving school.

The 1970s saw a reversal of the emigration trend, with the numbers returning being greater than those leaving. Of the 104,000 who returned to the Republic between 1971 and 1981, there were almost equal numbers of married men and women, but only half as many single women as men (Kelly and Nic Giolla Choille, 1990: 15). In the 1980s, however, economic recession in the Republic resulted in another huge outflow. It is estimated that at least 200,000 people left in the 1980s, and of those remaining behind, one-third live below the poverty line. Census figures indicate that more men than women have left, but the School Leavers Report, recently by the Irish Department of Labour (1990), shows that more girls than boys have emigrated at school-leaving age. A large proportion of the new exodus made Britain, and especially London, their destination, but a minimum of 150,000 Irish people have emigrated illegally to the USA since 1981. In both of these countries there is disturbing evidence to show that although young Irish women are frequently well educated, they often find employment only in those sectors traditionally open to the Irish, namely, domestic work and service industries, such as nursing and catering. Young Irish men also tend to be confined to their traditional area of employment — the construction industry. A survey conducted by the *Irish Voice*, the New York newspaper for the Irish community, found that in 1987, 64 per cent of Irish women were employed as home helps or au pairs, 28 per cent were waitresses and only 18 per cent were engaged in office or other types of work (Kelly and Nic Giolla Choille, 1990: 17). While their illegal status may be cited as a major cause of their low occupational status in the USA, a report by the *Guardian* on Irish women in 1987 stated, 'In fact young Irish women are among the best educated in London, though this is not often reflected in their employment status. Many are apparently unable to find jobs reflecting their educational skills' (2 September, 1987).

Putting down roots
Although there was a wide and varied geographical distribution of Irish-born migrants in nineteenth-century Britain, closely-knit communities in areas of heavy concentration, known as the 'Irish rookeries', probably sustained a sense of identity. There were also high levels of inter-marriage which maintained the social cohesion of the community. Gradually, as class differences made themselves apparent and a certain degree of upward

mobility took place, the Irish became more dispersed, but a notion of 'Irishness' was retained through the many immigrant organisations which sprang up, ranging from the political to the social, though all but a minority of these were closed to women.

Southwark Irish Literary Club (later Irish Literary Society), set up in 1883, and the Gaelic League, for example, admitted members of both sexes. Above all other institutions, it was the Catholic Church, formally restored in Britain in 1850, which occupied a pivotal position in the lives of Irish women immigrants. Some writers, such as Sheridan Gilley, assert that the Irish community in Britain was essentially constructed by the Church and that the survival of an Irish identity was crucially bound up with the survival of Catholicism in Britain (1988). Through fund-raising for vast church building programmes, parish devotional associations, sodalities, guilds, confraternities, welfare organisations and, not least, Catholic schools, the Church established strong links with the immigrants. While men dominated virtually all the secular organisations, women formed the backbone of church-based activities, and although a recent book on Irish Catholics in England in the period 1880—1939 does provide some glimpses (Fielding, 1993), the magnitude of their work is, as yet, hidden from history.

The extent to which women, and mothers in particular, are involved in the processes of integration (and possibly assimilation) of the Irish, especially of the second and subsequent generations, is rarely discussed, most commentators regarding the Catholic church and the labour movement as the significant agencies of assimilation of the Irish in Britain. Looking generally at the link between women, the state and the national or ethnic processes, Nira Yuval-Davis and Floya Anthias (1989: 7-9) suggest that the female role extends far beyond the biological reproduction of an ethnic or national grouping. Women also act as 'cultural carriers' of the group, since they are the main socialisers of children.

Reading through the case studies of Irish women immigrants presented in *Across the Water, Irish Women's*

Lives in Britain, it is difficult not to be struck by the extent to which this takes place. Noreen Hill recounts:

> When I was bringing up my children it was very important to me to try and pass on a sense of Irishness to them. I told them about Irish history, read Irish story books to them, tried to teach them a little bit of the Irish language, tried to teach them their prayers in Irish. I tried to tell them about the Famine, and things like that. But they were very young and I was the only one that could tell them, there was nobody else . . . They were fine while they were in the Catholic school. After that, the Irishness dwindled away, apart from what I was trying to inject into them (Lennon, McAdam and O'Brien, 1988: 99-100).

While the authors of *Across the Water* found that none of their interviewees considered themselves to have assimilated, all identifying themselves very much as Irish, and many clearly making strong efforts to transmit an Irish culture to their children, it is difficult to reconcile this evidence with Liam Ryan's argument that Irish assimilation into British society is amongst the fastest that occurs among immigrant groups anywhere in the world, being practically complete in a single generation (1990: 59-60).

Women and the churches

The role of religion in the lives of Irish women immigrants has yet to be researched and analysed. Traditionally, religion has been a source of strength and solace for many, as well as an outlet for their organisational abilities, most particularly in the nineteenth century when many political and social organisations barred them. The strength of women's allegiance demonstrates itself in a number of ways. Bronwen Walter's work on Irish women in Ealing shows that Irish-born women — predominantly southern and married — tend to drop out of employment in the child-bearing years at a greater rate than in other groups analysed in her report — 'white UK', 'Afro-Caribbean' and 'Asian' (1989b: 28). From this we can probably conclude that the exclusively familial role ascribed to mothers by church and state in Ireland can survive a different economic and social environment. At certain times, however, women are forced to confront the central paradox that their religion is, on the one hand, the embodiment of ideological and institutional sexism, and on the other, a consolation and an inspiration. This contradiction perhaps becomes most apparent to those who step outside accepted norms, when, for, instance, they become unmarried mothers or have abortions. Consequently, there is a strong tendency for women to remain silent, to depend on their own individual resources to resolve their predicament, and not to challenge the status quo.

There is also a long tradition of pregnant, single women leaving Ireland to give birth in Britain, and of others fleeing from broken marriages or domestic violence. Rarely do such immigrants appear in the annals of Irish migration, and if they do, it is as deviants. For example, Father McSweeney, Director of the Irish Centre in Camden Town, London, reported that the 1950s surge of emigrants contained an increasing number of what he termed 'social casualties', which included alcoholics, unmarried mothers, prostitutes and petty criminals who, he said, were a source of concern to church authorities (O'Briain, 1981: 122) The emigrant section of the Catholic Social Welfare Bureau, set up in Ireland in 1942, has produced annual reports based on its operations in Britain. A 1956 report stated, 'As in other recent years registry office marriages, laxity in attendance of religious duties and, in the case of young girls, irresponsible conduct and moral delinquency continue to provide the main case problems.' (Kelly and Nic Giolla Choille, 1990: 13). No comment was made on the morals of young Irish male immigrants.

Some of the traditional silence surrounding the taboo area of sexuality has been broken in recent years, with the official publication in Britain of yearly abortion figures indicating the numbers of Irish residents who have had abortions in private British clinics since the passage of the 1967 Abortion Act. In 1972, it was reported that 261 women normally resident in the Republic of Ireland obtained legal abortions in England and Wales during 1970. By 1986 the figure was 5,642 and it is widely believed that the real figure could be 10,000, given that many women give fictitious British addresses and are therefore included in the figures for England and Wales. The failure of progressive forces to secure an extension of the 1967 British Abortion Act to Northern Ireland means that considerable numbers of women from there also have to secure private abortions in Britain. In 1981, the Irish Women's Abortion Support Group (IWASG) was set up in London to give emotional and material support to Irish women who travel over from Ireland. IWASG members have stressed the importance of working in an organisation which has active political links with Ireland:

> Women choose to get involved in IWASG for different reasons. For some it provides the opportunity to continue their involvement in issues that they'd previously worked on in Ireland. For others of us it is a practical way of taking some action around an important issue. We are conditioned as women to be helpful, to look after other people, but there seems to be a contradiction in providing support for women having an abortion, as it would never be seen to be a good cause by either our families or the Irish state. It is a subversive activity — enabling women to have terminations undermines the dominant values of both the Church and State in Ireland (IWASG, 1992).

Issues of nation and race

Political links with Ireland have also been sustained through activities related to the national question. The extent to which historians have excluded women from Irish political history has been explored by Margaret Ward (1983) in her study of women in Irish nationalism, but women's involvement in Irish politics in Britain has yet to be excavated. Possibly one of the earliest all-women secular organisations to be formed in Britain was the Ladies' Land League. In response to the outlawing of the Land League in Ireland and the imprisonment of the leaders, Parnell and Davitt, under Gladstone's Coercion Act, Anna and Fanny Parnell set up the Ladies' Land League in Ireland in 1881. Being without the franchise and in certain respects regarded as minors, it was assumed that the women would not be subjected to the full rigours of the Coercion Act and thus could keep the organisation on ice until the men were released from jail. But Margaret Ward's work demonstrates that the Ladies' Land League did a great deal more than just that.

An Anti-Coercion Association containing a number of feminists was set up in Southwark, an area of south London where the Irish accounted for at least 10 per cent of the local population. In February 1881, the English radical feminist, Helen Taylor, organised a London branch of the Ladies' Land League and set about fund-raising for the sister organisation in Ireland. Further branches were opened in Southwark and Poplar in east London. By the summer of that year, the Ladies' Land League was reported to be making great headway and a group of English feminists went to Ireland at the invitation of Anna Parnell. By the end of the year the League had developed in Britain to such an extent that it could challenge the police without male support. By December it had caused sufficient disaffection to warrant its suppression by the British government (Russell, 1987: 17-21). No information exists on any other Irish women's political organisations until the 1970s. It is likely that Irish women became involved in British movements such as that for women's suffrage, and records of a few individuals like Frances Power Cobbe, an Irish feminist and reformer in Victorian London have been published (Kavanagh, 1983). Although a considerable amount of information is available on US labour leaders, such as Elizabeth Gurley Flynn and Mother Mary Harris Jones, records of Irish women labour leaders in Britain have still to be uncovered.

The current wave of British feminism coincided with the second major upsurge of Irish nationalism this century, and Irish feminists in Britain, together with British and other women, formed groups and campaigned on Irish issues. A 'Women and Ireland' group was set up in London in 1972 to discuss and publicise the war in Northern Ireland and to highlight the crucial role being played by women, especially in the nationalist community. By the early 1980s a network of Women and Ireland groups existed in twelve British cities, from Bristol to Dundee, campaigning on a number of fronts, but particularly on the issue of political prisoners. In 1980, the London Armagh Group was formed to work specifically on women prisoners, and after a long campaign the group was instrumental in securing the release of Pauline McLaughlin, a young prisoner in Armagh Jail who was seriously ill. An International Women's Day demonstration has been organised outside Armagh Jail each year, and the group has brought demonstrators from Britain and many other countries. A 'stop the strip-searches' campaign, initiated by the group, became active in Britain in 1983 and succeeded in gaining widespread opposition to the practice from a number of trades unions, and political and human rights organisations (*Women Behind the Wire*, 1981).

In the aftermath of the deaths of ten hunger strikers in Long Kesh Prison in 1981, a dramatic change took place in the politics of the Irish in Britain. The level of anti-Irish racism, amplified to hysterical proportions by the media, and echoed in many sections of British society, caused a mushrooming of organisations with an exclusively Irish membership. Given that British feminism at best provided only a marginalised space, struggles against the Prevention of Terrorism Act, the wrongful convictions of the Guildford Four, Maguire Seven and Birmingham Six, and, indeed, anti-Irish racism, Irish women-only groups were formed (Rossiter, 1992). A London-Irish Women's Centre came into being in 1983 which, among many other activities, hosts the annual Irish Women's Conference. Conference reports give some indication of the range of groups active in the London area alone, eg the Irish Lesbian Network, Irish Women's Housing Action Group, Irish Women with Children Group, Video na mBan and a wide range of cultural groups. The effect of the groups has been to raise the profile of Irish women, and especially feminists, in community activities and in the local Irish press, although the latter is still extremely hesitant over the issues of abortion and lesbianism. The lack of an Irish immigrant women's journal is keenly felt, but as Marian Larragy remarks:

> There is a growing debate between Irish feminists here
> and in the two parts of Ireland, and also vast areas of
> unresolved debate amongst Irish feminists in Britain,
> which need to be aired in print. We do not have the
> resources to develop a whole separate feminist media
> and, even if we did, most Irish feminists have no desire
> to retreat into total exclusivity (Larragy, 1990: 43).

It is, however, essential that Irish women in Britain,
North America, Australia, New Zealand and elsewhere
'come in from the cold' and ensure that their experiences,
unlike those of their sisters in past generations, are
committed to history.

References and further reading

Abortion in Northern Ireland: The Report of an International Tribunal. 1989.
    Belfast.
Barry, U. and Jackson, P. 1988. 'Women on the Edge of Time: Part-Time
    Work in Ireland, North and South'. In Buckley, M. and Anderson, M.
    (eds.), *Women, Equality and Europe.* Macmillan, London.
Brody, H. 1973. *Inishkillane, Change and Decline in the West of Ireland.* Allen
    Lane, London.
Casey, M. 1987. *Over the Water.* Macmillan, London.
Collins, B. 1981. 'Irish Emigration to Dundee and Paisley during the First
    Half of the Nineteenth Century'. In Goldstrom, J. M. and Clarkson, L.
    A. (eds.), *Irish Population, Economy and Society.* Oxford.
Commission on Emigration Report. 1954. Dublin.
Daly, M E. 1981a. 'Women in the Irish workforce from pre-industrial to
    modern times'. *Saothar 7.*
Daly, M E. 1981b.*Social and Economic History of Ireland since 1800.* Dublin.
Davin, A. 1972. 'Women and history'. In Wandor, M. (ed.), *The Body Politic,
    Writings from the Women's Movement in Britain, 1969-1972.* London.
Davis, G. 1991. *The Irish in Britain, 1815-1914.* Dublin.
Diner, H. R. 1983. *Erin's Daughters in America: Immigrant Women in the
    Nineteenth Century.* Johns Hopkin's University Press, Baltimore.
Engels, F. 1970. 'The origin of the family, private property and the state'.
    In *Karl Marx and Frederick Engels, Selected Works.* London.
Fielding, S. 1993. *Class and Ethnicity: Irish Catholics in England, 1880-1939.*
    Buckingham, Open University Press.
Fitzpatrick, D. 1989a. 'A curious middle place: the Irish in Britain, 1871-
    1921'. In Swift and Gilley, (eds.), *The Irish in Britain, 1815-1939.*
Fitzpatrick, D. 1989b 'A share of the honeycomb: education, emigration
    and Irishwomen'. In *Continuity and Change* 1,2 .
Fortnight: Voyages of Discovery, Exploring Emigration. Proceedings of a
    Fortnight Educational Trust Seminar. *Fortnight* 295, 1991, Belfast.

Gibbon, P. 1975. *The Origins of Ulster Unionism*. Manchester University Press, Manchester.

Gilley, S. 1988. 'Irish Catholicism in Britain, 1880-1939'. In *Catholics and their Church in Britain c. 1880-1939*, Warwick Working Papers in Social History, Warwick.

Hobsbawn, E. J. 1968. *Industry and Empire, The Pelican History of Britain*, Vol. 3. Penguin, Harmondsworth.

Hollen Lees, L. 1979. *Exiles of Erin, Irish Migrants in Victorian London*. New York.

— 1976. 'Mid-Victorian migration and the Irish family economy'. In *Victorian Studies* , Autumn.

Hvidt, K. 1975. 'Flight to America: the social background of 300,000 Danish emigrants'. In *Studies in Social Discontinuity* . New York.

Hynes, E. 1978. 'The Great Hunger and Irish Catholicism'. In *Societas*, 8, 2, Spring.

Irish Women's Abortion Support Group. 1988. 'Across the water'. In Smyth, A. (ed.). *The Abortion Papers: Ireland*. Attic Press, Dublin.

Jackson, J. A. 1963. *The Irish in Britain*. Routledge and Keegan Paul, London.

Jackson, P. 1984. 'Women in 19th-century emigration'. In *International Migration Review 18, 4* .

Kavanagh, P. 1983. 'Frances Power Cobbe — Irish Feminist andReformer in Victorian England'. In *Retrospect, Journal of the Irish History Students' Association*, Third Series No. 3.

Kelly K. and Nic Giolla Choille, T. (eds). 1990. *Emigration Matters for Women*. Attic Press, Dublin.

Kennedy, R. 1983. *The Irish: Emigration, Marriage and Fertility*. University of California Press, Berkeley, California.

Larragy, M. 1990. 'Looking back, looking forward'. In *Spare Rib*, No. 215, August.

Lee, J. 1988. 'Women and the Church since the Famine'. In MacCurtain, M. and O Corráin, C. (eds.), *Women in Irish Society, the Historical Dimension*. Arlen House, Dublin.

Lennon, M., McAdam, M. and O'Brien, J. 1988. *Across the Water: Irish Women's Lives in Britain*. Virago, London.

Lerner, G. 1979. *The Majority Finds Its Past, Placing Women in History*. Oxford University Press, Oxford.

Liddington, J. and Norris, J. 1978. *One Hand Tied Behind Us: The Rise of the Women's Suffrage Movement*. Virago, London.

Limerick Rural Survey: Third Interim report: Social Structure. 1962. Tipperary

London Irish Women's Centre. *Our Experience of Emigration*, Report of the London Irish Women's Conference, 1984; *Living in England*, Report of the Second London Irish Women's Conference, 1985; *Irish Women, Our Lives Our Identity*, Report of the 1987 Irish Women's Conference, 1987; *Irish Women Today*, Conference Report, 1988; *The Fifth London Irish Women's Conference Report*, 1989. (LIWC), London.

Luddy, M. and Murphy, C. (eds.). 1990.*Women Surviving: Studies in Irish Women's History in the 19th and 20th Centuries*. Poolbeg Press, Dublin.

McCrory, M. 1985. *The Water's Edge and Other Stories*. London.

MacGill P. 1982. *Children of the Dead End*. Brandon, Dingle.

Miller, K. A. 1985. *Emigrants and Exiles: Ireland and the Irish Exodus to North America*. Oxford.

Nolan, J. A. 1989. *Ourselves Alone: Women's Emigration from Ireland, 1885-1920*. Kentucky University Press, Lexington.

O'Brien, M. 1981. 'Irish Immigrants in London'. Unpublished M. Phil. thesis. The City University, London.

O'Brien, S. 1990. 'Lay-Sisters and Good Mothers: Working-Class Women in English Convents, 1840-1910'. In Sheils, W. J. and Woods, D., (eds.), *Women in the Church, Studies in Church History*, Vol. 27, Oxford.

O'Carroll, I. 1990. *Models for Movers: Irish Women's Emigration to America*. Attic Press, Dublin.

O'Sullivan, P. (ed.). 1992. *The Irish World Wide, History, Heritage, Identity*. Leicester University Press, Leicester..

O'Tuathaigh, G. 1985. 'The Irish in nineteenth-century Britain: Problems of integration'. In Swift and Gilley, (eds.), *The Irish in the Victorian City*, London.

O'Tuathaigh, G. 1978. 'The role of women in Ireland under the new English order'. In MacCurtain, M. and O Corráin, D. (eds.), *Women in Irish Society, the Historical Dimension*. Arlen House, Dublin.

Rhodes, R. M. 1986. 'Women and the Family in Post-Famine Ireland: Status and Opportunity in a Patriarchal Society'. Unpublished Ph.D. thesis. University of Illinois, Chicago.

Rose, E. J. B. 1969. *Colour and Citizenship. A Report on British Race Relations*. Oxford.

Rossiter, A. 1992. 'Between the Devil and the Deep Blue Sea: Irish Women, Catholicism and Colonialism'. In Saghal, G. and Yuval-Davis, N., *Refusing Holy Orders*. Virago, London.

Rossiter, A. 'In Search of Mary's Past: Placing 19th Century Irish Immigrant Women in British Feminist History'. In Grant, J. (ed.), *Silent Voices* . London. (Forthcoming).

Russell, D. 1987. 'Some early Irish movements in South London'. In *South London Record*, South London History Workshop, 2.

Women Behind the Wire: Bulletin of the Armagh Co-Ordinating Group. 1981. 1.

Ryan, L. 1990. 'Irish emigration to Britain since World War II'. In Kearney R. (ed.), *Migrations: the Irish at Home and Abroad*. Wolfhound Press, Dublin.

Seller, M. 1975. 'Beyond the stereotype: a new look at the immigrant woman, 1880-1924'. In *Journal of Ethnic Studies 3*. Spring.

Swift, R. and Gilley, S. (eds.). 1985. *The Irish in the Victorian City*. London.

Swift, R. and Gilley, S. (eds.). 1989. *The Irish in Britain, 1815-1939*. London.

Walter, B. 1989a. *Gender and Irish Migration to Britain*, Geography Working Paper, 4, School of Geography, Anglia Higher Education College Cambridge.

Walter, B. 1989b. *Irish Women in London: the Ealing Dimension*. London.

Ward, M. 1991. *The Missing Sex: putting women into Irish history*. LIP Pamphlet, Attic Press, Dublin.

Ward, M. 1983. *Unmanageable Revolutionaries: Women in Irish Nationalism.* Brandon, Dingle; Pluto, London.

Yuval-Davis, N. and Anthias, F. (eds.), 1989. *Woman-Nation-State.* Macmillan, London.

Discussion Topics

1 What would history be like if it were seen through the eyes of women and ordered by values they define? Is one justified in speaking of a female historical experience different from that of men?

2 The Act of Union, the repeal of the Corn Laws in 1846, and the British Industrial Revolution had a profound effect in marginalising women in nineteenth- and twentieth-century Ireland. Do you think this is a valid statement?

3 Traditionally, the Catholic Church (not the Protestant churches) is seen as the prime mover in the construction of a strongly puritanical Ireland in the nineteenth-century. Is this a reasonable assessment, or were the economic needs of the Irish peasantry of more fundamental significance in the creation of this type of society?

4 Evaluate the relative importance of economic pressures in Ireland ('push' factors), and the attractions of higher social status and a more liberal social environment overseas ('pull' factors), in women's decision to emigrate.

5 Debate the contradictions inherent in women's role as the ideological as well as the biological reproducers of ethnic and immigrant groups through their function as the transmitters of culture.

6 Discuss the seeming irreconcilability of the viewpoints which, (a) see exclusively Irish or black feminist groups as a form of ghettoisation, and contrary to the ideals of a universalist feminism, and (b) see such groups as essential for the Irish or black experience to survive in an Anglocentric feminist movement.

Moving Statues and Irish Women

Margaret MacCurtain

Context

In the summer of 1985 the series of episodes known as 'The Moving Statues' agitated Irish society in ways that were similar to the apparition of Mary, Mother of Jesus and St John the Evangelist in Knock, Co. Mayo in 1879. Over a hundred years ago on a rainy night in late autumn the people of a little village in remote Mayo collectively watched for over an hour a kind of tableau on the outside church gable depicting Mary, the Blessed Mother, the Lamb of God and St John the Evangelist. Brigid Trench, the oldest witness of the Apparition said: 'I threw myself on my knees . . . I went in immediately to kiss, as I thought, the feet of the Blessed Virgin, but felt nothing in the embrace but the wall.' On that occasion famine had again struck the West of Ireland, bringing hunger, eviction and emigration. It was a prelude to the land war which pitted tenant against landlord. The Knock apparition had a validity of spiritual experience which over decades confirmed it as a place of pilgrimage, and eventually as the centre of a national shrine for Roman Catholic believers. The moving statues episodes in the summer of 1985 are remembered as occasions which evoked puzzlement, confusion, but strangely not hilarity. Too many people experienced the suspension of normality, the disjunction of reality which permitted an alternative vision of another reality.

The moving statues ceased to move at the end of a long rainy season. They stayed in people's memories, associated with a series of humiliations that women underwent as the male public discourse about women's sexuality took place in the courts and Dáil debates. There was a sense of a community acknowledging chaos and trying to find some way of expressing it without resorting to violence. Thus it can be argued that the moving statues were sessions of mass therapy for a society deeply troubled by the fragmentation of cherished and private values.

Introduction

It rained all through the summer and early autumn of 1985, and the statues moved at Ballinspittle, Mount Mellery, Asdee, Ballydesmond, Courtmacsherry, and over thirty small Marian shrines in different parts of the country. There were reports of moving or speaking statues, ones that showed visions of heavenly light during that untowardly long spell of unceasing rain in July, August and September. By October the statues had become stationary again and the coach firms, the burger vans, the temporary benches and car parks around the grottoes gradually disappeared.

What was the spirit saying to the Irish Catholic Church? Can it even be assumed that the Spirit of God was speaking through a series of events? A number of journalists, some theologians and churchmen, and a group of psychologists gave the subject serious attention. The media, both Irish and British, including a remarkable photo-book taken during the last week in August, *Ireland, A Week In The Life Of A Nation* (Saunders and Shelton, 1986), covered the crowds at the different shrines intent on encapsulating the out-of-the-ordinary. Canon Denis O'Callaghan, parish priest of Mallow and former professor of moral theology at Maynooth College, addressed audiences on the subject, neither dismissing the crowds' eyewitness accounts superciliously nor yielding to any pressures to sanction their alleged authenticity.

The observers from the Applied Psychology Department of University College Cork offered a substantial explanation at the phenomenological level. They claimed in relation to the Ballinspittle statue of the Blessed Virgin (which attracted unusually large crowds during the night hours) that it was a problem of eye focus where the onlookers were unable to fix a bright object against a dark background. Staring at the statue fixedly gave the onlooker the experience of seeing it shimmering or moving backwards and forwards. This mass experience they termed the 'Ballinspittle syndrome', but they did not address the question why the power of the imagination to form such images occurred just then.

What the journalists thought

Journalists probed the reality of the phenomenon with acuity. Some had attended the gatherings as spectators in Ballinspittle or elsewhere, writing for newspapers and periodicals throughout Ireland and Britain. Colm Tóibín, a freelance journalist, assembled in book form the impressions of a group of journalists and invited other writers to contribute by analysing what was occurring on a cultural level to draw some inferences. Of the four women who contributed to the book, *Seeing is Believing* (1985), two, June Levine and Isabel Healy, had gone to Ballinspittle and they narrate the effect on the bystanders and on themselves of the moving, five-foot-eight statue of Mary, placed high up above the road. The other two women, Mary Holland and Nell McCafferty did not visit the shrine. In their contributions they endeavour to situate the reported sightings of the statues within the context of female experience in Ireland in recent years. For Nell McCafferty the moving statues of the Virgin Mary were symptomatic of 'the desolate situation of Irish women'. In Mary Holland's estimation, 'The crowds at Ballinspittle are a salutary reminder of how divided our society has become.' With the trained ears of sensitive journalists they sensed that the occurrences were in a subliminal way connected with issues that affected women's lives in the area of what Nell McCafferty termed 'the war of the womb'. Both referred to the aftermath of the 1983 Eighth Amendment to the Constitution, the incorrectly-styled Abortion Referendum. Both listed a series of tragic incidents connected with unwanted pregnancies, singling out the Kerry Babies Tribunal, which had occupied the media for months in 1985, as an example of the public humiliation that women in this country had to undergo. Both situated the moving statues of Mary in the context of female oppression in Ireland. For Nell McCafferty the occurrences were a predictable superstitious reaction; for Mary Holland, 'The crowds at Ballinspittle dramatise the problem facing the Church . . . for the yearning after the old certainties goes beyond religious practice to reflect an unease with the quality of life in Ireland and with a society which, it now seems to many people, has failed them materially as well as spiritually.'(McCafferty: 53-8; Holland: 45-8, in Tóibín, 1985). The stranger to Irish politics could well suppose that in the mid-eighties our society was traumatised around women's issues and that large sections of that society were caught between the competing claims of Catholic morality and secular modernisation of our civil legislation in the areas of birth-control, illegitimacy, marriage and divorce.

Not the full explanation
For other contributors to *Seeing is Believing*, explanation of the phenomena went wider. Notably in the essay by folklorist, Dáithí O hOgáin, 'A Manifestation of Popular Religion', there is an effort to place the sightings in the context of iconophily. He reminds the readers of the role statues have played in pre-Christain culture and traditions as heroic images, as representations of deity, as oracles that spoke or moved. After the death of Christ, the place of Mary in iconography of the mother-symbol, and the almost sacred character of the Icon and the 'Luke' portraits were firmly established in western religious consciousness. Parallel to the statues, in pagan and Christian memory, was the notion of prodigies, signs, portents, foretelling disaster, signs associated with the Apocalypse of John, indicating a popular perception of some approaching catastrophe. Because of the historical circumstances, statues in Ireland were a fairly recent introduction in Catholic worship associated with the building of churches from the mid-nineteenth century onwards, thus the phenomenon of moving statues, well-documented in western European religious history, is not familiar to the Irish psyche. O hOgáin concludes his observations by noting:

> It would seem to be of far greater value if we searched for the underlying causes which lead people to notice such things at some times and places rather than others. (O hOgáin: 66-74, in Tóibín, 1985)

Something certainly happened at the level of religious and psychological experience in Ballinspittle and found a response in men as well as women. Even if it can be decided that it was the imagination playing tricks on the crowds that gathered nightly, such an acknowledgement — that the imagination of hundreds of people was exploding in tantric or semi-magical images — allows us to comment on the event in a less dismissive way than if we approached it with an uncompromisingly scientific explanation. After all, the episodes were communal events, and many people who came there experienced simultaneously a sensation of a Marian statue swaying or dissolving into other images, such as St Joseph, Padre Pio for June Levine, a young rabbi. Not everyone was bewitched; but those who went realised that the social happening they witnessed had a significance that so far has defied a totally satisfactory analysis. To explain away the phenomenon in terms of a diagnosis consonant with 'normal' secular views of mental health is to miss the nuances. Some kind of fuse ignited the imagination around an object of popular devotion during those weeks, and there occurred a disjunction of spiritual vision, or a suspension of conventional faith. It took place in the context of lay devotion. No Catholic rituals, no masses, no official presence of Church authorities occurred at the grottoes. The statues that moved were of Mary, a woman, in a year that had not been kind to Irish women.

My purpose in the following pages is to follow the line of investigation opened by the women journalists and to examine what has been happening to the spirituality of Irishwomen as they encountered the challenge of secularisation and feminism.

Irish women in the 1980s

In 1969 the women's movement was entering consciousness all over the world. In Dublin a number of women met regularly in a support group whose goal was to launch the movement upon a society more open, more liberal than at any previous period in the twentieth century.[1] The 1960s had been a buoyant, optimistic decade in Ireland, north and south. The closing of Vatican Two in 1966 with its call for *aggiornamento*, had released spiritual energies among priests, laity, and religious women and men. The Catholic Church was seen to be part of the contemporary world. The weekly radio discussions of Seán MacRéamoinn from Rome and the television exposure of large sections of Irish society to the minds of the world's finest theologians contributed to a new awareness among Irish people. Irish society was about to take its place among the member-states of the European Community and it was to face, among other challenges, the hitherto unknown one of secularisation. For many Irish Catholics there was perplexity. To a society as highly sacramentalised as the Catholic Irish new demands of vernacular liturgy resulting from a changed model of Church caused bewilderment. There was a sense of loss which affected devotional practice and religious observance alike. It is in this period that Professor J. A. Murphy, a specialist in twentieth-century Irish history, perceives 'a collapse of the kind of solid Catholic church-going practices that were there up to 1960 or so' (Murphy, 1985).

The women's movement inserted an added tension into the Irish woman's faith-life. The splendid mutterings of the Latin Mass became the vernacular whose language was, to ears sensitised by consciousness-raising exercises, disconcertingly sexist. Confession was, throughout the 1970s, supplanted by the therapies — gestalt, co-counselling, psychosynthesis — and never regained its old ascendancy. As the decade moved on, the Catholic Church in Ireland began to be considered by groups of women, religious as well as lay, as unattractively male-dominated. Two alternatives presented themselves to women: they closed ranks around the Church they loved and clung to their familiar devotional practices; or they embraced the ideology of the women's movement wholeheartedly, and identified with feminism.

The search for feminist spirituality
Ursula Coleman (1985) examines the effects of dualistic thinking upon our experience of the sacred and the secular, sealing them off from each other. She applies her methodology to the women's movement in contemporary Ireland and arrives at the conclusion that feminism is, at

this point in time, perceived to be opposed to religion because it is identified with secular philosophy. She traces the growing polarisation which has occurred since our membership of the European Community. There is a better deal for women in paid employment, social welfare, equal work opportunity but, she adds, 'In the really contentious issues . . . the discussions relating to contraception, sex education, unwanted pregnancies, pre-marital sex, the abortion trail to England, the need for civil divorce, Irish people have divided.' As she views it the women's movement has become part of that divide, finding itself at odds with the Catholic Church. 'It was seen to be waging war against what was sacred. The response, therefore, was a defensive one. The Catholic Church and the women's movement became enemies.' Thus the 1983 referendum was a watershed in attitudes which polarised women among themselves.

Feminism is more than the women's movement, however: it is a way of interpreting life and it has a protean quality in its diversities. There is a radical agnostic, even atheistic feminism which rebels against male authoritarian structures and, unable to contain the critique from within the institution, forces the feminist to leave; or, as Hanna Sheehy Skeffington once declared, 'to read or think oneself out of the Church is a hazard of being a feminist'.

Feminism is also a 'therapy of the soul', to borrow a phrase from James Hillman, the psychoanalyst, and as such he insists 'it tends to ignore that gender question'. He sees feminism as a structure of consciousness, and like the ecology movement it has much to offer in perceptive insights. The soul, he argues, does not know whether it is rich or poor, learned or ignorant, male or female (Pozzo, 1984: 70-4). Feminism thus understood pertains to men as well as to women and it offers profound insights to the contemporary Church in its self-understanding of liberation.

Many Irish women who have left the devotional practices of their youth are now genuinely seeking a spirituality that meets both their search for a god who is not patriarchal, and for a continuing revelation of god's presence in the world not in opposition to past traditions but evolving out of them. In Ireland it is to Celtic models that the feminist search is turning more and more. One such model has been studied as a Leaving Certificate textbook by thousands of Irish women, unaware that in the person and autobiography of Peig Sayers there are to be found clues that lead into the heart of Celtic spirituality, and supply an agenda for becoming a free spirit (Sayers, 1978).

The faith-world of an Irish woman

Broadly speaking the religious experience of Irish women is uncharted territory. It may be discovered in diaries, letters, recorded conversations if researched carefully and it appears in the occasional autobiography that spans the century between 1870 and 1970, frontier decades for Irish women in their long stride towards self-awareness. 1878 bestowed on them the Intermediate Certificate; 1973 gave them entry into the equality of the European Community.

Following a tentative methodology, I shall endeavour to discover the faith-worlds of the Irish rural woman using whatever personal sources are at hand. Peig Sayers (1873-1958), in her autobiography and her subsequent *Reflections of an Old Woman*, gives us glimpses of the spiritual resources on which she drew, when as a young bride she came from the mainland to live on the large Blasket Island off the Dingle peninsula. It was an Irish-speaking world and she lived on that rocky island for over forty years of the present century as wife, mother and neighbour in a community which her own testimony has rendered famous. For Peig Sayers, her encounter with the supernatural was one in which she sharply differen-tiated her superstitious world of ghosts and spirits, of which she was a supreme story-teller, from the central mysterious path of her life. For Peig the significant guideline of her actions was always 'whatever God has destined for me, I will receive it': that as a young thirteen-year-old parting from her beloved mother for nearly three years. The note is clearer in the incident of her son's fatal fall from the cliff. Unable to leave the house because of her sick husband she cannot accompany the boats in their search for the body. 'It was they who were surprised when they found where he was, not hundreds of yards out to sea but high up on a smooth ledge, his exact size, and he was laid out as quiet and composed as if twelve women had taken charge. No living person knew he had happened on that ledge with the blue sea all around. No one but God alone.' (Sayers, 1963).

Peig's deepest conviction that she was 'a bauble in the hands of the Maiden and her Son' is reminiscent of Teresa of Avila, and another of her sayings is biblical: 'God always opens a gap of support'. When her son, Micheál, is going to the USA she enjoins on him: 'Let nothing cross you that would diminish the love of God in your heart.' Her faith in Mary's powers of intercession with her son was unshakeable; her identification with the Sorrowful Mother complete. She lost four children and her husband before middle-age. 'I remember bending to my work with my heart breaking. I used to think of Mary and the Lord the hard life they had. I knew I had a duty to imitate them and bear my sorrow patiently.'

Celtic spirituality

Peig Sayers' God was pre-eminently the spirit who infuses nature: she had an intense sense of the presence of God. Her favourite form of refreshing her own spirit was to be by herself looking over the harbour out to sea on a clear day, enjoying the waters that so often claimed the lives of the fishermen. This facility in contemplating God in nature is the essence of Celtic spirituality which John Macquarrie describes thus:

> The sense of God's immanence in his creation was so strong in Celtic spirituality as to amount almost to a pantheism . . . But perusal of typical Celtic poems and prayers makes it clear that God's presence was even more keenly felt in the daily round of human tasks and at the important junctures of life. Getting up, kindling the fire, going to work, going to bed, as well as birth, marriage, settling in a new house, death, were occasions for recognising the presence of God (Macquarrie, 1981).

On reading her autobiography the reader is left with a sense of a human being who has succeeded in integrating the different strands of her life in a meaningful way. Her ability to observe her own grief and to describe herself and the way of life on the Great Blasket was truly remarkable. She was esteemed by the other islanders for her neighbourliness and for her capacity to enjoy good company and laughter. Her sense of Heaven was that of the conviviality of friends gathered, talking together and telling stories; her concept of God as final judge daringly familiar: he was An Rógaire, The Rogue. There is a tenth-century poem called 'St Brigid's Heaven', translated by Seán O Faoláin in *The Silver Branch*, which finds echoes in many of Peig's reflections and epigrams:

I would like to have the men of Heaven
In my own house;
With vats of good cheer
Laid out for them . . .
I would like a great lake of beer
For the King of Kings.
I would like to be watching Heaven's family
Drinking it through all eternity. (Rogers, 1978)

Peig Sayers' life, like that of many country women, was of necessity one removed from church-going, frequency of mass and sacrament and from the hearing of sermons. Like her neighbours she lived, when times were bad, in poverty and frugality of food. What, then has she to offer the town-dweller in the way of getting 'to know God'?

The answer is in her life, written and lived. There is a sense in which the quest for feminist spirituality must veer towards the side of the oppressed and the poor if we want to find God. The world of the late-twentieth century, including Ireland, is one of structural conflict in which keeping large masses of people poor is the key element. Women and children suffer grievously in such circumstances. For women there is a growing recognition that the issue of oppression will not go away, has not disappeared, and needs to be confronted daily.

If Peig Sayers on her rocky island has any spiritual meaning for the contemporary Irish woman, it is about finding a knowledge of oneself that comes from with the soul and within the culture, one which steels the will and detaches the spirit from all sentimentality. To be a kindly neighbour sharing house and bread, to be steadfast in the face of loss as great as hers, to remain true to her roots which she discerned had to do with her essential identity, and to add to that, serene old age, and the reputation of being the best storyteller in Ireland: what more salutary antidote to a moving statue could there be than the spirituality of Peig Sayers?

Note

1 The best account of the early years of the women's movement in Ireland is in Levine, J. *Sisters,* Ward River Press, 1982. See also A. Smyth in this collection.

References and further reading

Coleman, U. 1985. 'Secularisation: A Healing Process'. *Studies,* 74.

Condren, M. 1989. *The Serpent and the Goddess.* Harper and Row, San Francisco.

Holland, M. 1985. 'Ballinspittle and the Bishops' Dilemma'. In Tóibín, C. (Ed.). *Seeing is Believing.*

McCafferty, N. 1985. 'Virgin on the Rocks'. In Tóibín, C. (ed.), *Seeing is Believing.*

McCafferty, N. 1985. *A Woman to Blame: The Kerry Babies Case.* Attic Press, Dublin.

Levine, J. 1982. *Sisters.* Ward River Press, Dublin.

Macquarrie, J. 1981. *Paths in Spirituality.* Veritas, Dublin.

Maher, M. (ed.). 1981. *Celtic Spirituality.* Veritas, Dublin.

Murphy, J A. 1985. 'What it means to be Irish'. In *Boston College Magazine,* Vol. XLIV, No. 3.

O hÓgáin, D. (ed.) 1985. 'A Manifestation of Popular Religion'. In Tóibin, C. *Seeing is Believing,*

Pozzo, L. 1984. *Interviews with James Hillman.* Harper Books, London.

Rogers, W. R. 1978. 'Introduction' to Sayers, P. *An Old Woman's Reflections,* Oxford University Press, Oxford.

Sayers, P. 1963. *Peig.* Comhlacht Oideachais na hEireann, Atha Cliath.

Sayers, P. 1978. *An Old Woman's Reflections.* Oxford University Press, Oxford.

Tóibín, C. 1985. (ed.). *Seeing is Believing.* Pilgrim Press, Dublin.

Discussion topics

1 If you were given a grant, how would you design a space and activities for a Spirituality and Resource Centre for Women?

2 All significant movements of popular culture have depth and power to the extent that they have been doing something else besides justifying sexism. What fears and hopes do you suppose the moving statues responded to?

3 Select six feminist theologians, one at least must live in Ireland, and write a booknote on one book.

4 If a feminist spirituality is one that is different from women's spirituality, in what ways would you distinguish its characteristics?

5 Explore the traditions of the goddess in religious experience, past and present.

6 Is Celtic spirituality 'wishful thinking'?

The Irish Travelling Woman:
Mother and Mermaid

Mary O'Malley Madec

Introduction

Some years ago I was walking through Eyre Square, Galway, when a young Traveller girl asked me for money. I bought her a bar of chocolate and we talked a bit. I had time to notice her red ribbons and it occurred to me that they were an important element of the mental image I had of little Traveller girls. I felt there was a mystery to be unlocked there. It was at that moment that I decided to find out more about the culture of this little girl and the community of approximately 20,000 Travellers to which she belongs.

The Irish settled population are reluctant to acknowledge the Travellers as an ethnic minority and this has serious consequences in the practical matter of providing for them in Irish society. Many prefer to regard the Travellers as a subculture of poverty, although an early proponent of this theory, Patricia McCarthy, retracted her thesis after Sinéad Ní Shúinéar presented her findings in the early 1970s.[1]

I am primarily interested in how the culture of the Travellers is reflected in their language. However, the relationship between culture and language is an extremely close one and leads me on this investigation as a folklorist. It remains for the professional folklorist to establish the relationship of the folklore of the Travellers to that of the settled people, resisting, as Propp (1984) advises, the temptation to draw premature conclusions.

The issue of origin is central to the debate on ethnicity. The popular view that the Travellers comprise family groups displaced during the English plantations and the great famine casts no light on the problem. However, Irish Travellers abroad provide an interesting foil, considering that they preserved a culture and language strikingly similar to that of the Irish Travellers at home and a culture, it has to be said, rather far removed from the culture of the settled people of their country of origin or of the countries in which they settled.[2] Since I have discussed this elsewhere I shall not dwell on it here (O'Malley, 1990). Instead I would like to focus on the part women play in building up and breaking down the culture, for it seems to me that women in any culture play a central role in inculcating its values and passing them on from one generation to another and, by the same token, are the first to call the culture into question in their search to find their own identity in it.

Those of us, settled people, who have had significant contact with the Travellers recognise women as the very backbone of Traveller society. They dominate in the camp and anywhere the family is not under public scrutiny; they are an important source of income (children's allowance and begging), and in recent years have become responsible for the education of young boys as well as young girls.

It would be easy to get lost in the 'quicksand' of asserting rights for them, but allowing Travellers to make their own way means, above all, helping them to get a picture of the past which is capable of informing the future. It is the task and the duty of the linguist, the sociologist and the historian and the folklorist to elicit the kind of information which in years to come the children of the Travellers will want to hear — the history of their race.

Customs relating to mother and child point to a rich distinct culture. They show how the world-view of the Travellers developed. My informants, all women, were chiefly from the Galway area in the West of Ireland, where the traditions of the Travellers have remained rather intact compared to other places. I did not set out to elicit information on maternity or childhood; rather it was my own pregnancy and my friendship with a young Travelling woman who was also expecting her first baby that opened the doors of their tradition to me.

When we take into account the precarious nature of life on the roads, even in our times, it is hardly surprising to find customs designed in essence to protect the mother and child — the most vulnerable people in such a lifestyle. However, this is not at all the full picture, as we shall see shortly. The protection of the woman is as much a factor of her power as her vulnerability and important for the welfare of the entire community.

My fieldwork on this material was done between 1986 and 1988. I set out knowing very little about these people. However, in the course of observing the group very closely, through my close friendship with one family in particular, I came to discover the centrality of women in the organisation of their society. The settled population tend only to see the very superficial situation of the women oppressed by the men, whereas close inspection shows that such oppression is the fruit of a particular fear of female power manifested in child-bearing and the power of seduction. Now, there are many reasons why this account is of interest. Most importantly it points to the existence in the Travelling community of rites to guarantee the ritual cleanliness of the group, rites which are best explained as symbolic of the relations between men and women within the group on the one hand, and between Travellers and settled people on the other hand. Secondly, this kind of ritual behaviour has not been previously reported by fieldworkers, one fieldworker going as far as to say that compared to the Gypsies 'Tinkers seemed to have no comparable customs.' (Court, 1985, p.43).

My success in gaining this kind of information was, I believe, a factor of the trust my informants had in me as a woman, and of the fact that when I began this field-work I was pregnant myself, which gave rise to many spontaneous questions and made natural conversation possible. In many cases it seems that material of this sort never comes to light because the anthropologists are male and are consequently not invited into this female world. In the case of the Travellers this is not altogether true in modern times since most of the people actively engaged in research are women. However, it is clear to me now from my knowledge of the social structures of the group that it was the fact that I was able to meet with women on their own that such subjects were permissible.

Of course there are undesirable political consequences in not documenting these realities. The Irish Travellers have never enjoyed the academic interest that Gypsy groups have commanded. Somehow they are regarded as inferior to them. This notion of their inferiority is due in part to the treatment of their language but also to the common belief that they do not constitute an ethnic minority in any recognisable sense (O'Malley, 1989). I hope that the facts in this chapter will set matters straight and open up the question again of the ethnicity of the Travellers.

Vladimir Propp spent his life asserting that 'for some people folklore will prove a valuable historical document by which the ethnographer can reconstruct both the social system and ideas.' (1984: 12). However, he wisely cautions against establishing a too direct or simplistic cause of the culture and social structure in the folklore because, 'reality is not reflected but appears through the prism of thought and this thought is so unlike ours that it can be difficult to compare a folklore phenomenon with anything at all.' (1984: 12). In this chapter I would like to look at some aspects of the folklore of the Irish Travellers which I believe indicate the ethnic identity of this group in terms of their social organisation and perception of reality. Since what I am going to focus on pertains in a particular way to women, the following story which is told by a settled Traveller in Artelia Court's book *Puck of the Drums* (1985), offers some insights into the particular prism of thought by which these people see the world today.

Bridget Murphy's story tells of a farmer who falls in love with a mermaid, captures her and removes her tail to expose her two legs: 'Her feet was only stuck into this cloak like a fish's tail but she was a plain woman within. He takes the cloak and he hides it above in the thatch and she never knew where he hid it.' (Court, 1985: 63-64) With the breaking of the spell in the loss of her tail the mermaid lives out the normal duties of a wife and mother. However, one day her daughter finds the tail and gives it to her; once the woman sees it she becomes enchanted again and is drawn back to the sea against

human reason, 'and the roaring of her and the crying of
her as she didn't want to go.' (1985: 64).

Of course Bridget Murphy's choice of story tells its
own tale. It dramatizes at one level the dilemma of a
woman who attempts the option for settled life but fears
eventually that the desire to travel and live the life that is
in her blood will overtake her. Moreover, in view of the
mother-daughter motif in the story, I believe that the
dilemma she addresses is particularly a female one
ouside of the male domain. It concerns the potential
power of the woman in the group to destroy, through her
sexuality, the family unit and therefore ultimately
threaten the group. Since the men are aware of this
power, they are afraid of it and therefore attempt to
control it. There is no doubt a sexual symbolism involved
with the mermaid who represents rather universally the
power of woman as enchantress and seductress. Because
of this fear the men have of the women, it is necessary to
adopt rites that control their sexual and reproductive
functions. The women must not, above all, be allowed to
enter into sexual relations with settled men, which is why
the control on teenage girls in the group is much stricter
than on teenage boys. It also explains why the loss of
female virginity is such an issue for Travellers. Unlike
the Gypsies there are no inspections before marriage, but
the social constraints on girls are for the most part so
great that the opportunity to engage in sexual activity
does not exist outside of marriage.

The attitude of the Travelling men to 'their' women is a
sure indicator of their attitude to settled people: they fear
the pollution that might ensue from the contact of
Travelling women with the settled population. This is
reflected in the ritual sexual control shown in the practice
of matchmaking. The manner in which matches are made
bears out the fact that they are rites serving a patriarchy.
First of all, the father of the boy is approached by an
'aunt' or older female and the girl's father. After this,
both sets of parents meet to discuss the proposition. The
young lad, that is the prospective groom, is then
approached and if he says Yes the girl is approached. The
girl has the right to refuse, in principle, although it is

unlikely she can ever marry if she exercises this right. We, in the settled community, are quick to make moral judgements on such practices. However, from the point of view of the women living in this system, it is a pragmatic solution and a positive response to a very difficult problem — getting a husband in an endogamous community.

Overall, Travelling women are more aware than their male counterparts of the tugs which the settled life all around them presents and they totter perilously between the values of their own culture and ours. Once we understand their point of view we are more able to appreciate the problems which genetic counselling, for example, involves for them. Many of us would consider that Travelling women are oppressed and are ready to deliver our solutions to them without taking the time to hear their perspective. For the settled community the most visible sign of the oppression of Travelling women is the practice of begging which is the formal contact between Travellers and settled life. However, I think we have to look at this oppression (evidenced most visibly in begging) as part of a cultural crisis involving male as well as female roles. Cultural evolution, it would seem to me, involves a process whereby male and female values are redefined; for the Travellers this is particularly difficult because their culture is derided on the one hand, and the system of education which we offer them is based on conforming to middle-class settled values rather than giving them support to find their own way forward. On the other hand, their belief in themselves as superior to settled people and therefore in risk of defilement through contact with them, makes any scheme which involves integration a failure.

Pollution and female function: maternity taboos and folk rites

There is probably no greater insult in Travelling society than to be called *clotty*. The word, which appears to be equivalent to the word *mochadi* among Gypsies, refers not to everyday grime but to ritual uncleanliness. It involves the separation of washing basins on the basis of whether they are used for the outer body or the inner body: Every

Traveller has a 'clean basin' for washing food, eating utensils and the towels used for drying them and a 'dirty basin' for the washing of the body and clothing. The reaction of Travellers to certain 'dirty' practices in the settled community is hardly surprising, given these facts. Some years ago on an RTE program broadcast from the Girls' Training Centre in Galway, a young Travelling woman expressed her disgust at the settled practice of 'washing babies' nappies in the sink'[3]. Travellers have also expressed to me their abhorrence of indoor toilets which represent another transgression in settled society of the code by which they live. Judith Okely provides an excellent documentary and explanation of such practices among the Gypsies which I believe also holds for Travellers, although up to the point of the present fieldwork there was no proof of it:

> The problems arising from this relationship [a relationship where they are constantly degraded and undermined] with the Gorgios [the settled population] are resolved and symbolized in the Gypsies' attitudes to the body. They make a fundamental distinction between the inside of the body and the outside. The outer skin with its discarded scales, accumulated dirt, by-products such as hair, and waste such as faece, are all potentially polluting. The outer body symbolizes the public self or role as presented to the Gorgio. It is protective covering for the inside which must be kept pure and inviolate. The inner body symbolizes the secret ethnic self. (Okely, 1975: 60).

The reason that women appear so central to the probem of ritual cleanliness has to do with the very nature of their bodies which allows the inside body into the domain of the outer body as in menses and childbirth. This is why in the Travelling community, reproduction is still seen as entirely the woman's function and proceeds without reference to or consultation with men. It would be unheard of for a man (including the father) to mention or allude to a pregnancy in mixed company, because doing so would be an acknowledgement of the act of sexual intercourse, which given the exchange of body fluids it entails, also involves a crossing of these two symbolic bodies and is therefore taboo. In the past, a man who dared to remark on a pregnancy would have been shunned by the other men and labelled *dirty*.[4] Although it is now common practice for a settled man to accompany his wife in labour, it is a very rare occurrence among Travellers. I have been told that it would be a 'crime' to do so. It is not only a primitive awe of the natural process which accounts for this attitude, it is also fear of the supernatural forces that may be experienced in this event of exposing the inner body.

In the past a mother always took certain precautions during her pregnancy as a duty to her unborn baby, but also as a duty to the community as a whole. Some of these measures were also known and practised among settled people, eg an expectant mother would take care not to kiss a corpse at a wake or go to a graveside for fear the baby would be 'cold at birth[5]. There were other customs practised by Travellers which were not, perhaps, as common among settled people, or if they were, the frame of reference was rather different. For example, the prospective parents were expected to avoid conflict, as they believed this could endanger the baby. Even today, the arrival of a handicapped baby is considered to reflect the sin of the father and mother who fought before he was born, or gave scandal before he was born, or at some time in their past lives. Diseases and defects in children are seen as a just retribution for this kind of immoral conduct. At the same time, the devotion they show such children suggests a healthy acceptance of the human condition.

Pregnancy and birth then, are both sacred and taboo. The mother's pregnant state and her act of giving birth are somehow seen to unleash supernatural forces in human life which pose a danger to everyone in the mother's entourage and particularly the male members of the camp. Quite recently, one of my informants explained to me that, 'if you had it on a campsite it would be too dirty'. Judith Okely's interpretation of a similar attitude among the Gypsies helps to clarify why, in light of all this, Travelling women today do not mind going to hospital to have their babies: 'But since hospitals are polluted places of death and disease, they are the best places for dealing with polluting rites of passage: childbirth and death . . . [which] used to take place on the perimeter of the camp.' (Okely, 1983: 251-3).

In the past it would appear that women gave birth away from the camp in some areas, although I am unable to establish whether this was a common practice throughout the country. Mr Nioclás Breathnach, who did some work for the Folklore Commision in the 1930s remembers a bridge between Newcastle West and Abbeyfeale under which the Travelling women went to give birth. The symbolism of giving birth under a bridge by a stream of water can hardly escape us and places the act again in context.

Also connected with birth were some dietary prohibitions but my informants were unable to say what foods were in fact disallowed. More generally, in living memory, there was also ritual fasting imposed on the new mother. There were also restrictions on the preparation of food. New mothers were not allowed to cook for the camp because, as one woman explained to me, 'there'd be no strength in the food she'd cook'. This restriction is of course related to the fact that food goes to the 'inner body' and must not be polluted by someone who is a participant in a rite of passage. This would also seem to explain the reluctance of Travellers to eat food offered by a settled person, particularly in a hospital.

The Travellers consider themselves Catholics and readily embrace the means of purification and protection which the Catholic Church offers. Baptism is still important, not as a rite of initiation, but as a rite which takes the baby out of her or his taboo state. A young mother explained that before baptism, 'the evil would be off it [the baby]'. This fear that the unbaptised baby might endanger the community is well illustrated in the practice of baptising miscarried babies of even three or four months, contrary to common Church practice.

I was surprised to learn that none of my informants believed in Limbo. When I asked them what happens the baby who dies before baptism, the answer they gave was the following: 'The baby has a place in Heaven but always in darkness because the sin the father and mother commit is still in the baby.' The baby's place of repose, then, is in the borderland of Heaven rather than in the 'borderland of Hell assigned to the unbaptised', as Limbo was defined in Catholic theology.

In the past, the Travellers, like the settled people, believed in the fairies and gave them the same name, the good people, in their own language *(ni:des go bori:)*. This, of course, is a curious title given the malicious tricks which these supernatural beings played on Traveller and settled person alike. Although the beliefs of these two communities were rather similar, the customs which were the expression of these beliefs, were somewhat different. I am not in a position to say whether the stories of the Travellers are variants of ones heard in the settled community or whether they represent a parallel though separate tradition. I heard the following stories from Travellers in counties Cavan and Galway in the period 1987—88. Some of them at least are original.

Since children are little beings only in the process of developing an 'outer body' they are particularly vulnerable and a danger to the community. This is why there many rites of protection for children and many stories which show the preoccupation the Travellers had with their welfare.

Some thirty years ago, a Travelling mother would have taken care not to put the clothes of a young baby out on the bushes to dry because she believed it would attract the attention of the fairies who would then come to abduct her baby and put a changeling in its place. The mother would not know immediately that her baby had been swapped for a changeling, because although the baby would have changed in nature, it would look the same. On November's Night a mother would take care to take in the clothes of all the family members so as to protect them from the fairies. This folk ritual would appear to reflect the fear of the exposure of the 'inner body' as in Bridget Murphy's story. And clearly the baby represents more 'inner' than 'outer body', in the sense that its arrival has brought the inside out, and had therefore to be particularly protected.

Many of the Travellers' means of outwitting the fairies

took advantage of their fear of water or fire. A Travelling woman assured me that a basin of dirty water left at the entrance to the camp afforded protection for all its members. However, such precautions did not always prevent the fairies from snatching very young babies but it was always possible to get them back by getting the better of the fairies in this way. One means of recovering a baby from the fairies, according to an account from Cavan, is to bring it in its cradle to a stream of water. There, the Travelling couple swing the baby over the water, threatening to drown the changeling. This threat is enough to ensure the safe return of the real baby to its parents. Again, the kind of symbolic world which this suggests is one about which we know nothing.

One of the signs by which changelings were recognised was crying. The following story is quite common among Travellers: There was once a woman who had twins who never stopped whingeing — a sure sign they were changelings. Her neighbour, a shoemaker, suspected they were changelings but had no way of proving it. One day the mother came to complain to him because she had been invited to a party and couldn't go because of her whingeing infants. The shoemaker offered to look after the babies and the woman accepted and went to the party. Now, she was only gone out the door when the babies revealed their changeling characteristics. They took down the violin and began to dance. The shoemaker was taking note of their antics all the time of their mother's absence. And as soon as they heard their mother returning, they hopped back into the cot and began to whinge once more. The shoemaker told the mother they were changelings so they decided that the best thing to do was to go to the fairy fort and claim back the human babies. This they did, threatening to burn out the fairies, if they did not return the babies at once. It goes without saying, given the nature of the threat, that the babies were promptly returned to their mother.

In another account by a young Traveller, the same principle applied: 'I often heard me grandfather telling this one,' he said. 'If a mother suspected her baby was a changeling, she should bring him to a three-road crossroad [modern T-junction], place the baby in the triangle of grass in the middle and shout and roar at him as if he was a changeling.' She would say, for example, 'the fort is on fire'. If the baby was traumatised by her shouting, she could be sure it was her baby and not a changeling and would quickly return to the camp with him. Presumably, the mention of fire was the effective element in the threat. It is interesting in this regard that fire still has some ritual force in the tradition of the Travellers who burn the caravans of their deceased. This burning would seem to have a protective function dependent on its purification properties. It serves to cleanse the community from the pollution of death, which, like other rites of passage, poses a threat.

The evil eye
Babies and children were in danger, not only from fairies, but also from the evil eye. The possessor of the evil eye was always a woman, often childless, and the victim was, at least in the accounts I got, a female child. The roles which the colour red plays in the customs of protection against the evil eye are unique. It is used primarily as a talisman, e.g. in certain families it is still customary to tie a piece of red cloth on a baby's cradle or clothes to protect the baby from the evil eye. This is also the reason why mothers, in the past, plaited the hair of their little girls with red ribbons and, although the protective function is rarely alluded to and even poorly remembered today, the fondness for red is still evident. The Travelling mother believed that the colour red brought a blessing on the child; it encouraged the admirer to utter the saving formula: 'You have a lovely child, *God bless him/her.*' Even today, a Travelling mother will demand an admirer who omits the blessing to say it so as to make good the admiration. This formula settled mothers have often heard on the doorstep and in the street from Travellers; it is very much their way of assuring the mother of the child that they wish no harm.

The belief in the evil eye might also help to explain the unkempt appearance of many Travelling children. Minturn and Hitchcock show that the custom of commenting on the beauty and health of a child has no place in a culture believing in the evil eye. Their case study is a community in northern India and they explain the connection as follows: 'Because of the belief in the evil eye, a visitor who followed the American custom of admiring the baby, praising its unusual healthiness, good looks, or well kept appearance, would cause panic rather than pride, and a village mother would no more show off her baby to the admiration of a visitor than an American mother would deliberately expose an infant to a contagious disease' (Minturn and Hitchcock, 1966: 111—112). The unkempt appearance of Travelling children has the same purpose: it can be thought of as a means of providing a kind of social anonymity which takes children out of the public eye and therefore out of the danger of pollution from outside. This is why many Travelling mothers feel angered by school authorities who insist on making their children take showers before going into class. Somehow, they fear the exposure it brings to the children and ultimately to the whole group.

A middle-aged Travelling woman from Galway told me of an incident which occurred in a public house in county Roscommon, 'not so long ago', which dramatises the fate of a child cursed by the evil eye. It concerned a Travelling couple accompanied by their little girl who went for a drink. In the course of the evening, an unknown woman admired the little girl twice without using the blessing suffix. That night the little girl died and the parents believed that her death was brought on by the woman who admired her without blessing her. 'That is why we will always ask a stranger to bless the child on the third time round', she explained. Of course, in reality the psychological value of such a belief to the distressed parents was inestimable. Alan Dundes explains that 'the evil eye serves an invaluable projectile function. When an infant becomes ill or dies, there is potentially a great deal of shame felt by the parents. The evil eye belief complex provides a nearly foolproof mechanism that allows the anxious parents to shift the responsibility and blame for the misfortune upon someone else, perhaps even a total stranger.' (Dundes,

1976: 129).

The colour red plays an important role not only in the tradition of the evil eye but also in the system of communication Travellers had among themselves on the road. It involved, among other things, putting rags of different colours on the bushes when leaving a campsite, e.g. red and white rags were positive communication indicating, for example, the generosity of locals, while black rags were a sign of trouble, for example, fighting with the locals or a death in the family. I was rather surprised, in light of what I discovered about the role of the colour red in the tradition of the evil eye, that it was used in a very different way here. In fact, red could mean good or evil depending on the circumstances, my informant told me.

Of course, the association of the colour red with death, the other world and the fairies seems to have been widespread in Irish antiquity.[6] What is curious about the beliefs of the Travellers, is that that which signifies the otherworld or death should be invoked to protect against it. This is not particularly rare in the case of animals — for example, the cow's milk supply was protected from the evil eye in Hungary and Ireland by attaching a red rag to her tail after parturition. However, I was unable to find examples of the protective function of red for humans other than in the Travelling community. To understand the protective function of red we have to look at the logic upon which such a belief is based. Alan Dundes' account of the colour blue in the Near East suggests an interesting parallel to the colour red in the Travelling community: '[The protective function] is based on the principle of homeopathic magic, in which a focus of a dangerous object is itself used as a prophylactic counteragent. In Turkey and surrounding areas, for example, blue eyes are considered to be dangerous, perhaps evil eyes. Yet the colour blue in the Near East is also regarded as protective against the evil eye.' (Dundes, 1976: 19). This principle of 'like against like' appears to operate in the Travellers' tradition of the evil eye — red, which is the sign of the otherworld or death, is the best colour to protect against it.

Conclusion

The folk history of the Travellers remains for now a maze of unanswered questions. However, there are many clues to the past in the living folk memory. I have attempted to address some of these here but there are many more — for example, their belief in transmigration, the extent and nature of their animal lore, and the hierarchies evident in their family disputes and in their language. Getting an overall picture of this past is a considerable challenge; yet it is crucial to the future.

The issue of women in the Travelling community has a lot to do with the ways in which their world is defined. It extends beyond the realm of the camp and since this social space never admits men, it is a source of great anxiety to them. Moreover, it is clear that many women in the Travelling community are experiencing the need to consider their role in their own society in light of new found means of self-determination through their contact with settled society. What all of this means in terms of the culture as a whole remains to be seen. However, one thing is clear: the crisis which the end of the twentieth century presents for their culture is the most significant in their history to date and only the freedom to work through it on their own can prevent their annihilation as a group.

Notes

1 See McCarthy, Patricia, 1971, 'Poverty and Itinerancy', unpublished Master's thesis, University College, Dublin; Sinead Ní Shúinéir's work (unpublished) is available in Aileen l'Amie's Resource Collection on the Irish Travellers, University of Ulster at Jordanstown.

2 See Jared Harper, 1969, 'Irish Traveller Cant: An Historical, Structural and Sociolinguistical Study of an Argot', Unpublished Master's thesis, University of Georgia.

3 This interview was carried out by Ciana Campbell for a Community Access programme in 1984.

4 As Artelia Court notes, 'dirty' was rarely an accusation made from one man to another but a common accusation among women. Nonetheless we have to note that a man's risk of defilement — that of becoming   dirty — comes only through the woman by transgressing the code of ritual cleanliness.

5 'Cold' does not mean dead. It refers to a medical condition known as white cyanosis.

6 See, for example, some early Irish texts where red features in this way: Eleanor Knott, (ed.). 1936. *Togáil Bruiche Dá Dearga*, 1936, Dublin, p.9; K. Meyer, 1919. 'Bruckstucke der alteren Lyrik Irlands', Abhandlungen der Prussischen Akademie d. Wiss. phil. hist, Klasse Berlin, VII, p.59.

References and further reading

Court, A. 1985. *Puck of the Drums*. California University Press, Berkeley.

Dundes, A. 1976. *Interpreting Folklore*. University Press of Indiana, Blomington.

Minturn, L. and Hitchcock, J. T. 1966. *The Rajputs of Khalapur, India*. John Wiley and Sons, New York.

Okely, J. 1975. 'Gypsy Women: Models in Conflict'. In Ardener, S. (ed.), *Perceiving Women*. John Wiley and Sons, New York.

1983. 'Why Gypsies hate cats but love horses'. In *New Society*, , February.

O'Malley, M. 1990. 'Emigration of Irish Travellers to Britain'. *Proceedings of the Labour History Conference*. Galway.

O'Malley, M. 1989. 'The Crux of Secrecy in Shelta, the secret Language of the Irish Travellers'. Paper presented to the American Conference for Irish Studies. Syracuse, New York.

Propp, V. 1984. *Theory and History of Folklore*. Manchester University Press, Manchester.

Discussion Topics

1 The author refers to the Travelling community as an ethnic minority. In what ways can they be said to constitute an ethnic minority, that is to say, are the differences between them and the settled community sufficient to merit a separate treatment?

2 'There is no possible way to release women from oppression in the Travelling community without destroying the culture of the group.' Discuss.

3 'Taboos are essential and protective for communication between the sexes in every society.' Discuss

4 The solution to 'the problem' of women in the Travelling community lies not so much in the education of the women as the men. Although the women are 'muted' in their own group, the settled community are familiar with their voices. In what ways can the men in the group be called forth without being called to judgement?

5 Given that the Travelling community lives on the fringe of settled life, their future very much has to be shaped by a dialogue with us. Can settled people presume to offer models of interaction betweeen the sexes that are better than theirs? How do you imagine the redefinition of the roles of men and women in the Travelling community occurring?

6 How would you see the relation of Travellers to mainstream religion, given the facts of this article? How do women fit into this picture?

Sex and Nation:
Women in Irish Culture and Politics

Gerardine Meaney

The aim of this discussion is to challenge the assumptions made by and about the women's movement in Ireland. It is to some extent a retrospective exercise, an attempt to analyse and respond to some of the ideas put forward in discussions in the series of LIP pamphlets published by Attic Press. It is, more importantly, an attempt to suggest directions in which Irish feminism can move in the future, an attempt to learn from the reverses and successes of the 1980s and to identify opportunities which will be available to Irish feminism in the 1990s.[1]

Many of the previous pamphlets in this series have made the point that, in Ireland, sexual identity and national identity are mutually dependent (Boland, 1989; Longley, 1990). The images of suffering Mother Ireland and the self-sacrificing Irish mother are difficult to separate. Both serve to obliterate the reality of women's lives. Both seek to perpetuate an image of Woman far from the experience, expectations and ideals of contemporary women.

The extent to which women only exist as a function of their maternity in the dominant ideology of Southern Ireland became apparent during the referendum on the Eighth Amendment to the Constitution. The constitutional prohibition on abortion which was the result of that referendum has proved entirely ineffective. The number of Irish women seeking and obtaining abortions in Britain has continued to increase. One is tempted to speculate that abortion itself was quite incidental to those who campaigned so vociferously for an unworkable constitutional ban. The only real effect of the Eighth Amendment has been to compromise any general or 'human' constitutional rights which might give precedence to the woman's rights as an individual over her function as a mother.[2]

That such a constitutional amendment was felt to be

necessary by conservative groups — and that they were able to mobilise an available reservoir of mass hysteria to achieve it — is indicative of the anxiety which changes in women's role and self-concept have induced in Ireland. The assumption that the law needed to intervene in the relationship between woman and foetus — to protect the so-called 'unborn child' from its mother — is indicative of a deep distrust and fear of women. This distrust and fear is paradoxically rooted in the idealisation of the mother in Irish culture as an all-powerful, dehumanised figure. On the one hand, the 1980s saw the Catholic Church and the Right expend very considerable energy in the attempt to contain women within their traditional role. On the other hand, it was that traditional role which excited precisely the fear and anxiety (in men *and* women) which the Catholic Church and the Right shared and exploited to induce an electorate to endorse a constitutional compromise of the rights of women.

The participation of women in the so-called 'pro-life' movement is indicative of an even more complex and contradictary response. Such women seek to perpetuate the idealised virgin/mother figure of woman so that they can *be* that figure. Such identification offers women one of the few roles of power available to them in patriarchy. The hard struggle for political and economic power and equality cannot yet compete with those consolations for many women. The attractions of the traditional feminine role, particularly as the Catholic Church defines it, are grounded in a deep distrust and loathing of femininity, however, and those women who identify with it are also expressing a form of self-hatred, a revulsion against themselves as women. They are unable to accept themselves as thinking, choosing, sexual, intellectual and complex ordinary mortals and instead cling to a fantasy of women as simple handmaids of the lord.

This inability is the product of centuries of education and socialisation of women into acceptance of restricted lives and poor self-concepts and it is exacerbated in this country by the churchs' continuing hold over education.[3] Patriarchy's strongest hold over women is its ability to promote this inner division, which inhibits women's will for change and recruits women damaged by patriarchal ideology to the cause of patriarchy itself and sets them campaigning and voting against their own interests.

The election of Mary Robinson as President has been welcomed by many as an indication that this pattern has finally been broken. Certainly the widespread identification by women with a woman who has so consistently opposed the conservative version of what it means to be an Irish woman indicates that that version no longer holds the same enchantments, even for the rural women so often seen as its most loyal adherents. Moreover, the celebration of Robinson's victory as a triumph for Irish women, in which so many women participated, is evidence of a new confidence and spirit of self-assertion. Attempts by political opponents to use Mary Robinson's sex as a weapon against her failed and the knee-jerk response of distrust and loathing of femininity was not forthcoming. The extent of the political fallout from Robinson's election suggests the potential of such a self-conscious and self-confident sense of common cause among women to effect change. The context in which her election victory was achieved must be recalled before we become too optimistic about the future, however. The common cause of women obviously benefits when left-wing and progressive groups in general make common cause. It is difficult to assess the extent to which public disgust at the unedifying spectacle of the Fianna Fáil/Fine Gael campaigns created a protest vote which was not so much for Robinson as against Lenihan and Currie. That such a protest occurred is in itself a hopeful sign, however, and it must be remembered that even prior to the Lenihan débâcle Robinson was doing better than anyone would have predicted.[4] Change, then, is on the political agenda, but before it can proceed it is important to assess the reverses of the 1980s, their causes and effects, and to analyse the most pressing issues facing feminism in Ireland in the 1990s.

Constituting Irish women
The choice of the Constitution as the vehicle for the attack on women's rights in Ireland in the 1980s was, as Ruth Riddick has pointed out in *The Right to Choose* (LIP

pamphlet, 1990), entirely in keeping with the spirit of that document and its original authors. The identification of the family (rather than, for example, the individual) as the basic building block of society is more than pious rhetoric in the Irish Constitution. In post-colonial southern Ireland a particular construction of sexual and familial roles became the very substance of what it meant to be Irish.

The Indian political philopsopher, Ashis Nandy (1993), has argued that a history of colonisation is a history of feminisation. Colonial powers identify their subject peoples as passive, in need of guidance, incapable of self-government, romantic, passionate, unruly, barbarous — all of those things for which the Irish and women have been traditionally praised and scorned.

Nandy points out that the subject people, in rebelling and claiming independence and sovereignty, aspire to a traditionally masculine role of power. The result is that colonised peoples, often long after colonisation itself has ended, tend to observe or impose strictly differentiated gender roles in order to assert the masculinity and right to power of the (male) subjects. This has been the case, Nandy argues, in his native India. It is readily identified as a trait of fundamentalist Islam and it is not difficult to trace this process at work in the sexual conservatism and political stagnation of post-independence Ireland. Anxiety about one's fitness for a (masculine) role of authority, deriving from a history of defeat or helplessness, is assuaged by the assumption of sexual dominance.

Women in these conditions become guarantors of their men's status, bearers of national honour and the scapegoats of national identity. They are not merely transformed into symbols of the nation. They become the territory over which power is exercised. The Irish obsession with the control of women's bodies by church, state, boards of ethics and judicial enquiries, has its roots in such anxieties, though it is arguable that any form of national identity must constitute itself as power over a territory defined as feminine.

That the experience of women is to be specifically

excluded from Irish national identity is inscribed in the Constitution in which the Republic of Ireland describes itself to itself. Women's 'duties in the home' are constitutionally re-enforced. The most basic 'civil right', the right to life is constitutionally compromised in the case of women — a circumstance which provides a grim gloss on an observation by one of the architects of the concept of civil liberties: Rousseau commented (ironically in his *Discourse on the Origin of Inequality*) that, for citizenship in his ideal republic, 'it must be men'. The consequences of the circumscription of one basic 'right' for women has been, as a series of High Court and Supreme Court judgements have made clear, very specific limitations on the right to freedom of information and free speech.[5] Women, in everything which is specific to them as women, are quite obviously not citizens of the republic.

Feminism and Unionism
Irish nationalism may have little to offer Irish women, but what can the relationship be between feminism and unionism? Mary Holland in an 'open letter' in her *Irish Times* column (30 May, 1990) to the Unionist MP, John Taylor, articulated, tentatively and sceptically, what has long been a furtive wish of liberal forces in the south — an alliance between those forces and Ulster Protestantism. Holland welcomed Taylor's intervention in the dispute over the future of the Adelaide Hospital, the last remaining Protestant hospital in the Republic.

There have been repeated attempts to use Unionist opinion as a lever to put pressure to reform on conservative nationalism. During the divorce referendum the point was unsuccessfully made that a vote against divorce was a vote against pluralism and as a consequence a vote against unification. Since the electorate seems to have responded, not to such abstract principles, but to fear of dispersing family landholdings, it is difficult to make assumptions about the priority of Catholic moral teaching over nationalist aspirations. Nonetheless it is even more difficult to avoid the conclusion that the majority in the south is unwilling to concede that any form of united, federated or more closely integrated Ireland must also be a more hetero-genous Ireland. A second referendum on this issue seems likely in the near future and it will be interesting to observe how far the southern electorate has moved towards a more pluralist notion of Irishness. It is unlikely that any such shift in public opinion will be a product of a re-consideration of the Northern situation.

It is likely, however, that Unionist alienation will be once again invoked by those seeking change as a spectre to ward off the worst excesses of groups such as Society for the Protection of the Unborn Child (SPUC) and Family Solidarity. That invocation has, in the past, created some confusion and misunderstanding of the Unionist position. Part of this confusion stems from a more fundamental confusion in the south of Ireland between what has become known as 'the Protestant ethos' (associated in the public mind with the Adelaide Hospital, compassionate medicine and liberal attitudes to social and sexual matters, in that order) and the perceptions and beliefs of Northern unionism. The former is to some extent identifiable with the Church of Ireland, but it really represents the residue of a secular, humanist tradition which was not and is not exclusively of that faith. It is part of a cultural heritage which feminism elsewhere has had to fight, but which in Ireland might be a significant ally if only it were stronger, a little less complacent and a lot less conservative. It added an important leaven to the dreadful dough of the confessional southern state from the 1930s to the 1960s. It is, in many important respects, part of the culture and the self-concept of the Republic.

Northern unionism is quite distinct from this amorphous cultural 'ethos'. It has a different class base and a different denominational orientation. It has no history of aristocratic guilt: politically it has an unrepent-ent, recent and continuing record of civil rights abuses and intimidation. That record is rooted in a distrust and fear of nationalism which glib generalisations about the 'Protestant ethos' and reconciliation at best obscure and at worst entrench further. It is not a likely ally of any group in the south and its brand of Protestant fundamentalism will not be comfortable with liberalisation. To suggest otherwise is to ignore the facts and to contribute, not to reconciliation, but to further misunderstanding and antagonism. As Holland, in her address to John Taylor, pointed out, 'many, many unionists' opposed the decriminalisation of homosexuality. Unionists and nationalists appear to be able to make common cause against the extension of British abortion legislation to Northern Ireland. Whatever other divisions there are, Ireland, north and south, is united in its denial of women's right to choose.

It is not just nationalist Ireland which exhibits the traits of sexual conservatism and social stagnation. Unionism is, if anything, more insecure and equally prey to the sexualisation of political identity, even if this takes different forms. The fundamentalist streak in Northern Protestantism is as hostile to feminism as is Catholicism. American feminists have had long and bitter experience of evangelical and fundamentalist Protestantism's efforts to combat feminism and to use the concept of the right to life of the 'unborn' to restrict the rights of women. If southern feminism has nothing to say to women in the unionist community in Northern Ireland beyond an assurance that they would be worse off if they were Catholics, then it really will have been defeated by nationalism. Preoccupation with the ill effects of nationalism will have induced a moral and political blindness which obscures other ills. For many women, particularly in Northern Ireland, both feminism and (at least some variants of) nationalism are positive forces for change in their society.

Edna Longley's denial in her LIP pamphlet (1990) that it is possible to be both feminist and republican is not only an historical absurdity. It runs the risk of making Irish feminism no more than a middle-class movement directed towards equal participation by privileged women in the status quo. For a feminism which refuses to engage with the hard realities of Ireland can be no more than that. A feminism based on exclusion will continue to be itself excluded. A feminism which participates in the translation of political into moral categories which bedevils discussions of Ireland, north and south, will itself continue to fall prey to such translations.

Feminism must interrogate nationalism, must maintain its own interests and women's interests against any monolithic national identity which perpetuates patriarchy. In engaging with nationalist women, it must point out how little nationalism and republicanism have promoted or protected women's interests, how much they have done to denigrate and oppress women. Nonetheless, if feminism in the south continues to regard nationalism and republicanism as contagious diseases and to protect itself from contagion by a refusal to engage with either it will also continue to occupy the political margins and to lose referenda. Instead of increasing the isolation of republican women and pushing them further into a ghetto where violence is the only form of political expression left, we have an obligation to enter some kind of dialogue. Instead of lecturing them on their political and moral failings as women we might pause to listen. Perhaps they could teach us to address those women for whom the myth of Mother Ireland is still a powerful enchantment. Perhaps they know better than academics, writers and pamphleteers how to expose and destroy that enchantment.

Feminism needs to address women in *both* communities in Northern Ireland. It will not succeed in doing so by sentimentalising unionism on the one hand and scurrying away from the civil rights issues raised by the treatment of women prisoners on the other. If feminism abroad understands strip-searching as flagrant abuse of civil rights and deliberate sexual degradation, then it is not because it does not understand the circumstances, but because it does understand the principle. It is because it is not so obsessed with distancing itself from one form of political violence in Northern Ireland that it has become blind to all others. Feminism has reason to fear hi-jacking by nationalist and republican groups, but it cannot allow that fear to paralyse it. Moreover, it is time for feminism to ask if it has not already been hi-jacked by its more respectable political allies. Liberal forces in Fine Gael and the Labour Party may have been on our side in the battles on divorce and on the abortion amendment, but that support is in the end less significant than the failure of that support to be effective. They helped us to lose. The nomination of and support for Mary Robinson by Labour in conjunction with the Workers' Party, Greens and others was obviously more effective, but feminism cannot afford to lose any more ballots in Ireland and some caution is necessary.

Feminism cannot, in attempting to see women outside their traditional role as symbols of the nation, be content to merely impose a revised role on them, a role as victims of the nation or of history. The work of contemporary continental feminist thinkers, with its emphasis on the way in which we are produced by and produce the dominant culture and the internal complexities of any programme of cultural and psychological change, may offer a way out of the twin stereotypes into which any analysis of women in Irish culture so easily falls. An analysis which emphasises how deeply we are involved in patriarchal culture and in our idealisation as symbols of the nation denies us the moral high ground — we are not the innocent victims of Irish or any other kind of historical circumstance. Women are not, as Edna Longley suggests in her pamphlet, essentially more peacable, less dogmatic, uninfected by bloodthirsty political ideologies. Women have been actively involved in every possible variant of both nationalism and unionism. They too have 'been prejudiced and brought their children up to be prejudiced. Women have supported and carried out violent actions. They have gained and lost from their involvement. If patriarchal history has portrayed us as bystanders to the political process, it has lied. We have always been implicated, even in our own oppression.

A dangerous consensus

Any analysis of feminism in Ireland needs to take note of an observation by Angela Carter quoted by Clodagh Corcoran (1989) in the LIP series:

> The notion of a universality of human experience is a confidence trick and the notion of a universality of

female experience is a clever confidence trick.

Irish feminism has sometimes perforce played such tricks. In the 1980s it appeared to progress, where it progressed at all, by stealth, disguising its demands for women in assertions of human, individual or civil rights.

It may be a shocking thought for some that the Irish woman reading Irish writing finds in it only a profound silence, her own silence. It is certainly a painful thought for an Irish woman writer and the talents of many of them must have been dissipated or lost in evading such pain. The exclusion of women was constitutive of Irish literature as it was consitutive of the Irish Republic. In her pamphlet, Boland confronts that exclusion, but even her title, *A Kind of Scar*, is testament to its disabling legacy (1989). 'Mise Eire,' her own poem from which Boland takes that title, revised Pearse's poem of the same name. Pearse's refrain of 'I am Ireland' became, in Boland's poem, 'I am the woman'. The myth of Mother Ireland was countered by an insistent feminine subjectivity. Boland's LIP pamphlet counters another cultural cliché: Yeats's 'terrible beauty' is contrasted with a vision of 'terrible survival'. (The centrality of the famine rather than the vagaries of nationalism to Boland's sense of her identity as an Irish woman writer is an interesting indication of the different shape Irish history may take when women have reconstructed their part in it.)

The common insight of Clodagh Corcoran and Eavan Boland is that even where Irish literary and political culture opposes the dominant ideology of church and state it often merely re-presents the emblems and the structures of that ideology in more 'enchanting' forms. One consequence of this is the cultural hegemony which the women's movement has found particularly difficult to shatter.

Rewriting the script
If women are to renegotiate their relation to Irish culture, much work needs to be done. The work of analysing and theorising women's relation to Irish culture, of criticising and changing that relation, of providing a critical, political and historical context for Irish women's writing

is an exciting and necessary task which, as yet, has scarcely begun. The work undertaken by feminist scholars elsewhere can be of invaluable assistance in this task and can expand the horizons of Irish sexual and national identity.

The American feminist critic, Nina Baym (1986), has discussed the way in which nationalism influenced and often constituted the definition of 'American Literature'. That definition was produced by (male) academics eager to legitimise not only American culture, but also their own status as professionals and the equals of their European counterparts. As Baym points out, 'the search for cultural essence' which ensued excluded women and ethnic minorities almost entirely, working on the basis that the experience of these groups is not 'normal', ie masculine, white, 'the same', and is therefore 'inessential'. On these criteria, the work of white, male and predominantly middle-class artists was regarded as that which best expressed the essence of American culture. Work by such artists and writers was thus deemed to be not only the mainstream, but the best.

Baym identifies the myth of the artist as hero, struggling against the odds to create his 'own' work as the myth which legitimised the 'artist' for American culture, reshaping 'him' in the familar mould of a culture which valorised action and 'truth' and was ambivalent about art and artifice. Art became macho. The writer became the prototypical hero, his writing a pioneeering exploration of new territory which he made his own. Effectively he became a literary imperialist.

The myth of the Irish artist is a different myth, but it is equally masculine in its terms and equally concerned with the legitimisation of a particular view of national culture. Two forms of the myth of the (literary) hero predominate. He may be a 'true son' of 'Mother Ireland': this view has very much gone out of fashion. The current myth of the literary-subversive-in-exile (epitomised by Joyce) is no less masculine in its terms, however, and has certain similarities with the American myth, for he too is a 'son' escaping from the 'nets' of 'Mother' church, 'Mother' Ireland and, perhaps, 'Mother' tongue.

If the male Irish writer must speak from this Oedipal place of exile, what position as speaking and writing subject is available to the Irish woman? According to Nuala Ní Dhómhnaill, 'We've all internalised this patriarchal thing. It would be a lie for me to say that I'm out of the woods, because I'm not'. (1986).

Ní Dhómhnaill here echoes the imagery of the French novelist and theorist Hélène Cixous. Cixous sees language as an agent of the internalisation of 'the whole patriarchal thing' and argues that 'as soon as women begin to speak they're taught that their territory is black: because you are Africa, you are black, your continent is dark. Dark is dangerous' (1976). The image of the feminine as a colonised territory has now become almost banal, but Cixous's association of language and colonialism is particularly resonant in an Irish context.

For both Ní Dhómhnaill and Cixous the language of patriarchy colonises women's self-concept and world view. It presents the masculine as the norm and the feminine as an aberration. Words abound for experiences which are exclusive to or predominantly those of men. The public domain, which was for so long the domain of men, is also the domain where discourse proliferates. The private domain, women's traditional 'sphere', is very often the realm of the oblique and unspoken. (Compare, for example, the proliferation of technical vocabularies in the twentieth century — mechanical, electronic, computer languages and jargon — with the scarcity of words relating to the experience of childbirth.) How then can women use language, particularly how can women write, without succumbing to the inherent masculine bias in the languages of patriarchal cultures? According to Ní Dhomhnaill the woman must write — and the man who would break out of the strait-jacket of patriarchal repression and 'linguistic schizophrenia' must write — in 'the language of the Mothers' which she calls Irish.

This latter assertion has caused considerable controversy. Ní Dhómhnaill herself admits, 'There's a level of hurt involved in the language.' This is especially so for women. The question of Irish identity and the question of feminine identity often — as we have seen — have mutually exclusive answers. Moreover the political exclusion implicit in this valorisation of the Irish language is undeniable and runs the risk of a return to the same old insular Irishness. The most productive way to understand Ní Dhómhnaill's assertion is as an attempt to revise the significance of the language she chooses and an assertion that she has a choice. The use of Irish by a woman poet to write in ways which challenge the basic assumptions and myths of patriarchy is an attempt to wrest authority, not only from patriarchy and misogynist myth, but from that formulation of national identity to which the Irish language and the silence of women were fundamental. That is an exercise which can only be beneficial to those many women writers in Ireland who do not see Irish as their mother tongue and who instead grapple with the problem of looking back through literary mothers who are as often as not Anglo-Irish and excluded from that narrow definition of Irishness which Ní Dhomhnaill challenges.

Analogies: The international context

Women on either side of the political divide in Ireland share with the women of many developing countries the burden of the social and sexual conservatism which stifles societies which are insecure in their origins and haunted by civil strife. If we look for analogies to the position of Irish women, it might perhaps be to the Arab nations where, as in Ireland, women are too often the scapegoats of national and religious identity.

We must be wary, however, that we, from our position on the margin of European culture, do not colonise other women's marginality, their history, literature and experience, for our own ends. European feminism poses major problems for Third World women who perceive it to be ethnocentric in its approach to their specific cultural and economic dilemmas. It is important to keep those reservations in mind, even as we look forward to becoming part of a new European feminist movement. Political alignments and the locus of power are shifting and those changes offer opportunities to escape old political polarities. Ireland is not the only European country where feminism and nationalism are in conflict. It is worth noting that one of the first groups which demonstrated in large numbers against the new, united German state were women protesting at the threat to abortion and childcare faciltities, previously guaranteed in East Germany.

The resurgence of nationalism and ethnic strife in Eastern Europe makes it more urgent than ever that feminism not only re-examines its relation to nationalism, but that it actively seeks to change the nature of national and ethnic identity and how we experience them. A particular construction of sexual identity has, in Ireland and elsewhere, given form and substance to national identity. Women have been denied a role in the life and history of nations and been reduced to symbols of the nation. As women claim and change their role and seek a different identity for themselves as women, they will also change the meaning of national identity. According to Eavan Boland, 'Irish poems simplified most at the point of intersection between womanhood and Irishness' (1989). Irishwomen, now that they are breaking their silence, will complicate and change Irish culture at precisely that point of intersection.

The double marginality of Ireland-European, but sharing a history and experience with post-colonial states elsewhere, never quite one thing or another — may yet provide a space in which Irish women can make and say something different of ourselves as women and of the many traditions which are our burden and our inheritance. No longer the territory over which power is exercised, women, in exercising power, may re-define the territory.

Notes

1 This chapter appeared in part in my Lip Pamphlet: *Sex and Nation: Women in Irish Culture and Politics.* Attic Press, Dublin, 1991.
2 The analysis of the strength and agenda of the anti-choice lobby which follows obviously refers to the situation preceding the Supreme Court ruling in the X case and the subsequent referendum in November 1992 which guaranteed the rights of travel and information and where an amendment to restrict further the limited circumstances in which the Supreme Court found abortion to be

constitutionally permissible was rejected.

3 The even more sinister influence exerted by the Catholic Church over the practice of medicine in the Republic has become apparent in the aftermath of the X case judgement and the attempt to use the concepts of medical ethics and professional propriety to pre-empt legislation on abortion.

4 The Labour Party, which was Robinson's major backer as a presidential candidate, subsequently did better than at any time since the foundation of the state in the 1992 general election. The same election produced a significant increase in the number of women TDs in the Dáil. See F. Gardiner in this collection.

5 See note 2 above.

References and further reading

Baym, N. 1986. 'Melodramas of Beset Manhood: How Theories of American Fiction Exclude Women!' In Showalter, E. (ed.), *The New Feminist Criticism*. Virago, London.

Boland, E. 1989. *A Kind of Scar: The Woman Poet in a National Tradition*. Lip Pamphlet. Attic Press, Dublin.

1987. 'Mise Eire'. *The Journey*. Carcanet, London.

Cixous, H. 1976. 'The Laugh of the Medusa'. Translated by Cohen K. and Cohen P. *Sigus*, Vol. 1, No. 1.

Corcoran, C. 1989. *Pornography: The New Terrorism*. LIP Pamphlet. Attic Press, Dublin.

Longley, E. 1990. *From Cathleen to Anorexia: The Breakdown of Irelands*. LIP Pamphlet, Attic Press, Dublin.

Nandy, A. 1983. *The Intimate Enemy: Loss and Recovery of Self Under Colonialism*. Oxford University Press, Delhi/Oxford.

Ní Dhomhnaill, N. 1986. Interview with Michael Cronin. *Graph*. No. 1, October.

Riddick, R. 1990. *The Right to Choose: Questions of Feminist Morality*. LIP Pamphlet. Attic Press, Dublin.

Rousseau, J. J. 1973. 'Discourse on the Origin of Inequality'. In *The Social Contract and Discourses*. Translated by Cole, G. D. H.; revised edition Brumfitt, J. H. and Hall, J. C. Everyman, London.

Discussion Topics

1 What is the relationship between feminism, nationalism and unionism in Ireland?

2 Why is Irish society sexually conservative?

3 Why do women support anti-feminist measures and movements?

4 Has feminism in southern Ireland been damaged by its unwillingness to confront the northern situation?

5 What role can women's writing play in changing Irish culture?

The Women's Movement In The Republic Of Ireland 1970 —1990

Ailbhe Smyth

The Origins of the contemporary women's movement
The origins of any social movement are complex, and it is clearly beyond the scope of this chapter to examine the root causes of the women's movement in Ireland in a detailed way.[1] Many of the reasons why the movement arose as and when it did are, broadly speaking, applicable to most Western countries, although in each case there are socially and culturally specific factors which must be taken into account (Andreason et al, 1991; Ryan, 1992). [2]

Drude Dahlerup explains what she calls 'the revival of feminist protest' as follows:

> [It] is rooted in the fundamental changes that have occurred in women's position in Western industrialised countries since the Second World War. During the period of economic boom, this new generation of women, better educated than any generation before them and enjoying greater personal freedom . . . entered or planned to enter the labour market but found themselves up against the old image of women as housewives (the unpaid Madonna) or sex objects . . . The social change in women's position and women's resources explains why a new generation of women started to revolt (Dahlerup, 1986).

The profound transformation of Irish society that has occurred since the 1940s is clearly reflected in the changing socio-economic situation of women. It would be difficult to claim that Ireland experienced a 'sexual revolution' in the 1960s in the same sense as it occurred elsewhere in the West. Nonetheless, sexual mores have evolved significantly since that time. And although women's entry into the labour force has occurred at a slower pace in Ireland than in most other Western countries, the number of married women in paid work has increased by almost 500 per cent since the 1960s (see

245

Daly in this collection). Irish women now marry younger, have fewer children and live longer. They are far better educated than their mothers, and are much more likely to have professional or vocational qualifications.

Illustrating the dramatic changes which have taken place in women's lives from one generation to the next, Jenny Beale quotes Maura, a Dublin teacher in her early thirties:

> My mother came from a very primitive cottage in the West of Ireland. She went to national school in her bare feet. She showed us a picture of her class — all shaved heads and bare feet. She came up to Dublin when she was eighteen. It must have been amazing for her to live in a nice house with taps and hot water. She had no qualifications whatsoever as she had left school very young, but she got into the civil service. Then she married and lost her job because of the marriage bar. She had five children and never took a job again. And me, how different my life is! I was born in Dublin. I've been to university and I was in a women's group there. I am a teacher, and I am still working although I have a child. There isn't a little pattern I can slot into — I have to make decisions and choices for myself that my mother didn't have to make (Beale, 1986).

The impact and example of the women's liberation movement in America and Europe was strong, in an Ireland becoming rapidly less insular and parochial, and reinforced Irish women's sense of unrest — Betty Friedan's 'strange stirring'. June Levine comments:

> . . . if one had been a mite more sensitive, it would have been possible to recognise the anger that was mounting under the surface as the decade [the 1960s] went on. It was female anger, subtle, veiled, but there. It was an anger the cause of which I only partly recognised or understood. It was a hang-over, an almighty international hang-over . . . I had looked with sympathy upon the oppression of the Red Indian, the American black, the Northern Ireland Catholic. Now here in Ireland I began to feel terribly, terribly angry (Levine, 1982).

The civil rights movement in the USA, anti-Vietnam

protest, student rebellion in America and Europe, the strengthening of radical protest generally in the West during the 1960s, and, obviously, the emergence of the women's movement, were influential contributory factors in generating a climate of change and protest in Ireland.

Although the organised Left was, and is still, weak here, and there was little radical protest or direct action at that time, the example of the civil rights movement in the North, and the resurgence of republicanism were also catalysts for the women's movement in the South. Several of the women who were to be prominent in the Irish Women's Liberation Movement (IWLM) were active in or had connections with the republican and civil rights movements, while others had become politicised as a consequence of the turmoil of the late 1960s.

The increasingly political work of women in trad-itional women's organisations during the late 1960s in particular was to be a further factor in the emergence of the women's movement (Tweedy, 1992). In 1968, ten traditional women's organisations, including the Irish Housewives' Association, the Soroptomists, and the Irish Countrywomen's Association formed an *ad hoc* committee to investigate discriminations against women in Ireland. They subsequently presented a detailed memorandum to the government calling, among other things, for the establishment of a commission on the status of women. The government did in fact set up such a commission in 1970. What is interesting about this particular event is that it was initiated and carried through by women who were fairly or even very active in public life, but certainly not noted for their radicalism. And yet their action was to have a significant impact over the following decade. The Commission on the Status of Women, chaired by Dr Thekla Beere, the only woman to become secretary of a civil service department, made an interim report on equal pay in 1971, and a full report containing forty-nine detailed recommendations just over one year later.[3] The Council for the Status of Women was formed in 1973 to monitor the implementation of these recommendations, and to act as an umbrella or co-ordinating body for women's organisations.[4]

It is difficult to decide whether the 1968 *ad hoc* committee was a *catalyst* for the emergence of the more radical 'liberation' feminism of the early 1970s, or whether it actually marked the beginning of the movement. Clearly, it was liberal/reformist in both its ideology and its tactics, and it is fair to say that the orientation of the Council for the Status of Women is still broadly similar today. When it began in 1970, the IWLM was specifically — and self-consciously — radical and leftist, and thus distinguished itself carefully from the reformist 'women's rights' feminism of the earlier group. Nonetheless, although it is important to observe and maintain that distinction, the two ends of the feminist spectrum have from the beginning frequently joined together in common cause in Ireland, with many individual women moving from one to another at different stages. A number of 'reformist' feminists have, over time, developed a more radical politics while the reverse is also true — some feminists took fright at the more flamboyant actions of the IWLM or IU (Irishwomen United) and took refuge in a more liberal praxis. The blurring of the boundary lines between radicalism and reformism is, I think, a distinctive feature of the movement in Ireland, and one which requires closer analysis. In any event, I would suggest that the 1968 *ad hoc* committee laid the groundwork for many of the legislative reforms and other measures which did help to bring about changes for the better in women's lives over the course of the ensuing decade. It also meant that established — or establishment — women, many of them in prestigious posts or occupations, developed a specifically political awareness of the multiple discriminations practised by the state against women. That awareness, translated into action, has been an important element in the growth of contemporary feminism in Ireland.

Discussing the differences between 'women's rights' feminism and the women's liberation movement, Drude Dahlerup argues that:

> Political reform, that is, reform effected through the political establishment, has never been the main strategy

of the Women's Liberation Movement. Its main focus was and is on women, not the state. The goal is to change people's way of thinking and acting (Dahlerup, 1986).

I agree in principle. In practice, it has to be said that in Ireland, while radical feminists have used mainly direct action tactics and developed alternative, non-traditional strategies which effectively by-pass the state apparatus, there has also been a willingness from the very beginning to use state machinery, especially the legal process, to achieve radical change. The dialogue this entails between radicals and reformists has not been foreclosed here, which is not to say that there is not tension, and often some difficulty, in keeping the channels open. One of the factors which may partly explain the existence of this dialogue indicates, paradoxically, both a strength and a weakness of the women's movement in Ireland. Pauline Jackson has suggested that:

> Lacking, with notable exceptions, the support of female intellectuals, the women's movement failed to explore in depth many cultural, political and ideological issues during (the) early years (Jackson, 1986).

The 'failure' to confront real ideological differences might also be construed as the pragmatic ability to disregard them. There has been a tendency over the years to get on with the task in hand, without overmuch reflection and analysis. This has meant that practical, tangible, 'survival' issues have been dealt with, while the ideological superstructure has not, until recently, been extensively challenged.

Chronology of the women's movement

> The Women's Movement is a creature of ebb and flow — a chameleon (Anne Speed, in Smyth et al, 1987).

No social movement is static — indeed, if and when it reaches a point of stasis, if it ceases to *move*, it fades away and dies. The women's movement in Ireland has continuously evolved over the past two decades, which is a positive dimension, a necessary pre-condition of continuity and growth. And it is as important for us to accept its 'ebb and flow', the periods of high and low energy, as it is to understand the connection between different moments or phases of the movement as it develops over time. Changes of shape and substance within the movement are clearly related to the overall social and political context in which it evolves, although that relationship and the interaction between them is not always precisely measurable. The emergence and development of the movement up to 1990 seem to me to fall into four phases, although the distinctions are not in any sense absolute and sharp. One stage fades into and merges with the next. Nevertheless, obvious trends and patterns of activity are discernible. The first stage runs from about 1970 to 1974, a period of growing politicisation and mobilisation. The second phase runs from 1974 to 1977, which was a time of high energy and radical action. From 1977 until 1983, the movement both consolidated the achievements of the preceding years and began to diversify significantly. From 1983 to 1990 there was an experience of severe repression, socially and economically, accompanied somewhat surprisingly by an unprecedented blossoming of cultural expression by women. The end of 1990 marked a turning point in the movement. The election of a feminist lawyer, Mary Robinson, as President of Ireland generated a strong sense of renewed belief and optimism among feminist activists and Irish women generally (Smyth, 1992a; 1992c). Although it is still too early to assess the impact over time of this election and its many reverberations, in the 'abortion' controversy which marked 1992, feminist voices and actions were clear and strong (Smyth, 1992b).

In those twenty years, Ireland has moved through a period of relative ease and prosperity to the severest economic crisis since the foundation of the state. The hegemony of the Roman Catholic Church in social and moral matters, which appeared to be in decline during the 1970s, surged up with renewed vigour and resilience after the referendum on abortion in 1983. The national question reached crisis point with the hunger strikes in 1981, and remains a dominant theme, along with the economy, in Irish social and political life. Emigration dramatically increased in the 1980s, coming close to the depression levels of the 1950s.

In short, the optimism and relative comfort of the late 1960s, the volatile but still promising 1970s, were followed by a bleak decade of hardship.

1 Beginnings: consciousness-raising and mobilisation, 1970-1974

The Irish Women's Liberation Movement was founded — or came together — early in 1970, in a mood of euphoria and excitement. Ideologically, it contained a plurality of perspectives, and in terms of tactics it may often have seemed chaotic, but the sense of vigour and resourcefulness were extraordinarily powerful. A small group of women succeeded, in a remarkably short space of time, in attacking the sacred cows of social and political life in Ireland. They caught the attention of the media as no group of Irish women had ever done before, shocking, controversial, galvanising substantial numbers of women to take action — or to publicly voice their support — on a whole range of new issues.

The original founding group of what was later to become known as the Irish Women's Liberation Movement (IWLM) was initiated by about a dozen women. They met informally, first in Bewley's Café in Westmoreland Street, later in one of the founder member's houses, and finally in Margaret Gaj's restaurant in Baggot Street. Although by no means all middle-class, professional women — especially journalists — predominated. Articulate, literate, familiar with the media, their presence within the group meant that the IWLM would develop a public profile more rapidly and effectively than in many other European countries — and this despite Irish conservatism and parochialism. Several of the founder members had been, and were still, active in and around left-wing and nationalist politics, which would later lead to accusations of male infiltration of the group, problems relating to structures and organisation and to pressures on the IWLM to affiliate to left-wing and nationalist movements and campaigns.

During 1970, the group functioned partly as a discussion group and partly as a business and planning collective. June Levine describes the group as working within a classic radical feminist mode:

> We were trying to be a structureless, leaderless group, following the main organisational method of groups during those years (1982).

Reading between the lines of June Levine's account of these early meetings, one nonetheless has a strong impression that structures were quickly imposed, if not actually spelled out. It is also possible to detect signs of what were later to become the sources of more serious divisions and conflict within the group — between reformist and radical perspectives, socialist and radical feminists, nationalist and non-aligned women:

> With such a diverse collection of people, it was inevitable that interests varied, priorities differed and disagreements were passionate (Levine, 1982).

Early in 1971 there was nevertheless a sufficient degree of consensus for the group to define its aims and to publish a manifesto — *Chains or Change? The Civil Wrongs of Irish Women.* The thirty-two page pamphlet detailed discriminations against women in the law, employment, education and taxation, analysed the problems and inequities suffered by 'women in distress' (widows, deserted wives, unmarried mothers, single women). In retrospect, it seems ironic that a section dealing with such issues as the absence of childcare and contraception should have been entitled 'Incidental Facts.' The aims of the IWLM echoed these same themes:

1 One Family, one House
2 Equal Rights in Law
3 Equal Pay Now; Removal of the Marriage Bar
4 Justice for Widows, Deserted Wives, Unmarried Mothers
5 Equal Educational Opportunities
6 Contraception — A Human Right.

While the major focus of the pamphlet was the chains that bound Irish women, the aims did emphasise areas in which change was vitally and urgently needed if women were to gain even minimal independence and autonomy.

The focus on the nuclear family, on 'liberal' themes

such as equal rights and educational opportunities, the low-key treatment of contraception and the absence of any reference to abortion, the lack of any analysis of sexuality or of sexual politics, these all seem surprising now in the 1990s. This in itself is an indication of the extent to which the women's movement has stimulated discussion and action in areas once considered unspeakable, if not unthinkable, and now taken for granted. In the Ireland of 1971, the IWLM manifesto was perceived as radical, challenging and deeply subversive of the status quo. The aims also, of course, reflected the concerns of the women who formulated them. There is a fundamentally middle-class/liberal preoccupation with legal reform and equal rights, while the social-ist/republican element is discernible in the demand for 'one family, one house'. Máirín de Burca, who had been involved in the Dublin Housing Action Committee, claimed that 'equality would mean very little for women who lived in overcrowded, unsanitary and insecure conditions'. (R. Conroy, private archive).

It is interesting to compare the aims and concerns of the founders' group with those of the Sutton (Co. Dublin) IWLM group, outlined in their magazine *Succubus* (May 1971). The Sutton group proposed to picket the Eurovision Song Contest and distribute leaflets on contraception; to picket against the housing of three priests in three separate houses costing £25,000 when many families in Dublin were still living in one room, to meet 'Ballymun housewives' to discuss with them their living and housing conditions, and to organise a twenty-four hour emergency baby-sitting service.

Following the publication of *Chains or Change*, there was considerable pressure from within the founders' group to develop outwards and away from the potential if not actual élitism of the small group structure towards a mass movement. Some members believed it was too soon to do so, that the group was not equipped to deal with the ideological, organisational, and tactical problems such a shift would entail. It is difficult (and doubtless irrelevant) to know even now whether or not the 'correct' decision was made, but in the event, the IWLM became a public entity on 6 March 1971, when the controversial TV chat show, *The Late Late Show*, devoted an entire programme to the Women's Liberation Movement. The effect was electric. The IWLM women on the panel raised hitherto unspoken issues and taboo topics for women (indeed everyone) in Ireland on a range of social and sexual matters — single mothers, working mothers, the 'helpless dependency of the Irish wife', the miseducation of girls, social conditioning and so on. June Levine (1982) recounts that a 'free for all screaming match' took place. The issue of liberation had been well and truly raised and placed on the social and political agenda. Women's silence would never be quite as absolute as it had been.

When the founders' group organised a mass meeting in the Mansion House a few weeks later, there was an attendance of almost 1,000. The organisers could barely cope with the number of women who came forward to speak, and who wanted to set up local IWLM groups. It was by all accounts an extraordinary evening — moving, exhilarating and liberating, a moment when it seemed possible to change the world inside out and round about.

There then followed a period of direct action, involving relatively few women, but producing maximum impact. There were pickets, demonstrations, and other flamboyant and spectacular protests. The activities seem to have occurred fairly spontaneously in a euphoric mood, rather than as part of a concerted programme of action.

The number of activities and the mushrooming of local groups quickly became a source of pressure and tensions between the founders' group and local structures began to emerge. At a seminar in May 1971, although it was agreed that the IWLM aims would remain as originally formulated, there was heated discussion and argument over the divisive housing issue. In August of that year, the Sutton group demanded a general meeting between all local groups and the founders' group 'on specific women's issues as opposed to general or social issues'. The founders' group tried to delay what they foresaw as a confrontation but were overruled. At the general meeting in September, one of the original members resigned following a sharp disagreement over political affiliations. In retrospect, there appears to have been real difficulty over this issue within the founders' group from the beginning and more generally, an inability to break clearly with male — and specifically left-wing — structures and modes of activity. Underlying this and other disagreements, one senses the shadow of republicanism — always present, but rarely allowed to surface directly and explicitly.

There was more conflict over the contraception issue. Two founder members had originally disagreed with its inclusion in the 'aims', especially for single mothers. Following the 'contraceptive train' action in 1971, a founding member resigned, allegedly accusing the IWLM of being 'anti-America, anti-clergy, anti-government, anti-ICA, anti-police, anti-men'. It seems extraordinary now that a woman would call herself a feminist and still oppose contraception. This position was a representative one which can only be understood in the context of the authoritarianism of Irish Catholicism and its primordial role in shaping values, attitudes and behaviour.

Gradually, the founders' group, succumbing to tension, conflict and — no doubt — exhaustion, began to disband:

> During the above period women were drifting in and out of the movement, numbers were dropping dramatically in the groups, mainly because of friction, disillusionment, radicalism. ('Outline of Conflict in the Irish Women's Liberation Movement 1971' (R. Conroy, Private archive).

It was virtually inevitable that the energy and momentum of these beginnings would eventually dissipate, and direct action all but ceased at this time. For whatever complex of reasons, a peak of activity in the movement in Ireland, lasting from one to two years, tends to be followed by a plateau or levelling-out period in which energies are recouped, forces regroup, ideas settle and — becoming more acceptable — are integrated by a broader layer of women, some of whom subsequently assume the responsibility of militancy. I use the term 'responsibility' because so very many feminists do indeed conceive it to be their social and political 'responsibility' to initiate and maintain a certain level of activity.

The major issues of the first year or so of the IWLM concerned housing, equal rights, recognition of single motherhood and — although more problematically — contraception. They were to remain firmly on the feminist agenda (with the exception of housing) over the ensuing years, although the style or *modus operandi* of the movement changed very significantly. Although a number of women continued to meet in a consciousness-raising/discussion-group mode over the next two years or so (the 'Fownes Street' group, who also briefly produced a journal), the main preoccupation of the movement in 1972 shifted to the development of self-help, aid and single-issue groups. Many of these functioned in a necessarily contradictory manner, seeking to gain a measure of respectability and thus concrete recognition from the establishment, while at the same time posing a threat to the status quo by providing social services for women, clearly considered irrelevant by the state and its agencies. AIM (Action, Information, Motivation) was founded in 1972. A pressure group lobbying for family law reform, it was (and is still) also an advice and information centre for women. The emphasis was on legal reform and helping women in practical ways to deal with the reality of their situation. AIM, and other aid groups did not, on the whole, directly challenge the institutions and mechan-isms which produce and reproduce gender oppression. Many of these groups, both in the early 1970s and in later years, were modelled fairly obviously on similar groups in the USA and UK, as their names indicate — Women's Aid, the Rape Crisis Centre, even the 'Women's Right to Choose' group, as Pauline Jackson has pointed out (1986). Both ideology and practice were adopted, and then adapted, to suit the Irish social context, with the result that there was relatively little theorising around their areas of concern. Some action-research has emerged, especially from AIM, the Rape Crisis Centre and Women's Aid, but has tended to remain fairly scarce until very recently.

Cherish, a self-help pressure group set up by single mothers was from the outset radical and outspoken, no doubt because the experience it set out to deal with had for so long been denied as a reality in women's' lives in Ireland. It has remained an important force for change, legally and attitudinally. Also around 1972, the Women's Political Association, committed to working for the election of women to the legislature, was gathering momentum, and the Council for the Status of Women was established. One of the difficulties that the Council — an umbrella group for women's organisations both traditional and radical — has had to face since its inception is that its own structures are modelled directly on those of the organisations and institutions it sought to both influence and challenge — with a chairwoman, executive committee, delegate representation, and so on. Again, in the case of the Council, the dilemma of the dual function, seeking to change the system while working from within, is clearly marked and is still largely unresolved.

All of these activities occurred at about the same time, following the disintegration of the IWLM, and indicate a readiness to engage more directly with the state, or the establishment, and the availability of a certain 'layer' of women, mainly middle-class, to mobilise in the name of a more conventional 'women's rights'- style feminism.

2 Radicalisation and direct action: 1974-1977

Some time late in 1974 radical feminism surfaced with renewed vigour and determination, this time with a slightly younger generation of women, the majority of whom had no connections with the original IWLM, and came to the movement from student revolutionary and radical left groups, the republican movement, community action projects and the trade union movement. This new generation of feminists had a more coherent and developed sense of revolutionary ideology and practice, incorporating a clearer analysis of the gender and class systems.

The loose grouping of women which came together formally in April 1975 called itself Irishwomen United

(IU). They included one or two women who had been involved in the IWLM, members of Revolutionary Struggle (RS), the Movement for a Socialist Republic (MSR), People's Democracy (PD) and a number of students. Several had trade union affiliations. Nell McCafferty, who was herself involved, described them with her customary verve:

> Irishwomen United was composed of trade unionists, professional women, and the unemployed, who had scarcely heard of motherhood. They insisted on self-determined sexuality and lived with women or men, as the fancy took them, with nigh a thought for marriage (1979).

The IU Charter covered seven points and was noticeably more radical than the IWLM 'Aims':

> Preamble: At this time, the women of Ireland are beginning to see the need for and are fighting for liberation. This is an inevitable step in the course of full human liberation. Although within the movement we form diverse groups with variant ways of approaching the problem, we have joined together around these basic issues. We pledge ourselves to challenge and fight sexism in all forms and oppose all forms of exploitation of women which keep them oppressed. These demands are all part of the essential right of women to self-determination of our lives — equality in education and work; control of our own bodies; an adequate standard of living and freedom from sexist conditioning. We present these demands as the following women's charter.
>
> 1 The removal of all legal and bureaucratic obstacles to equality...
>
> 2 Free legal contraception...
>
> 3 The recognition of motherhood and parenthood as a social function with special provisions...
>
> 4 Equality in education — state-financed, secular, co-educational schools with full community control at all levels...
>
> 5 The male rate for the job where men and women are working together...
>
> 6 State provision of funds and premises for the

establishment of women's centres in major population areas to be controlled by the women themselves . . .

7 The right of all women to a self-determined sexuality . . .

(Summary: Back Page of *Banshee*, Vol. 1, no. 1, n.d.)

IU were to be extremely active over the course of the following eighteen months or so, organising, for example, pickets of all-male clubs and pubs, protests and campaigns on contraception and equal pay, supporting women strikers, holding seminars, discussions and so on. A discussion paper prepared for one of the regular IU teach-ins, addressed the central question 'How to build a women's movement', and provides us with some insight into the group's political theory and its praxis. Broadly, the collectively-written paper emphasises:

- the need for an *autonomous* women's movement.

- that the IU charter should be seen as a starting point for the construction of 'an on-going movement which will combat the whole sphere of women's oppression in Ireland'. If attention is paid to women's precise and immediate needs — here identified as contraception and equal pay — the basis for a more all-embracing and profound radicalisation on all issues will have been constructed.

- that the issues which need to be confronted urgently include discussion about the scale and kind of growth envisaged in IU: should it develop in linear fashion as a mass organisation or retain its small group identity; discussion about the recruitment and induction or ;integration' of new activists into the group.

- the need to analyse the specific role of IU — mobilisation and radicalisation.

- auto-critique of previous activities — principally the attempt 'to initiate too many activities in relation to our strength'.

- IU's relation to the state in general as a 'vanguard' feminist group and, more specifically, IU's stance with regard to women politicians.

(*Irishwomen United* (n.d.); 'Discussion Paper for Teach-in of Irishwomen United: How to Build a Women's Movement'. (Private archive, R. Conroy).

The issue of equal pay enabled the group to demonstrate that 'action on the part of women themselves was very important', although they noted that the difficulty of bridging the gap between the women's movement and the trades unions was a lesson that had been learned as a result of the equal pay campaign.

The crucial importance of the contraception issue is accentuated throughout the discussion paper. It was perceived and presented as the issue most central to women's lives in Ireland, and the one most likely to mobilise and/or radicalise the broader mass of women. Abortion, significantly, had been excluded from the IU charter on the basis not only that it would alienate many women from the movement, but also because there were women within IU 'who were not clear what their own position was, and that was something that was very instructive because we were all these so-called radical women — and suddenly we were confronted with the Irish reality' (Interview with IU activist, cited in Gaudin, 1983). Individual IU activists nonetheless did raise and debate the issue publicly:

> Today Irish women are organising to fight for the right to control our own bodies — that fight we will win — and throughout the fight we will stay united and organised — this time we will win our full liberation. (Monica Adams. Report of a meeting in University College, Dublin, on abortion, December 1976.) (Private archive, R. Conroy).

Irish feminists did indeed try to remain 'united and organised' during the abortion amendment campaign of 1982/83, but were ultimately defeated not only by the fundamentalist backlash but also by the forces of 'good sense' and political expediency who advocated that the anti-amendment campaign be fought on mainly medical and legal/constitutional grounds rather than around women's right to control reproduction (Barry, 1988). A decade later, during the 1992 abortion referendum campaign, it was clear that feminist activists had learned the lesson of political dilution. Groups such as the feminist-led Alliance for Choice and the Women's Coalition successfully campaigned on an unambiguous 'pro-choice' basis (Smyth, 1992b).

Of no less significance in the IU teach-in paper referred to was the almost total exclusion of any discussion of sexuality. The 'right of all women to a self-determined sexuality' appeared in the IU charter as the seventh and final point. Neither heterosexuality nor lesbianism was addressed in the discussion paper, although it is clear from IU minutes that the issue was raised at meetings. LIL (Liberation for Irish Lesbians) was not to form until 1978 (Crone, 1988). The interaction between feminism and lesbianism were first broached in issue No. 3 of *Banshee*, the IU magazine, but in an article by American feminist Robin Morgan, while in a short piece on sexuality in the same issue, lesbianism is not once referred to:

> I think that the lesbian feminist separatists used to meet outside of IU to discuss lesbian politics (Jennings, 1985).

Eight issues of *Banshee* were published in IU from about March 1976 until some time in 1977. Three thousand copies of the first issue were printed, and 2,500 sold, making a profit of £100! The articles covered a wide range of themes, more or less related to the IU charter, and reflecting a variety of political perspectives. Liberal, radical and socialist feminist positions co-existed without editorial comment or intervention. Contraception, equal pay, women and the law, education, sexism in the media, women and the church, Celtic mythology, the patriarchal family, wages for housework, news from abroad — these are some of the areas included in the generally unsigned articles. Lesbianism, abortion, the national question are noticeable by their absence. Were they evacuated or elided by common but tacit consent? Some topics were clearly too dangerous, because too divisive, to raise:

> All the tension then, about lesbianism, about being involved in working class movements, about taking on campaigns that were important for Irish society, about republicanism, came up (Jennings, 1985).

The fragmentation of IU during 1977 was again, as in the case of the IWLM, a gradual process rather than the result of exploding conflict or confrontation. It seems to have happened for a number of reasons, some pragmatic (exhaustion; professional and personal responsibilities;

emigration; diversification into other actions and projects) some ideological (republicanism; lesbianism, socialist versus radical feminism, etc.)

> In the spring of '77 IWU did have this day workshop on where we are now, where are we going, and so on, because everybody knew that there was, not cracks, but exhaustion. Nobody knew what to do abut it (Jennings, 1985).

3 Consolidation and diversification: 1977-83

Nothing much could be done about the disintegration of IU because it had, in an important sense, fulfilled its role. Had the massive equal pay campaign not forced the trades unions to confront the issues raised, it is doubtful whether the Irish government would have implemented equal pay legislation in 1977, the EEC directive notwithstanding. The Contraception Action Programme (CAP) was instrumental in keeping the issue on the political agenda. IU had succeeded, via its participation in these two major campaigns and by a series of imaginative, witty and effective direct actions, in mobilising large numbers of people (a remarkable 36,000 signatures were gathered in ten days for the equal pay petition) and in re-infusing energy and a sense of passionate commitment into a movement which had become lacklustre, even complacent. Its disintegration was to be followed by another 'plateau' period of consolidation and diversification.

A number of feminist conferences were held over the following years, opening up or developing reflection, discussion and exchange on the whole gamut of feminist issues. The first 'All-Ireland' feminist conference took place in Belfast in 1977, quickly followed by another in Dublin. A women's conference on lesbianism was held in 1978 in an attempt to 'break down the barriers of silence and ignorance surrounding lesbian sexuality'. The conference 'tradition' was maintained over the following years, with a major thirty-two counties national women's conference taking place in 1984, for example. The Trade Union Women's Forum organised several conferences, published pamphlets and maintained a high level of activity both within the trades unions and in the women's movement.

The campaign for a women's centre began in October 1978, leading eventually to the opening of the relatively short-lived Dublin Women's Centre in 1982. The first rape crisis centre had opened its doors in Dublin in January 1977, and actions and campaigns around rape legislation and violence against women were initiated. In fact, violence against women was probably the major mobilising issue of this period with an astonishing 6,000 women taking part in a 'Women Against Violence Against Women' torchlight procession in October 1978.

Irish Feminist Information, founded in 1978, published a wall calendar recalling the main events of the movement over the preceding years, while in 1979, Pat Brennan wrote an article for *Magill* magazine in which she outlined the history of the contemporary movement.

The women's movement was far from moribund, but it had again changed in style and character, becoming more diffuse and diversified. During this period, there was a marked tendency on the part of the state, and political parties in particular, to co-opt feminism generally and individual women. In the 1977 general election 'women's vote was canvassed as never before . . . and the two major political blocks nearly fell over each other to proclaim their dedication to the cause' (Murphy, 1978). The Women's Political Association continued and expanded its activities, while the Women's Talent Bank lobbied for the inclusion of women on state and semi-state bodies, without marked success, it must be said:

> It could be called the new feminism, women not asking or demanding any more, but getting into the thick of things and doing it for themselves. It's a slow process and we've a long way to go, but it's where the future is at (Murphy, 1978).

The apotheosis of 'state feminism' can be located in 1982 with the appointment by the new coalition government of a minister of state for women's affairs and family law reform — the combination of these two briefs being in no sense coincidental or insignificant. 'Women's affairs' had become legitimate — although neither cabinet status nor adequate financial resources were allocated to further the realisation of women's liberation to any real extent.

4. Repression/expression or denying the backlash: 1983-90

While it is important not to dismiss the activity of the 1977-83 period, it is clear that the revolutionary ardour of the early and middle years had been dimmed. It was to be well-nigh quenched by the fundamentalist repression and the economic recession of the mid-1980s. These were to be difficult and demoralising years, leading many feminist activists to a point of weary disenchantment. In retrospect, the encounters of the 1970s over contraception, rape, equal pay, appeared as mere skirmishes, a phoney war, prior to the battles of the 1980s against the serried ranks of church and state, staunch defenders of the faith of our fathers and the myth of motherhood.

The litany of defeats, and of victims — some known, the vast majority unnamed and nameless — is shocking: abortion — already a criminal offence — declared unconstitutional in a 1983 referendum; divorce — still prohibited by the Constitution despite attempts to introduce an amendment in a 1986 referendum; Eileen Flynn lost her job as a teacher (in a Catholic convent school) for being pregnant and living with a married man; Sheila Hodgers died in agony, without painkillers, shortly after giving birth to her baby because no-one had told her of the danger of pregnancy in her cancerous condition; Ann Lovett, aged fifteen, died in the open air, in front of a shrine of the virgin mother, while giving birth to her stillborn child, alone and apparently without the knowledge of anyone in the small country town where she lived; Joanne Hayes, aged twenty-four, concealed the birth and death of her baby and subsequently 'confessed' to the murder, by stabbing, of another baby, despite contrary forensic evidence; during the course of the longest public tribunal of enquiry in the history of the state, Joanne Hayes, accused of no crime, was subjected to the most appalling interrogation and humiliation. High Court judgements were handed down, on foot of actions brought by right-wing extremists, rendering abortion counselling or the dissemination of information about abortion illegal (O'Reilly, 1991; Smyth, 1992b) and so on, and on.

During the 1980s, women were subjected to unprecedented social, psychic, and moral battering. Pauline Jackson comments:

> I think there has been, certainly, a very real experience of depression . . . and I would argue that hard-core activists in the unions have been put up against the wall on so many issues — for example, low pay, equality, parttime work, the right to unionise, the rights of younger women workers, and so on. These issues are being projected as luxuries during the recession (Smyth, Jackson, McCamley and Speed, 1987).

The various feminist groupings which coalesced during the abortion amendment campaign in 1982/83 conferred a sense of strength and cohesion on the movement which was to prove somewhat illusory when measured in terms of success in the public arena. It proved difficult for women to come together — and to maintain momentum — to campaign on major issues, as the experience of the June 1986 divorce referendum, the failure of the government to implement the EC social security directive within the deadline, and the 'defend the clinics' campaign demonstrated.

Paradoxically, although the movement was less forceful and unified in campaigning terms, extraordinary energy was channelled into the development of what amounts to a new feminist 'counter-culture'. In an environment as hostile to political and social change as the 1980s, feminist energies tended to focus on educational, cultural and creative projects. The work of women artists and writers became increasingly visible and their claims for recognition more insistent (Smyth, 1989). Feminist publishing, with its roots firmly in the earlier years of the movement, played a crucial role in the development of women's creative and political expression.[5] Women's Studies and research developed with remarkable speed and solidity within adult education and local settings and in the universities, despite the absence of state funding or firm institutional support (Smyth and Healy, 1987; Mulvey, 1992). Debate on key feminist issues emerged more strongly, in new spaces created by feminist activism.[6] Divisions and differences between women were more openly acknow-ledged and discussed, while previously 'difficult' topics were confronted with a greater degree of openness.

Poverty, class and sexuality, the national question were some of the major concerns on the feminist agenda, and as Anne Mulvey (1992) remarks:

> . . . it is simply not accurate to see feminists in Ireland as having a monolithic or homogeneous view on North/ South political issues, on women's issues, or how to prioritise and address them.

In an important sense, the 1980s were the decade in which the women's movement recognised, sometimes haltingly, the complexity of the task it was embarked on and the diversity of strategies and organisational forms necessary to continue with that task. The election of Mary Robinson as President, in 1990, did not come from nowhere. It was rooted in the subtle socio-political shifts which had continued to reverberate through the 1980s, despite the recession and the battery of anti-feminist repressive strategies. With the election of Mary Robinson, the tide was on the turn and Irish women were once again signalling their desire for change and their determination to bring it about (Smyth, 1992a; 1992c).

Conclusion

The women's movement has been a positive force for change for more than two decades. During that time, some demands have been met and some grievances at least have been partially resolved. Greater numbers of women are now involved in policy-making than was the case in 1970. Most importantly, women's awareness of gender-based oppression, exploitation and injustice has sharpened and spread far beyond the small circle of women active in the very early years of the IWLM. Consciously and unconsciously, the effects of feminist practice and theory have premeated women's everyday lives.

It would require another chapter (at least) to assess the impact of the women's movement on the everyday, material conditions of women's lives, on state policy and social institutions, and I shall not attempt such an evaluation here. There is so much recording and remembering, reflection, and research which requires to be done before we can begin to fully appreciate the difference the contemporary women's movement has made to our lives. We need to undertake this work urgently so that we may have a clearer understanding of the movement now, and of its potential to generate the new visions of our future freedom.

Notes

1 For analyses of first wave feminism in Ireland, see Owens (1984) and Ward (1983). There is no detailed published history of the contemporary women's movement, although see, for example, Barry (1988); Crone (1988); Jackson (1986) on specific aspects. June Levine's personal account of her involvement with the IWLM (1982) is an invaluable resource. I am indebted to many women who helped to locate information for this brief account, and to one private archive (R. Conroy) in particular.

2 This chapter deals only with the Republic because I consider the development of the women's movement, North and South, to be distinctive, although with common points of reference, in both historical and contemporary terms. For discussions of the movement in the North, see Ward (1987); Evason (1991); Roulston (1989); Collective (1989).

3 The government established The Second Commission on the Status of Women in 1991. The Commission's report, published early in 1993, makes numerous recommendations, many of them in relation to areas or issues still invisible or profoundly unspeakable in the early 1970s.

4 About one hundred women's groups and organisations were affiliated to the CSW in 1993.

5 Arlen House, founded in 1975, continued to publish feminist work until the 1980s. Irish Feminist Information (IFI), founded in 1978, ran two training courses for women in publishing, which led directly to the setting up of Attic Press and of Women's Community Press. KLEAR, the North Dublin-based adult education group, published collections of students' work both on its own and with Women's Community Press.

6 Attic Press's LIP Pamphlets, beginning in 1990, were commissioned specifically to stimulate debate on a range of contemporary feminist issues and controversies. See G. Meaney's chapter in this collection.

References and further reading

Andreason, T. et al. 1991. *Moving on: New Perspectives on the Women's Movement.* Aarhus University Press, Aarhus.

Barry, U. 1988a. 'Abortion in the Republic of Ireland'. In *Feminist Review*, No. 29, Spring.

Barry, U. 1988b. 'Women in Ireland'. In *Women's Studies International*

Forum, Vol. 11, No. 4.

Beale, J. 1986. *Women in Ireland. Voices of Change.* Macmillan, London/Dublin.

Brennan, P. 1979. 'Women in Revolt'. *Magill,* Vol. 2, No. 7.

Collective. 1989. *Unfinished Revolution: Essays on the Irish Women's Movement.* Meadhb Publishing, Belfast

The Crane Bag. 1980. Special Issue: *Women in Ireland.* Vol. 4, No 1.

Crone, J. 1988. 'Lesbian Feminism in Ireland'. *Women's Studies International Forum,* Vol. 11, No. 4

Dahlerup, D. 1986. 'Is the New Women's Movement dead? Decline or Change in the Danish Women's Movement'. In Dahlerup, Drude, (ed.), *The New Women's Movement.* Sage, London.

Evason, E. 1991. *Against the Grain: The Contemporary Women's Movement in Northern Ireland.* Attic Press, Dublin.

Gaudin, E. 1983. 'Les Femmes dans l'évolution de la société contemporaine en République d'Irlande'. Thèse de 3ème cycle, Université de Lille, France.

Irish Feminist Review '84. 1984. Women's Community Press, Dublin.

Jackson, P. 1986. 'Women's Movement and Abortion: The Criminalisation of Irish Women'. In Dahlerup, Drude, ed., *The New Women's Movement.* Sage, London.

Jennings, M. 1985. 'Discussion about Irishwomen United'. *Trouble and Strife,* No. 7, Winter.

Levine, J. 1982. *Sisters. The Personal Story of an Irish Feminist.* Ward River Press, Dublin.

Loughran, C. 1986. 'Armagh and Feminist Strategy'. *Feminist Review,* No. 23.

McCafferty, N. 1979, December 28, *The Irish Times.*

MacCurtain, M. and O Corráin, D. (eds.). 1978. *Women in Irish Society: The Historical Dimension.* Arlen House, Dublin.

Mulvey, A. 1992. 'Irish Women's Studies and Community Activism: Reflections and Exemplars'. *Women's Studies International Forum,* Vol. 15, No. 4.

Murphy, C. 1978. 'The New Feminism' *The Irish Times.* January.

O' Reilly, E. 1991. *Masterminds of the Right.* Attic Press, Dublin.

Owens, R. C. 1984. *Smashing Times: A History of The Irish Women's Suffrage Movement.* Attic Press, Dublin.

Rose, C. 1975. *The Female Experience: The Story of the Woman Movement in Ireland.* Arlen House, Dublin,

Roulston, C. 1989. 'Women on the Margin: The Women's Movement in Northern Ireland, 1973-1988'. *Science and Society.* Vol. 53, No. 2.

Ryan, B. 1992. *Feminism and the Women's Movement: Dynamics of Change in Social Movement Ideology and Activism.* Routledge, London/New York.

Smyth, A. (ed.). 1989. *Wildish Things: An Anthology of New Irish Women's Writings.* Attic Press, Dublin.

Smyth A. (ed.), Jackson, P., McCamley, C., Speed, A. 1987. 'Feminism in the South of Ireland: A Discussion'. *The Honest Ulsterman,* No. 83.

Smyth A. and Healy G. 1987. 'Women's Studies — Irish Style'. *RFR/DRF*, Vol. 16, No 4.

Smyth A. 1992a. '"A Great Day for the Women of Ireland": The Meaning of Mary Robinson's Presidency for Irish Women'. *Canadian Journal of Irish Studies*, Vol. 18, .1.

Smyth, A. (ed.). 1992b. *The Abortion Papers: Ireland*. Attic Press, Dublin.

Smyth A. 1992c. 'Hail Mary — A President of Women'. *Trouble and Strife*. No. 23.

Tweedy, H. 1992. *A Link in the Chain: The Story of the Irish Housewives' Association 1942-1992*. Attic Press, Dublin.

Ward, M. 1987. 'Feminism in Northern Ireland: A Reflection'. *The Honest Ulsterman*, 83, Summer.

Ward, M. 1983. *Unmanagable Revolutionaries*. Brandon Books, Dingle/ Pluto Press, London.

Discussion Topics

1 Do you see women as much better off today compared with twenty years ago or as only slightly better off? What aspects of our lives are most significant in making such judgements?

2 How do women from different economic classes or ethnic groups differ in our perceptions of feminist issues? To what extent have such differences been acknowledged by the Irish women's movement?

3 Discuss the issues which you consider to be most crucial for the women's movement in the 1990s.

4 In your view, which organisational forms and strategies are likely to be most effective for the women's movement in the 1990s?

5 To what extent do you think Irish feminism is now exploring in depth 'significant cultural, political and ideological issues'?

6 'There has always been a women's movement this century'. Does this apply to Ireland? And what are your predictions for the next century?

About the Contributors

Anne Byrne is currently working in the Department of Political Science and Sociology, University College Galway where she teaches Women's Studies courses amongst other things. She is a feminist, a mother and loves statistics, dogs and hens.

Mary Daly is a sociologist and former head of research with the Combat Poverty Agency in Dublin. She is at present affiliated to the European University Institute in Florence. Her publications include *The Hidden Workers* (1985), *Local Planning* (1987) with Laraine Joyce, *Moneylending and Low Income Families* (1988) with Jim Walsh, and *Women and Poverty* (1989).

Eileen Evason is a Senior Lecturer in Social Administration at the University of Ulster at Coleraine. She has been involved in many different campaigns on women's issues and has written numerous articles and books, including *Against the Grain: The Contemporary Women's Movement in Northern Ireland* (1991).

Frances Gardiner, a founder member of Women's Studies in UCD, now teaches in the Department of Political Science at Trinity College, Dublin. She is a member of the EC Expert Network 'Women in Decision-Making' and has published on women and politics. Research interests include a cross-cultural study of women and parliament, religion and politics and interest groups.

Madeleine Leonard is a lecturer in the Department of Sociology and Social Policy at Queen's University, Belfast. She is currently working on a book examining 'Informal Economic Activity in Belfast'.

Margaret MacCurtain lectures in Irish History in the Department of History in University College Dublin. She has written on the role of religion in Ireland and has contributed studies of Irish women in their historical dimension in two books of essays: *Women in Irish Society* (MacCurtain and O Corráin, 1978) and *Women in Early Modern Ireland* (MacCurtain and O'Dowd, 1991).

Monica McWilliams is a lecturer in Social Policy and Senior Course Tutor for Women's Studies at the University of Ulster, at Jordanstown. She has been a participant in and a researcher of the women's movement in Northern Ireland. More recently, she has jointly completed a research project on domestic violence in Northern Ireland, (with Joan McKiernan) which has been published by the DHSS.

Gerardine Meaney lectures in English at University College Dublin. The author of *(Un)Like Subjects: Women, Theory, Fiction* (Routledge, 1993), she also writes fiction.

Jo Murphy-Lawless is a feminist sociologist who works with NEXUS Research Co-operative. She is also a member of the Centre for Women's Studies, Trinity College, Dublin.

Mary O'Malley Madec was born in County Mayo and educated at University College Galway, where she did an MA in Old English. After doing extensive fieldwork on the Travellers, she started a doctoral program in linguistics at the University of Pennsylvania in 1990. She is now in Ireland conducting research to complete her doctorate and teaching part-time at UCG.

Mary Robinson was called to the Irish Bar in 1967, where she was a Senior Counsel when this chapter was written. Reid Professor of Constitutional and Criminal Law, Trinity College, Dublin, from 1969 to 1975, she also lectured there in European Community Law. Mary Robinson was elected to Seanad Eireann in 1969 and served as a Senator until 1989. She was elected President of Ireland in November 1990.

Ann Rossiter, from Bruree, County Limerick, has lived in London for over thirty years. She has been an activist on Irish issues for two decades and is writing a book on Irish feminism in Britain.

Ailbhe Smyth is Director of the Women's Education, Research and Resource Centre (WERRC) at University College Dublin, where she co-ordinates the BA, MA and Adult Education Women's Studies programmes. She is a co-editor of *Women's Studies International Forum*. Other collections she has edited include *Feminism in Ireland* (1988), *Wildish Things: An Anthology of New Irish Women's Writing* (1989), and The *Abortion Papers: Ireland* (1992).

Margaret Ward is a feminist historian. Her work includes *Unmanageable Revolutionaries: Women and Irish Nationalism* and *Maud Gonne: Ireland's Joan of Arc.* She grew up in Belfast but now lives in Bristol, where she teaches history at the University of the West of England. She is currently writing a biography of Hanna Sheehy Skeffington.

Acknowledgements
and sources of chapters

The editor and publisher are grateful to Pergamon for permission to include: 'The Silencing of Women in Childbirth or Let's Hear it from Bartholomew and the Boys' by Jo Murphy-Lawless, first published in *Women's Studies International Forum*, 11: 4, 1988; 'Women and the Law in Ireland' by Senator Mary Robinson, first published in *Women's Studies International Forum*, 11: 4, 1988; 'The Women's Movement in the Republic of Ireland' by Ailbhe Smyth, an earlier verson of which appeared in *Women's Studies International Forum*, 11: 4, 1988; to Ron Marken, editor of CAIJS, for permission to include an amended verion of 'Political Interest and Participation of Irish Women 1922-1992: The Unfinished Revolution' by Frances Gardiner, first published in *Canadian Journal of Irish Studies*, 18, 1, 1992; to Open University Press for permission to include 'The Church, The State and the Women's Movement in Northern Ireland' by Monica McWilliams, an earlier version of which appeared in Hughes, E. (ed.), *Culture and Politics in Northern Ireland*, 1991; to Routledge for permission to include a substantially revised version of 'Bringing the Margins Into the Centre: A Review of Aspects of Irish Women's Emigration' by Ann Rossiter, first published in Hutton, S. and Stewart, P. (eds.), *Ireland's Histories: Aspects of State, Society and Ideology*, 1991. 'Suffrage First Above All Else! An Account of the Irish Suffrage Movement' by Margaret Ward, was first published in *Feminist Review*, 10, 1982; an earlier version of 'Revealing Figures? Statistics and Rural Irish Women' by Anne Byrne first appeared in UCG *Women's Studies Centre Review*, 1, 1992; 'Women and Poverty' by Eileen Evason was first published in Davies, C. and McLaughlin, E. (eds.), *Women, Employment and Social Policy in Northern Ireland: A Problem Postponed?* Policy Research Institure, Queen's University, Belfast, 1991; 'Moving Statues and Irish Women' by Margaret MacCurtain first appeared in *Studies*, 76: 302, 1987; 'The Irish Travelling Woman: Mother and Mermaid' by Mary O'Malley Madec was first published in *UCG Women's Studies Centre Review*, 1, 1992; 'Sex and Nation: Women in Irish Cultire and Politics' by Gerardine Meaney is extracted from the LIP Pamphlet of the same title, published by Attic Press in 1991; 'The Relationship Between Women's Work and Poverty' by Mary Daly is extracted from Daly, M., *Women and Poverty*, published by Attic Press in 1989.

Index

Abortion 73, 74, 105-107, 195-200, 205, 209, 230, 236, 238, 243-244, 250, 253, 26-261, 264-271
Act of Union 101, 182, 202
Adelaide Hospital 234, 235
Adult education 142, 265, 267, 271
Agriculture 124, 131, 142, 154, 155, 169, 170, 181
AIM 102, 256
Airey, Josie. 101
Anglo-Irish Treaty 49
Apparition 203, 253, 257
Armagh Jail 98, 198
Asquith, Prime Minister 22, 26, 31
Attic Press 43, 44, 76, 106, 160, 201, 230, 244, 267, 268, 269, 271

Backlash 260, 264
Ballinspittle 204-206, 213
Barry, U. and Jackson, P. (see also Jackson) 138, 190, 199, 267
Beere, Thekla 51, 247
Bennett, Louie 26, 27, 35, 42, 43
Bernadette Devlin (see Mc-Aliskey)
Birmingham Six 198
Birth Control 52, 87, 88, 158 *see also Childbirth*
Byrne, Anne 116, 140-160, 269-270

Campaigns 22, 29, 34, 37, 41, 43, 44, 64, 68, 69, 80, 81, 88, 90, 93, 94, 115, 117, 198, 259, 260, 262, 265

CARE 115
Cat and Mouse Act 32, 33, 36
Celtic 210, 211, 213, 261
Censorship of Publications Act 50
Census 24, 143, 144, 150, 155, 182, 187, 191, 192
Central Criminal Court 114
Central Statistics Office (CSO) 144, 148, 149, 151, 154
Charter 258, 259, 260, 261
Cherish 102, 256
Childbirth 9-13, 15, 17-19, 86-87, 158, 222, 241
Forceps 17, 18
Childcare 70, 84, 85, 103, 126-128, 138, 139, 141-145, 152, 153, 158, 160, 170-173, 243, 252
Chenevix, Helen 26
Church 46, 51, 58, 59, 78-89, 93, 99, 185-186, 193-196, 200-205, 208-209, 212, 222, 231, 233, 235, 239-240, 243, 250, 261, 264
Church and state 78, 85, 88, 99, 194, 196, 239, 264
Citizenship 30, 34, 37, 41, 42, 201, 234
Civil Rights Movement 90, 247
Civil Service 51, 69, 86, 100, 106, 190, 246, 247
Civil Service Act 51
Class systems 257
Combat Poverty Agency 150, 156, 160, 269
Commission for the Status of Women 51-53, 74, 106, 145, 149, 157, 160,

Common Agricultural Policy (CAP) 60

Conditions of Employment Bill 50

Constitutional 21, 28, 30, 35, 36, 50, 52, 103, 190, 230-234, 260, 264, 271

Contraceptives *see birth control*

Corn Laws 182, 202

Costello, Mr Justice 107

Council for the Status of Women (CSW) 257, 267

Cousins, Margaret 23-26, 43

Cultural 18, 45, 63, 108, 121,193, 198, 205, 219, 235, 238, 239, 240, 242, 249, 250, 265, 269, 270

Cumann na mBan 22, 39, 40-44

Dáil 42, 47-48, 51-54, 64, 66, 74-77, 203, 244,

Daly, Mary 122-139, 141, 147, 160, 182, 189, 246, 269, 270, 272

de Burca, Máirín 101, 253

Despard, Mrs 26

de Valera, Eamon 50, 76, 78, 106

Dependence 166, 168, 169, 171, 172, 175, 181

DHSS 163, 270

Diplock (non-jury) 95

Disability 125, 153, 155, 169, 172

Discussion Topics 19, 44, 78, 99, 106, 121, 139, 160, 176, 202, 213, 229, 244, 269

Divorce 59, 80, 87, 94, 100, 150, 151, 161, 190, 206, 209, 234, 238, 264, 265

Domestic service 183, 187, 190

Earnings 92, 124, 128, 130-132, 134, 135, 138, 154, 164, 169, 173, 174

European Community (EC) 52, 56, 69-71, 75, 101, 104, 126, 128,130, 137, 150, 154, 155, 174, 265, 270

Economic crisis 250

Economic power 231

Emigration 37, 143, 144, 150, 160, 177-181, 185, 188-191, 199-201, 203, 229, 250, 261

Employment 24, 50, 53, 84-86, 103, 106, 122, 123-134, 137-140, 142-144, 153, 154-160, 164, 169, 172-175, 180-187, 190-194, 209, 252

Equality Act 53

Equality Agency 102, 138, 139

Education
    Adult education 142, 265, 267, 271
    Third-level 128

Equal pay 130, 169, 174-175, 247, 258-259, 261-264; campaign 259, 262

Equality 45, 52, 53, 61, 72-78, 101-106, 133, 137-139, 166, 182, 199, 210, 231, 253, 258, 265; directive 137

Ethnic 73, 179, 187, 193, 201, 202, 214, 217, 220, 229, 240, 243, 269

Eurobarometer 56-60, 72, 76

Evason, Eileen 162-177, 268, 270, 272

Fairies 223, 224, 225, 227

Family Income Support Schemes 157
Family planning 87, 98, 140, 142, 158, 159, 160
clinics 140, 142, 158,
Famine 14, 180, 184-187, 189, 194, 199, 200, 201, 203, 214, 239
Farrell, Mairéad 84, 97
Feminism 15, 20, 27, 38, 43, 49, 98, 99, 121, 179, 197, 198, 202, 207-230, 232, 234-239, 242-244, 248, 257, 261, 263, 267, 268, 269, 271
Feminist theory 20
Flynn, Eileen 264
Folklore 214, 217, 219, 222, 229
Force-feeding 32, 47
Franchise 22, 23, 27, 30, 32, 39, 42, 44, 55, 196
Free State 47, 188

Gaelic League 193
Gardiner, Frances 45-78, 270, 272
Gender 47, 49, 55-58, 62, 64, 70-76, 99, 106, 110, 121, 129, 138, 140, 147, 160, 171, 172, 179, 190, 201, 209, 233, 256, 257, 266;
differences 56, 58, 72, 73;
gap 55, 58, 59, 72, 73;
Gladstone, Prime Minister 20, 196
Guildford Four 198

Hamilton judgement 101
Haslam, Anna 23
Hayden, Mary 29, 30
Health Board 145, 147-151, 159-161

Heterosexual 119
Hierarchy 11, 45, 56, 131, 133, 139, 154, 186
High Court 80, 97, 104, 105, 234, 264
Hodgers, Sheila 264
Home Rule 20
House of Commons 21, 25, 27, 44, 115

ICTU 53, 91, 98
Ideology 79, 85, 88, 108, 190, 208, 230, 232, 248, 256, 257, 268, 272
Illigitimacy 14, 102, 185, 206
Irish Marketing Suvey (IMS) 55, 65, 77
Incest 89, 93, 114, 115, 159
Independence 20, 21, 30, 40, 42, 47, 49, 50, 69, 189, 190, 233, 252
Infant mortality 147-149
Information 74, 91, 92, 93, 98, 105, 140, 143, 145, 147, 149, 151, 153, 156-158, 189, 197, 215, 216, 234, 243, 256, 263, 264, 267
Intercourse 110, 111, 114, 220
International Women's Day 198
Irish Centre London 195
Irish Feminist Information (IFI) 263, 267
Irish Parliamentary Party 49
Irish Suffrage Movement 20, 43, 44
Irish Women's Franchise League (IWFL) 22-32, 34, 37, 40-42, 44
Irish Women's Reform League (IWRL) 26, 40, 41

Irishwomen United (IU) 248, 257-262, 268

Irish Women's Suffrage and Govern-ment Association (ISLGA) 23, 29

Irish Women's Liberation Movement (IWLM) 247, 248, 251-258, 261, 267

Jackson, Pauline 185, 200, 249, 256, 265

Jackson, Pauline and Barry, Ursula 138

Judiciary 80, 81, 100, 102, 105, 112-114, 119

Juries Act 52

Jury selection 101

Justice Costello 107

Kerry Babies Tribunal 205

Labour Court 105

Labour force 50, 53, 70, 71, 80, 101, 122, 123, 126, 131, 134-136, 138, 142, 144, 151-156, 160, 173, 186, 190, 245: survey 123, 134-136, 142, 144, 156; trends 144, 151-154

Labour market 125, 133, 154, 160, 189, 245

Ladies' Land League 32, 196, 197

Larkin, James 24

Law commission 110

Legal System 109, 111, 114, 119, 120, 121

Leonard, Madeleine 107-121, 270

Lesbians 198, 261, 262, 268

Live Register 136, 137

London Irish Women's Centre 179, 200

Lovett, Ann 264

MacCurtain, Margaret 49, 77, 106, 200, 203-213, 268, 270, 272

MacCurtain, Margaret and O Corráin, D. 106, 268

MacSwiney, Mary 32, 39

McAliskey, Bernadette 84

McCafferty, Nell 86, 99, 106, 205, 206, 213, 258, 268

McGivern, M. T. and Ward, Margaret 88, 92, 98

McWilliams, Monica 79-99, 175, 270, 272

Maastricht Treaty 73

Magee Case 101

Maghaberry prison 116

Maguire Seven 198

Market 'Research Bureau of Ireland (MRBI) 55, 59, 60, 63, 71, 77, 152, 160

Markievicz, Constance 40, 41

Marriage 14, 50, 51, 79, 80-87, 94, 101-104, 110, 111, 126, 147-151, 158-161, 164, 168, 176, 177, 183-187, 192, 200, 206, 211-218, 246, 252, 258

Married Women 53, 54, 85, 86, 111, 123, 126, 132, 136, 149, 156, 164, 165, 167, 172, 190, 245

Maternity 10, 13, 128, 135, 140, 142, 148, 149, 155, 157, 215, 219, 230; hospitals 10, 13; leave 128, 135

Meaney, Gerardine 230-244, 271, 272

Means Test 172

Medical Card 142, 158

Medical Power 10

Midwives 11-14, 16, 18, 191
Migration 177, 178, 195, 200, 201
Mother and Child Scheme 51
Mother Ireland 83, 84, 87, 230, 237, 239
Murphy-Lawless, Jo 9-18, 271

National Health Service 172, 191
Nationalism 20, 21, 23, 25, 27, 28-34, 37-41, 43, 44, 47-49, 78, 79, 81, 83, 91-95, 98, 99, 196, 197, 201, 234, 235-240, 242-244, 250-252, 260, 266
NESC 143, 144, 160
NHS 172,
Northern Ireland 79-97, 98-100, 110, 115-117, 164-176, 190, 196-199, 236, 237, 246, 268-271
Northern Ireland Women's Rights Movement 81, 94, 98
Notes 17, 97, 184, 188, 213, 228, 243, 267

O'Malley Madec, Mary 214-229, 237, 271, 272
Obstetric Science 16
OECD 86, 137
Old Bailey 112

Pankhurst, Emily 23, 44
Party Affiliation 65, 66
Patriarchal 58, 84, 94, 107, 110, 114, 119, 182, 190, 199, 201, 209, 231, 238, 241, 261; attitudes 114
Pension 135, 155, 157, 173, 174
Political science 270
Pornography 115, 116, 120, 121, 244

Post-Famine 14, 184, 186, 199, 201
Poverty 15, 16, 23, 59, 88, 89, 93, 98, 99, 102, 122, 124, 126, 127, 128, 130, 131, 133, 135, 138, 139-141, 143, 147, 150, 154, 156, 157, 159, 160, 162-166-170, 172-176, 192, 209, 212, 214, 228, 231, 266, 270
Prevention of Terrorism Act 95, 198
Prisoners 31, 33, 92, 98, 157, 198, 237
Prostitute 114
Protest 31, 33, 34, 36, 47, 50, 81, 98, 232, 236, 245, 247, 254, 259
Protestant 42, 45, 47, 61, 84-88, 91, 92, 95, 96, 98, 184, 202, 234, 235

Quaker 43

Rape 73, 89, 93, 101, 102, 107-121, 140, 142, 159, 160, 256, 263, 264;
Rape myths 107, 108, 115, 121;
Rape within marriage 110, 111
Rebellion 48, 247
Recession 54, 191, 264-266
References and Further Reading 18, 43, 75, 98, 120, 138, 160, 175, 199, 213. 229, 267
Referendum 106, 205, 209, 230, 234, 243, 250, 260, 264, 265
Representation of the People Act 47

Republicanism 49, 237, 247, 255, 261
Robinson, Mary 100-106, 232, 238, 250, 266, 268, 271
Rossiter, Ann 177-202, 271, 272
Rotunda 9, 13-18
RTE 102, 220
Rural 24, 71, 84, 128, 140-146, 148-151, 153, 155-160, 170, 181, 189, 191, 210, 232; women 141-143, 145-147, 151, 153, 155, 158, 159, 181, 210, 232

Sayers, Peig 210-213
Sectarian 42, 88, 91, 93, 95, 117
Sex role 119
Sexual assault 110, 159
Sexuality 18, 108, 112, 113, 119-121, 195, 203, 218, 253, 258, 260, 261, 262, 266
Sheehy Skeffington, Hanna 23, 29, 34, 40-42, 44, 47, 78, 209, 271
Sinn Féin 27, 32, 41, 49, 64, 94
Smyth, Ailbhe 68, 74, 78, 106, 200, 213, 245-269, 272
Social
  change 80, 82, 86, 96, 101, 105, 106, 245, 249, 265
  Employment Scheme 129
  Insurance 125
  Movement 75, 245, 268
  Policy 51, 162, 170, 171, 175, 176, 270
  Security directive 265
  Welfare 63, 101, 106, 125, 130, 137, 142, 143, 156, 157, 195, 209
Socialist 43, 87, 90, 252, 253, 258, 261

Sociology 18, 270
Spirituality 207-213
SPUC 105, 235
Statistics 111, 124, 137, 140, 141, 143, 145, 148, 149, 151, 152, 155-161, 166, 170, 176, 270
Stereotypes 108, 119, 238
Sterilisation 86, 87
Strategy 18, 25, 73, 85, 89, 97, 104, 105, 173, 175, 248, 268,
Strip-searching 91, 95, 98, 116, 117, 237
Students' Union 97
Supreme Court 52, 234, 243
Symbolic 51, 216, 220, 224, 233, 238, 243

Taboos 219, 229
Tax 128, 165
Technology 121, 136
Test cases 101, 105
The Irish Citizen (IC) 29-31, 33, 34, 38, 39, 40, 42
Trade Union 96, 105, 139, 198, 257, 260, 262
Travellers 214-223, 224, 225, 227-229, 271
Treaty 42, 49, 73
Trinity College Dublin (TCD) 23, 270, 271

UN Decade for Women 51
Unemployment 92, 96, 99, 103, 123, 126, 129-131, 136-138, 141, 152, 169, 172, 258
Unionism 20, 23, 200, 234-238, 244
University 18, 19, 29, 44, 74, 76, 77, 90, 99, 120, 121, 160, 175, 176, 199, 200, 201, 204, 213, 228, 229, 244, 246, 260, 265, 267, 270, 271, 272

University College Cork (UCC) 204
University College Dublin (UCD) 29, 34, 76, 77, 270, 271

Violence 80, 81, 111, 195, 270
Violence against women 107, 108, 119, 121, 263
Voting 22, 25, 27-29, 31, 44, 54-56, 60, 65, 67, 78,

Wages 101, 128, 131, 139, 167, 169-172, 181, 216
Ward, Margaret 20, 44, 78, 111, 112, 121, 169, 171, 177, 196, 197, 201, 211, 271
Wollstonecraft, Mary 17
Womb 205
Women candidates 48, 51, 54, 64-66, 68, 74
Women of Europe 56, 62, 71, 78
Women's Aid 80, 91, 93
Women's Centre 89, 263

Women's Education Project 91
Women's International League for Peace and Freedom 41
Women's Law and Research Group 81, 101
Women's movement 38, 51, 79, 90, 93, 96, 99 105, 122, 230, 239, 247, 251, 259, 260, 262, 263, 266-270, 272
Women's News 84, 98, 99
Women's Political Association (WPA) 52, 263
Women's studies 105, 160, 265, 267, 268, 269, 270-272
Women's Suffrage Federation (WSF) 33
Women's Support Network 91, 97
Women's Social and Political Union (WSPU) 23-26, 28, 29, 31, 33-38, 44

X case 73, 243, 244